CHOICE AGAINST CHANCE

An Introduction to Statistical Decision Theory

JOHN AITCHISON
University of Glasgow

ADDISON-WESLEY PUBLISHING COMPANY
Reading, Massachusetts · Menlo Park, California · London · Don Mills, Ontario

This book is in
the Addison-Wesley Series in
BEHAVIORAL SCIENCE: QUANTITATIVE METHODS

Frederick Mosteller, *Consulting Editor*

PREFACE

One of the disturbing, and at the same time fascinating, features of our human existence is the pervasiveness of uncertainty—disturbing since we often feel at the mercy of a capricious puppeteer, Chance, and fascinating because life without uncertainty would be incredibly dull. Indeed our recognition of chance is a prerequisite to our appreciation that we possess a freedom of action that would be impossible or meaningless in a deterministic world. We have to accept the reality of chance but, as compensation, we can usually exercise choice among some set of alternative actions. This tension of choice against chance forms our subject for study—decision-making under uncertainty or statistical decision theory and its applications. This book is thus concerned with the basic problems of how we may best use our accumulated knowledge and our ability to observe chance or nature at work, so to exercise our choice against chance that we come as closely as possible to desirable goals.

Prerequisites. One of the main compulsions for the writing of this book has been the strong belief that the recent theories of decision-making developed over the last two decades are readily accessible not just to skilled mathematicians and statisticians but to anyone who is prepared to think. Thus no deep knowledge of any mathematical technique is needed for an understanding of this book. Little more is required than a knowledge of the basic operations of arithmetic and an appreciation of what a graph is. For the rest it is sufficient to appreciate that concepts and quantities have to be given names, labels or symbols so that arithmetical operations can be carried out on them. In technical terms only finite mathematics (and hence no calculus) is used; high school algebra is certainly sufficient.

The following are the distinctive features claimed for this book.

1. The book is self-contained, the language of uncertainty (Chapters 2, 3), the theory of games (Chapter 4) and statistical inference (Chapter 5) being developed in a particularly simple form suited to the exposition of statistical decision theory in Chapters 6 and 7.

2. There is an insistence throughout that theory and practice must go hand in hand; that theory is necessary to provide insight into the essentially simple structure of the subject and to reveal similarities in apparently diverse problems; that application is required to allow assimilation and consolidation of theory. The exercises at the ends of sections provide an immediate test of understanding and the reader is recommended to work through most of them.

3. All concepts, ideas and principles are motivated by concrete situations and by the need to resolve realistic problems. A novel feature here is that at the outset in Chapter 1 a number of problems in decision-making under uncertainty are presented as a challenge to the reader and used throughout for motivation and illustration. The approach from simple to complex situations is made gradually, idea by idea.

4. The reader is encouraged to recognize that he is model-building, that there is a correspondence between entities in the real world and concepts in his model. The translation problem–the construction of a model of a given real world situation—is the area where students of the subject are most hesitant—and so particular emphasis is laid on developing an ability in translation by worked example and exercise.

5. Statistical decision theory is of wide applicability and this is reflected in the variety of fields from which the examples and exercises have been constructed, from golf to medical practice, from gem-cutting to locating machine faults, from water-divining to wage and price contracting. A main aim has been to make these illustrations as stimulating, meaningful and realistic as possible. Only where I have felt that the student should first familiarize himself with structure or computation, free from translation difficulties, have I inserted a formal or contentless exercise. Urns, coloured balls, dice and decks of cards play no part in the problems.

6. The importance of the design or choice of the informative experiments is brought out in §§ 6–11, 6–13 and 7–1 in a number of examples.

7. Since the consequences of an action can often only be assessed in terms of the outcome of some future experiment the importance of the notion of *prediction* and *prognosis* has been explicitly recognized in Chapters 5 and 7, and integrated with standard decision analysis.

8. An elementary account of step-by-step or sequential decision-making is presented in Chapter 7 and the usefulness of the dynamic programming tech-

nique illustrated. The reader is thus brought close to current research developments.

While the book has been designed for a one-year course and written to be read as a whole and in sequence, there are a number of subroutes which may serve a useful purpose. Chapters 2 and 3 by themselves provide an elementary (finite-mathematical) account of probability theory. Chapters 1, 2, 3 and 5 comprise a first course in probability and statistical inference. A course in basic statistical decision theory, omitting the predictive and sequential aspects, is formed by §§ 1–1 through 7–3 (omitting §§ 5–5, 5–6).

While the book is primarily intended for students with minimum mathematics I hope that its emphasis on the structure of problems will prove of interest to more sophisticated mathematicians. For them there remains the nontrivial challenge of the exercises and of deriving for themselves the extension of my finite mathematical presentation to the infinite and continuous cases.

Notation. Care has been taken to produce a simple notation to match terminology so that remembering the meaning of symbols is made as mnemonic as possible. Thus *a* represents an *action*, *R* a *record*, *s* a *strategy*, *state* of nature or *success* probability (in different contexts), *U* utility, *W* worth, and so on. Only one Greek letter (pi) is used, π for *plausibility* to allow an easy distinction between it and the related concept of *probability* for which the italic equivalent *p* is used.

Numbering system. Tables and figures are mainly of local interest in this book and are numbered serially within chapters. Thus Table 5–3 is the third table in Chapter 5, Fig. 6–8 the eighth figure of Chapter 6. Definitions, theorems and displays, whose influence is more widespread, are numbered serially within sections. For example, Definition 3–7–2 is the second definition in §3–7, Theorem 3–9–2 refers to the second theorem of §3–9 and a reference (3–7–2) indicates the second numbered display of §3–7. Such references may be located quickly by the use of the current section numbers displayed at the top of each page.

Glasgow   J.A.
March 1970

CONTENTS

CHAPTER 1

PROBLEMS OF DECISION-MAKING
UNDER UNCERTAINTY

1–1 INTRODUCTION

Any reader who has never been called upon to make a decision in the face of
uncertainty is almost certainly a newly arrived visitor from outer space. He has
undoubtedly been living in an environment radically different from ours. The
restaurants he frequented employed cooks who never spoiled the broth nor
oversweetened the custard; he chose what he fancied without fear that the
selected dish might by chance be unsavory. In his extraterrestrial marriage he
was blessed with a perfect wife; in selecting her birthday present he had never to
worry that it might not please her. The spatial climate was so equable that he
had never to choose between his antimeteoric raincoat and his anticosmic-ray
glasses before leaving for work.

   The natural conclusion to be drawn from these opening remarks is that the
vast majority of my readers are already, to some extent and with some ability,
decision-makers under uncertainty. Their everyday conversation strongly
supports such a conclusion. "It will probably be worth my while," "It was a
calculated risk which came off," "We must guard against the worst that may
happen," "The prognosis is good if we act now," "We must chance it and hope
for the best," all–too–familiar phrases, are the words of someone who is faced
with uncertainty and is about to make, or has already made, a decision.

   Do such inveterate decision-makers require a book to help them to face such
trivial decision problems as choosing a meal, buying a birthday present, or
selecting outdoor apparel? The direst consequence of any wrong decision for
these situations is probably only temporary indigestion, a cool reception, or a
summer drenching, and no doubt my readers are managing to avoid lives of

abject misery by making sensible decisions on a largely intuitive basis. Life would be intolerable if we had to analyze carefully and cautiously and consciously every little decision problem that came our way. Indeed, persons who are so extremely indecisive as to enter into detailed consideration of even trivial matters are soon labeled neurotic by society.

Other personal decision problems we regard as more serious, and we often find our intuition less able to cope with these. Which of the houses offered for sale should I buy; should I perhaps wait for further houses to come on the market? Should I retain my three-year-old car for a further period or should I trade it in for a new car now? Should I devote the next year of my spare time to the writing of this book or to the reconstruction of my neglected garden? A sense of added responsibility asserts itself when the decisions are less personal and affect the lives of a number of people. Should I, as a consultant heating engineer, advise the use of gas, electricity, oil, or solid fuel for the heating of this building? Which of five new drugs, each showing some success and some side effects, should my pharmaceutical firm develop further? Should my industrial group open a new factory and, if so, in which location? Which of the qualified applicants to this college should be offered the restricted number of available places? Which alterations should I, as Secretary of the Treasury, make in my next budget?

While the reader may feel adequately equipped for the smaller personal decisions of life, he may admit to being perplexed by the more complicated and less personal ones. Our purpose in this book is thus to attempt to make clear the precise nature of the difficulties that arise in decision-making under uncertainty, to investigate what assumptions and knowledge are required to overcome these difficulties, and to follow through the analysis to the stage of actually making a decision. A number of interesting and challenging examples will be used to illustrate the concepts, principles, and practice of decision-making. In such an assignment we are essentially presenting an elementary account of statistical decision theory and its applications.

We have already emphasized that we do not regard statistical decision theory as a necessary tool for the solving of trivial personal problems. Nor, on the other hand, can we possibly make the claim that if the Secretary of the Treasury only studied this book, all the nation's financial worries would be over. The present state of the theory and practice of statistical decision theory is not sufficient for the handling of such a complex problem. But there are many situations, especially in business, industry, and technology, where a careful analysis of the process of decision-making is undoubtedly beneficial. An understanding of statistical decision theory not only pinpoints which problems are immediately amenable to solution but also highlights those aspects of other problems which require further investigation before a truly satisfactory solution can emerge.

1–2 PREFERENCES AND UNCERTAINTIES

A Problem of Choice Let us consider in more detail the trivial problem of deciding between fish and steak, the only two dishes available, for my restaurant lunch. We shall suppose that the chef has good days on which he serves savory fish and tender steak, and bad days when he produces oily fish and tough steak. In order to make a decision I must be able to formulate my preferences clearly for all conditions that may obtain. Now, I prefer

1. savory fish to tender steak;
2. tough steak to oily fish.

If the waitress tells me that the chef is in good form today, then I have no hesitation in choosing fish. If she tells me that the chef is off form today, then again my decision is easy: I choose steak. If the waitress cannot give me this inside information about the chef's present state, then I am faced with a more challenging problem, one of *decision-making under uncertainty*.

Scales of Preferences The first point that emerges from this new complication is that I require a much more detailed picture of my preferences. Since I detest oily fish I can readily take the necessary first step of putting the four possible dishes in order of preference:

> *Order of preference*: Savory fish, tender steak, tough steak, oily fish.

It is, however, easy to demonstrate that such an ordering of preferences, with no indication of the strengths of these preferences, is not sufficient for the purposes of decision-making under uncertainty. Suppose, for the moment, that I am sufficiently introverted to be able to assign units of enjoyment (*whoopees*, say, for brevity) to the four possible dishes. For example, the two assignments or *scales* of preferences in Table 1–1 both lead to the *order* of preference already stated.

TABLE 1–1

Scales of preferences measured in whoopees

Chef's state of mind	Scale 1		Scale 2	
	Fish	Steak	Fish	Steak
Good	25	10	25	20
Bad	1	2	1	10

The Effect of Chance We can envisage circumstances of uncertainty which, for these scales, lead to different decisions. Suppose that I intend to visit the restaurant every Saturday over a long period, say of *N* weeks, during which my scale of preferences does not alter. Suppose further that I know that the chef has about as many good days as bad days, but I do not know his frame of mind on any particular Saturday. Suppose, for the moment, that I wish to choose the *same* dish on every Saturday. What is my best choice, fish or steak? If my preferences follow scale 1, then the choice of fish every Saturday will bring, on the $\frac{1}{2}N$ good days, $\frac{1}{2}N \times 25$ whoopees and, on the $\frac{1}{2}N$ bad days, $\frac{1}{2}N \times 1$ whoopees, making $13N$ whoopees in all. By similar calculation the choice of steak every Saturday will bring in all $(\frac{1}{2}N \times 10) + (\frac{1}{2}N \times 2) = 6N$ whoopees. Clearly on scale 1, I would decide for fish. On the other hand, on scale 2 fish provides altogether $13N$ whoopees while steak gives $15N$ whoopees. With this scale, therefore, I would decide for steak. Thus the *order* of preference is not a sufficiently detailed scheme of preferences to allow for rational decision-making under uncertainty. Something much more detailed, such as a specific *scale* of preferences, is needed.

Note that this fixed choice of dish for every Saturday brings me the greatest attainable pleasure. Any policy of varying my order from Saturday to Saturday (for example, fish on two-thirds of the Saturdays and steak on the remainder) will yield, on scale 1, an amount of enjoyment which is a "weighted" average of $13N$ and $6N$ whoopees (in our example, $\frac{2}{3} \times 13N + \frac{1}{3} \times 6N = \frac{32}{3}N$ whoopees), and so less enjoyment than the $13N$ whoopees attainable with fish every Saturday.

The Effect of Changes in Uncertainty Suppose now that I have determined for myself a specific scale of preferences, say scale 2 of Table 1–1. We have seen that when the chef's good and bad days are equally likely a decision for steak is indicated for overall long-term maximization of enjoyment. Suppose, however, that my information about the vagaries of the chef is different and suggests that about three-quarters of his days are good and the remainder bad. A decision for fish would then provide $\frac{3}{4}N \times 25 + \frac{1}{4}N \times 1 = 19N$ whoopees compared with $\frac{3}{4}N \times 20 + \frac{1}{4}N \times 10 = \frac{35}{2}N$ whoopees for steak. With this different information I would be led to decide for fish each Saturday. Thus we see that this form of decision-making depends not only on my scale of preferences but also crucially on quantitative knowledge of the chef's propensities to good and bad days.

It is most pertinent to ask the source of the information on which I must base my assessment of the uncertainties about the chef's state of mind. It may be that I have had a long enough experience with the restaurant to enable me to arrive at a reasonable assessment. Perhaps some habitué has offered me his assessment. In the latter case I may wish to perform the experiment of visiting the restaurant several times to provide myself with direct information. Such an informative experiment may cause me to adjust the habitué's assessment before I proceed to make my future decisions. I may even attempt to reach my decision on the basis of my experiment alone, discounting the habitué's assessment as quite unreliable. The important lesson at this stage of our discussion is the realization that I must make some quantitative assessment of the uncertainties of the situation before I can hope to make a sensible decision.

The Possibility of Wrong Decisions   One particular point worth emphasizing is that a good decision policy may lead to a wrong decision for the particular occasion of its application. For example, with scale 1 and equally likely good and bad days for the chef, I will ask quite sensibly for fish; but it may happen to be a bad day for the chef and I would then have been better off with steak. Such wrong decisions are unavoidable when we have to contend with uncertainty. Failure to realize this important fact of life often retards appreciation of statistical argument. In the world of sport we have such a failure in the person of the "results-player," who when defeated resorts to complaint and protest instead of straightforwardly accepting that a bad result can arise in chancy conditions from a good strategy. What we must do when faced with uncertainty is to choose our decision policy so that in some sense we minimize the evil consequences of any wrong decision which may arise from its application.

The dilemma of this simple homely example—the need to reach some compromise between my preferences on the one hand and the uncertainties of the situation on the other—is to be found in all decision-making under uncertainty. For example, the problem of selection of drugs already mentioned contains an element of uncertainty; for on any one occasion we may not be in a position to say whether or not the drug will act successfully and whether or not there will be side effects, although we may have information from previous trials about the proportions of successes and side effects. Here again in the process of decision-making we must consider this information in relation to the importance of success, the costs of the drugs, and the demerits of side effects.

Summary   To sum up, we see that the formulation of a problem of decision-making under uncertainty requires two basic steps:
1. a quantitative assessment of the uncertainties of the given situation;
2. an evaluation of a scale of preferences for the available courses of action. This evaluation must not only take account of basic aims but must also weigh usefulness against cost for each of the available actions in every possible circumstance.

The resolution of the problem then depends on how in our analysis we bring together these two aspects to point out a sensible course of action.

EXERCISES

1. The refrigeration plant at my favorite bar is unfortunately unreliable. I have noticed that on one-third of my frequent past visits it has been out of order, and warm beer

and warm lager have been offered instead of the more usual cold beer and cold lager. My choice between beer and lager is governed by the following scale of preferences, again measured in whoopees:

	Beer	Lager
Cold	16	20
Warm	13	2

Follow the argument of this section and suggest what I should order.

My companion has a different scale of preferences:

	Beer	Lager
Cold	25	20
Warm	3	14

What should I order for him?

My companion has persuaded me to accompany him to his favorite bar where, he claims, the refrigerator is three times as likely to be working as broken down. What orders should he place for us?

Can you quantify the long-term advantage to me of changing to my friend's favorite bar?

2. My car often fails to start, the cause invariably being either a low battery or moisture in the distributor (never both), the former cause being three times more frequent than the latter. My knowledge of motor mechanics is practically nil and I cannot easily tell which is the cause of any particular failure. The choices of action which face me are to hand-crank the engine or to dismantle and dry the distributor. I have very decided views on the degrees of annoyance associated with the various failure–remedy combinations:

Cranking for a distributor fault	40
Drying the distributor for a low battery	16
Drying the distributor for a distributor fault	8
Cranking for a low battery	4

Follow the argument of this section to arrive at a reasoned choice of action for me.

Imagine yourself foolish enough to have bought my car. Formulate your own scale of annoyance and discover your own best course of action.

I borrow my son's car which has the same failings, but a low-battery failure is only twice as frequent as a moist-distributor failure. Will I behave differently with this borrowed car?

1–3 SOME CHALLENGING PROBLEMS

We present in the remainder of this chapter a number of decision problems of different types and from different areas of interest. In each a short discussion of the general problem precedes the posing of simple illustrative examples for the reader's consideration. These eleven illustrative problems and the challenge of finding solutions which are intellectually and practically satisfying will provide the motivation for statistical decision theory in this book. Since we shall restrict ourselves to simple finite mathematics, it is inevitable that some of these problems will appear oversimplified in spite of all attempts to dress them in reality. Despite this necessary oversimplification, they do in fact contain all the essential elements of more complex situations which can only be dealt with by more sophisticated mathematics and computing facilities. Their advantage is their ability to display the structure of statistical decision theory without blinding the reader with irrelevant technicalities of mathematics.

We emphasize that in this chapter these problems are presented simply to stimulate thought. No solutions will be sought at this stage. After each problem we indicate the sections of the book in which the problem is further analyzed.

1–4 BUSINESS DECISIONS

Business decisions are invariably, and at times almost overwhelmingly, beset by uncertainties.

Which of three suggested new products should be developed? Will all three prove to be technically feasible? Which of the technically feasible products will be attractive to the public? What market research should be undertaken to obtain information on likely demand for the products?

Is it worth my company's while to open a new factory, and, if so, where should it be located? Will the better labor supply probably available in location *A* more than offset the likely advantage in the easier supply of raw materials to location *B*? Will location *A*'s better position for the export market prove more of an advantage than *B*'s nearness to the main home market?

Which of a number of suppliers of raw material should be chosen? How are we to balance the differing standard and variability of quality against the different prices asked? Is it better to pay a high price for high quality than a lower price for low quality?

The businessman reader could no doubt fill the remainder of this book with even more perplexing decision problems. We shall illustrate the decision problem here with the following two extremely simple examples.

Problem 1. Introducing a New Product

Consider the following simplified version of the problem of whether to start mass production of a new product. We are aware that a proportion of the items of the new product will be defective, but we do not know which particular items. It is, however, possible to test the items at some cost as they come off the production line, if we so wish. We guarantee to replace, and pay a penalty for, any defective item sold. Our various research sections have arrived at what they regard as reasonable assumed prices and costs. The selling profit—that is, selling price less cost of production and distribution—is 3 per item; the cost of replacing a defective item, including production, dispatch and penalties, is 7 per item; the loss from scrapping an item (computed as production cost less scrap value) is 1 per item; the cost of testing any item is 1.

What other assumptions or information, if any, do we need before we can reach a decision? What is our best course of action?

For the analysis of this problem see Sections 4–3 through 4–11.

Problem 2. Replacing Capital Equipment

In a certain production process the output from one operation with present equipment may be one of three qualities priced at 1, 2, or 3. The cost per operation is k, and experience has shown that the proportions of these qualities are as in Table 1–2. New processing equipment is now available for hire at a rental of h per operation, and we are interested in the relative merits of retaining the present equipment and renting the new equipment. To investigate this we arrange to examine the output of 50 trial operations with the new equipment, the resulting qualities being shown also in Table 1–2. The scrap value of present equipment is reckoned to be nil.

TABLE 1–2

Performance of present and rented equipment

	Price			Row sums
	1	2	3	
Proportions with present equipment	0.1	0.6	0.3	1.0
Numbers with rented equipment	4	21	25	50

Should we continue with the present equipment or rent the new equipment? Alternatively we may phrase the question: What is the maximum rental per operation which makes hiring worth while? (See Section 7–6.)

1–5 CLASSIFICATION PROBLEMS

In many fields of investigation (medicine, literature, machine repair, archaeology) it is very convenient to be able to classify individual units (patients, unsigned texts, machines, specimens) into categories (diseases, authors, sources of fault, periods). The observable aspects (symptoms and signs; lengths of sentences, frequencies of specific words; breakdown symptoms such as overheating, eccentricities of output, increase in fuel consumption; materials used, and radioactive count) vary considerably for individual units within a given class, and it is difficult, costly, and time-consuming to carry out the exhaustive examination and tests which might lead to an undisputed classification. For some individual units it may in fact be impossible to extract all such information; for example, an archaeological specimen may be a mere fragment of the original object.

The difficulties of classification can be simply illustrated graphically. Suppose that we have available information on two aspects (for example, oral temperature and blood pressure of each of a number of units (patients) which we know to have been properly classified into one of two classes (diseases). Each of these units can thus be represented by a point in the (x_1, x_2)-plane, the x_1-coordinate measuring oral temperature and the x_2-coordinate measuring blood pressure. Fig. 1–1 shows a typical configuration. The uncertainties of the situation reveal themselves in the scattering of class points. The basic problem is then the following: How should we classify a new individual unit with measurements (x_1, x_2), taking into account the consequences of possible misclassification? We would have little hesitation in placing new points such as A in class 1, but what of new points such as B? Clearly classification depends on the extent to which class clusters overlap, the scattering within clusters, the relative position of the new point to the clusters, and the relative disadvantages of misclassifying a unit of class 1 in class 2 and of misclassifying a unit of class 2 in class 1.

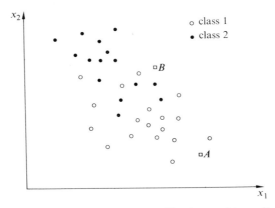

Fig. 1–1 Configuration of a typical classification problem. Do the units represented by A and B belong to the o class or to the • class?

In most applications the number or dimensionality of aspects of individual units may be large and there may be considerably more than two classes. For example, in medicine, even the presence of some major symptom may still allow a number of possible diagnoses which necessitate detailed further investigation of other aspects. Moreover, there may be a mixture of qualitative aspects (such as presence or absence of a rash, a headache) and quantitative aspects (such as pulse rate, blood pressure). These situations are undoubtedly more complex, largely because we are unable to enlist the visual aid of a two- or three-dimensional representation; nevertheless, the concepts remain the same. The study of classification problems is still the subject of vigorous research, and the rewards, particularly in devising more routine procedures of medical diagnosis, may be substantial. There are many extremely interesting questions which pose themselves. How many characteristics are required to obtain effective diagnosis? How much information is given by the various characteristics; would some subset be sufficient for all practical purposes? Measurement of some of the aspects involves costly tests. With information on the cost and time of the tests, what is the best order in which to conduct them to reach a careful diagnosis at reasonable cost within the shortest possible time?

Note that there are many allied problems of a nature similar to, and often confused with, the problem of classification. One such is that variously referred to as division, dichotomization, or cluster analysis, where the basic problem is first to identify the classes or clusters. If, for example, we are given the array of points in Fig. 1–2, how many classes are we justified in recognizing and how should we set about allocating units or points to these classes? This is essentially the nature of many taxonomic problems.

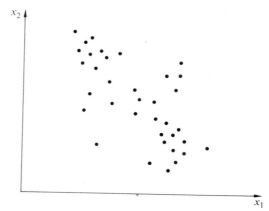

Fig. 1–2 The problem of taxonomy. Do the units represented here fall into two or more classes and, if so, which units fall into which classes?

In the following two simple illustrative problems, in machine repair and medical diagnosis, a single qualitative aspect is involved. Nevertheless, the examples serve to pinpoint the difficulties and the nature of the resolution of such problems.

Problem 3. Locating a Machine Fault

There are just two locations—the engine and the gearbox—where the cause of faulty operation of a certain machine may lie. There are just two symptoms of faulty operation—overheating and irregular traction. Unfortunately, there is not a one-to-one correspondence between locations of fault and symptoms of faulty operation, which would allow positive identification of the location of fault. Extensive past records, however, establish the proportions of breakdowns displaying the various symptom combinations for each location of fault; see Table 1–3.

TABLE 1–3

Proportions of past breakdowns

Location of fault	Symptom combination			Row sums
	Overheating only	Irregular traction only	Overheating and irregular traction	
Engine	0.1	0.4	0.5	1.0
Gearbox	0.5	0.3	0.2	1.0

The costs of examining, and where necessary repairing, the engine and gearbox are 1 and 2, respectively, and the charge made to the customer for any repair is 4. What should workshop practice be? In other words, devise a suitable set of working rules for determining the order of examination to locate the fault from the symptoms present on any occasion of breakdown. (See Sections 5–1 through 5–3 and 6–1 through 6–11.)

Problem 4. Medical Screening

In an attempt to diagnose early a certain metabolic disorder in babies a new screening method has been proposed. It has been found that there is a tendency for babies with this abnormality to have a higher concentration of a certain kind of steroid in the urine than normal babies. The proposed test uses an eight-point scale for level of concentration of steroid, and can determine quickly and inexpensively which of these eight levels applies to a particular baby. The steroid level varies from baby to baby, even within the same category (with the disorder or without), but extensive past records have established the proportions having

the various steroid levels for each of the two classes of babies. These are repro-
duced in Table 1–4. The proposed method of screening is that all babies with
steroid level 5 or higher will be subjected to the further expensive diagnostic
tests necessary to establish unequivocally whether a baby is abnormal or not.
Do you consider the proposed test a good one, and if so, why? What other
information would you require before deciding on a screening method? (See
Sections 2–9, 5–8, 7–3.)

TABLE 1–4

Proportions with different levels of steroid

Category of baby	Level								Row sums
	1	2	3	4	5	6	7	8	
Normal	0.05	0.35	0.45	0.10	0.04	0.01	0.00	0.00	1.00
Abnormal	0.00	0.00	0.01	0.07	0.24	0.47	0.15	0.06	1.00

1–6 SAMPLING INSPECTION OF QUALITY

It is frequently uneconomical to test every item from some mass-production
process to ensure that the overall quality of items does not fall too low. The
alternative is to use some form of sampling inspection whereby an attempt is
made to infer this overall quality from the testing of a subset or sample of the
items in question. The feature of uncertainty here arises from the need to sample,
and is deliberately introduced by the statistician through the device of "random
sampling" to ensure the validity of his inferences. The precise technical definition
of "random" and its practical implications need not concern us for the present.
To illustrate this aspect of uncertainty, suppose that from a batch of 100 items a
"random sample" of 10 items is selected and tested, and that exactly 3 are found
to be defective. All that we can deduce about the constitution of the entire batch,
conveniently expressed as (number of defectives, number of effectives), is the
exclusion of the following possibilities: (100, 0), (99, 1), (98, 2), (97, 3), (96, 4),
(95, 5), (94, 6), (2, 98), (1, 99), (0, 100). All other constitutions are possible,
though some, for example (30, 70), may appear more plausible than others, for
example (3, 97). Another view of this uncertainty is obtained when we ask
what may happen if this sampling experiment of selecting and testing 10 items
from the batch of 100 items is repeated, provided this is physically possible.
Whatever the specific technical meaning of the word "random," it clearly
implies that we will not necessarily obtain the same 10 items as in the first
performance. Two batches of the same constitution may yield samples of
different constitutions.

Sampling inspection procedures are widely applied in industry and marketing with varying degrees of success. Successful application depends on reaching a balance between the satisfactoriness of the product and the rigor of the test of quality applied: sampling inspection cannot by itself turn an indifferent product into a good one, although it can, of course, be used to weed out defective items. Sampling inspection procedures are, or should be, as multifarious as industrial products themselves. It is wise to tailor any procedure to the special features of the particular process and product and to avoid off-the-peg formulas. The procedure adopted will depend on the nature of the test of quality, whether it destroys, debilitates, or leaves unharmed the item tested; on the cost of the test and the time it takes to complete; on the nature of the process, whether it is a batch process, or a continuous conveyor-belt process; on what types of sampling are physically possible or convenient, whether to sample every tenth item, whether to test items until the sixth defective one is found; on the relative costs of testing and of replacement of defective items; on whether the product is fairly uniform or rather variable; and on the judgment of what is a tolerable range for the value of some characteristic in the case where the test measures such a characteristic. The following example illustrates some of these considerations.

Problem 5. Choice of a Batch-Sentencing Rule
A batch of three items (the number in this illustrative example is small simply to provide easy calculations) awaits sampling inspection. Untested items, whether effective or defective, can be sold at a profit of 2 per item, but the replacement cost of a sold defective item is 5. The test of an item determines whether it is effective or defective but is debilitating and reduces the profit obtainable to 1 per tested item. The loss involved in scrapping any item is 1 and the cost of testing an item is 0.06. What we have to decide is how many items it is advisable to test and what batch-sentencing rule should be used. For example, if we decide to test two items, should we place the batch on the market if and only if both items are effective, or should we destroy the batch if and only if both items are defective? Do we perhaps need more information before we can arrive at satisfactory answers to those questions? (See Sections 6–12 and 6–13.)

1–7 ESTIMATION

We are often called upon to provide estimates of some unknown quantity. Our estimate may have to be inferred from the imperfect knowledge that accompanies the time- and cost-cutting technique of sampling. For example, an opinion poll attempts, by eliciting the intentions of a small proportion of voters, to estimate the strength of support for a particular political party among the whole electorate. Another example is provided by a nationwide sample survey of 100,000 households. Suppose that among these we find 1240 households in which an old person is living alone. How reliable is 1.24 as the percentage of all the nation's households which consists of single old persons? How reliable an estimate of the average weekly income of such old-person households can be obtained from information collected over four weeks from each of the 1240 households? Is a sample of 100,000 households large enough to give reliable information? Is it perhaps too large and too costly for the purpose it serves?

Again, to "determine" a quantity, for example the potassium content of a new fertilizer or the bacterial infestation of suspect meat, we may need to perform some experiment, such as a quantitative chemical analysis or a microscopic sample count. In all likelihood there is "experimental error"; repeated determinations yield different results. The question then is: How do we estimate the potassium content or the bacterial infestation from the results of these repeated experiments?

How we use the information available to construct an estimate naturally depends on the nature and pattern of the uncertainty in the given situation. But we must also take account of the consequences of the estimate's missing the target or true value. In business estimation we have to balance carefully the advantages and disadvantages of overestimating and underestimating. If our estimate is high we may lose our customer, if it is too low we may make little, if any, profit.

The following elementary example gives some of the flavor of estimation problems.

Problem 6.   Estimating a Number of Cells

The number of "intruder cells" in an organism may be 0, 1, or 2, but the actual number cannot be determined without destroying the organism. One possible way of estimating the number is to carry out a certain nondestructive test on the organism. Extensive investigations with such organisms have shown the pattern of positive reactions to the test given in Table 1–5. Past experience has also shown that the proportions of organisms with 0, 1, 2 intruder cells are 0.2, 0.5, 0.3.

The test is repeated three times on an organism and produces exactly one

TABLE 1–5

Pattern of reactions

Number of cells in the organism	Proportion of positive reactions
0	0.3
1	0.6
2	0.7

positive reaction. What criterion of good estimation of the number of intruder cells should be adopted? On this criterion, what is the best estimate? (See Sections 5–4, 5–9 through 5–11.)

1-8 TREATMENT SELECTION

The need to compare the effects of different methods, treatments, or factors arises in many disciplines. Which of four antihistamines is most effective in the treatment of hay fever? Is the use of a teaching machine more effective than a human teacher for a particular course of technical instruction? Which combination of five fertilizers and three spraying techniques provides the highest yield of wheat? Satisfactory answers to such questions can be found only by obtaining relevant information from a properly designed trial or experiment. Controlled clinical trials and agricultural field trials are familiar forms of such experiments. The reader must have heard discussions on the ethical problems of the former, and seen in the countryside the patchwork fields of differing varieties so characteristic of the latter.

In such experiments the treatments (drugs, teaching methods, fertilizers) are assigned in some defined random manner to experimental units (patients, pupils, plots of ground) and the response (degree of improvement, score in examination, yield) of each experimental unit is measured. The problems can be very complex. For example, in the screening of new drugs, the "treatment" may be multidimensional, since not only the type of drug, but also its strength, the duration of its application, and the site of its introduction into the experimental unit are of importance. Considerable care and ingenuity are often required to devise an experiment which will allow the investigation of all the relevant factors.

Such situations involve an underlying uncertainty in the variability of response of different experimental units to the same treatment; no two persons react identically to the same drug. There is also a further imposed uncertainty in the random assignment of treatments; this deliberate introduction of uncertainty is essentially the means of counteracting unconscious bias in experimentation and ensures the validity of any significant conclusions.

While the selection of a treatment must thus depend on a sound assessment of these uncertainties, it should also take account of the different costs of different treatments. If an expensive treatment appears more effective than a less expensive one, is the disadvantage of greater cost, and so restricted availability, more than offset by the greater effectiveness?

The following examples show clearly the features of such problems.

Problem 7. Introducing and Comparing Treatments

Introduction of a new treatment. Advances in technology have made the introduction of a treatment of a certain type of material possible. All applications of the treatment, however, do not always lead to success. The cost of treatment is estimated as k and the return from a successfully treated piece of material is l. If the treatment fails the return is 0. The process has been carried out on n pieces of material and x applications have been found to be successful. Should the treatment be introduced?

Comparison of two or more treatments. Suppose that two treatments, 1 and 2, are available and that the costs per application are k_1 and k_2, the return from a successfully treated material being l as before and 0 if the treatment fails. We have studied n_1 and n_2, independent applications of treatments 1 and 2, and have found x_1 and x_2 successes, respectively. On the supposition that one of the two treatments will be adopted, which one should it be?

In both the above examples, we may pose the very pertinent question as to whether we have conducted our experimentation in the most sensible way. (See Sections 7–7 and 7–11.)

Problem 8. Selecting a Quality Improver
Units, which can be of quality 1 or 2, may be processed by one of two treatments, and the outcome of the processing may be a unit of quality 2 or 3. The choice of treatment is under consideration and an informative experiment has been performed. Units have been allocated to treatments 1 and 2 "at random" as they were produced and the resulting quality observed. The results are shown in Table 1–6. The costs of treatments 1 and 2 are 0.1 and 0.2 per unit, and the selling prices of units of quality 1, 2, 3 are, respectively, 1, 2, 3. Which treatment should be adopted in the future? (See Section 7–8.)

TABLE 1–6

Qualities produced by the two treatments

Treatment 1		Treatment 2	
Initial quality	Final quality	Initial quality	Final quality
1	2	1	2
1	2	2	3
2	2	2	2
1	3	1	3
2	3	2	3
1	2	2	2
1	2	1	2
1	2	2	3
2	2	1	3
1	3	1	2

1–9 NEGOTIATING CONTRACTS AND TARIFFS

In commerce and industry, and indeed in domestic life, we are often offered a number of alternative tariffs, price arrangements, wage agreements, or hire scales. For example, an electricity board offers its commercial consumers the choice of

1. a general block tariff, based only on the total amount of electricity consumed;
2. a monthly demand tariff, calculated for each month on the amount of electricity consumed and on the peak instantaneous demand during the month;
3. an annual demand tariff, calculated for the year on the amount of electricity consumed and on the peak instantaneous demand during the year.

Here the cost structure is well defined for each of the tariffs, but the demand for electricity (and particularly the instantaneous demand) varies from month to month and year to year. The problem is how to assess this variability, say from past records, and match it with the different tariffs to judge which tariff is most advantageous.

The following examples present similar problems of negotiating price contracts and wage rates.

Problem 9. Choosing Between Contracts

A manufacturer has found that the loads of raw material he uses to produce a large batch of components fall into two categories, 1 and 2, recognizable in the distribution of quality of the finished components. These proportions are shown in Table 1–7. Unfortunately it is not possible to recognize the category

TABLE 1–7

**Proportions of components
with different qualities**

Category	Quality	
	Low	High
1	0.5	0.5
2	0.3	0.7

of a load early enough during the production run before it is necessary to sign a price contract for the batch. However, it is known that loads of categories 1 and 2 arise with relative frequencies 0.6 and 0.4. In practice the qualities of only five components can be determined before one of three contracts must be accepted. These contracts are as follows:

1. a flat rate of 1.6 per component;
2. 1 per component of low quality, 2 per component of high quality;
3. 1.4 per component of low quality, 1.8 per component of high quality.

For a production run just started the five test components have produced one of low quality and four of high quality. Which of the three contracts should the manufacturer accept for this batch? (See Sections 5–6 and 7–4.)

Problem 10. Negotiating a Wage Rate

Wage negotiations are in progress, and the following alternatives have been offered by management:

1. a flat rate of 4 per day;
2. a flat rate of 1.6 per unit of production;
3. a flat rate of 1 per unit of production together with a bonus of 1, 2, or 3 if the day's output is assessed to be of quality 1, 2 or 3.

Records of the past production on each of 100 days are shown in Table 1–8. Which wage structure should the workers choose? (See Section 7–5.)

TABLE 1–8

Number of days with specified production pattern

Quality of day's output	Number of units produced		
	1	2	3
1	4	18	21
2	–	31	16
3	–	–	10

1–10   THE PROBLEM OF CONTROL

Although a process may be subject to random fluctuation or disturbance, we may yet be able to exercise some element of control over it. Everyday examples of this are central heating systems, where a thermostat measures the present state of the room and adjusts the rate of heating when necessary to maintain an even temperature; and our own bodies, where temperature can be adjusted to some extent by such controls as clothing, food, perspiration, and shivering. From information about the progression of a process to date we may wish to alter the controls so that the process has a better chance of more nearly reaching some desirable goal. For example, automatic control of an aircraft may be a continuous process of readjustment activated by feedback of information from its present position and state of motion. In market gardening the growth of a crop is governed by many chance factors, and the successful gardener will be continually monitoring his crop, and will be prepared to use the controls of watering, fertilizing, weeding, and insecticide-spraying in order to increase quality and yield. In his attempt to cure a patient a doctor re-examines the patient several times and is ready to adjust his treatment on the basis of the changes for better or worse that he discovers in his patient, with the aim of completing the cure. Those are all, to a greater or lesser degree, problems of statistical control, and in order again to point to the structure of the problem and to obtain some idea of how it may be tackled, we present the following simple example as our final challenge to the reader.

Problem 11. Attempting to Reach a Target
1. A process is aimed at producing a commodity of quality index 9 from a commodity of quality index 0. Improvement of the commodity can be regarded as taking place in a sequence of independent operations. At each of these operations, regardless of the present quality of the commodity, there may be an addition of quality to the existing index of 1, 2, or 3 units, and past records have shown that the relative frequencies of these additions are as in Table 1–9.

TABLE 1–9

Relative frequencies of different additions to quality

Addition to quality	1	2	3	Row sum
Relative frequency	0.4	0.2	0.4	1.0

At most five operations of the process are allowed. Each operation costs 10 units, and the loss from attaining a final quality q instead of the target value 9 is $(q - 9)^2$. (Note that undershooting and overshooting the quality target are

TABLE 1–10

Relative frequencies of different additions to quality

Type of operation	Addition to quality			Row sums
	1	2	3	
1	0.7	0.1	0.2	1.0
2	0.2	0.6	0.2	1.0
3	0.1	0.3	0.6	1.0

equally punished.) Is there an optimum procedure for such a process? (See Section 7–9.)

2. For another process, with the same loss from missing the target quality, three operations of types 1, 2, 3 are available at costs of 1, 2, 3 per operation. The relative frequencies for additions to quality from past records are shown in Table 1–10. What procedure with a maximum of five operations will best exploit the three types of operation? (See Section 7–10.)

CHAPTER 2

THE LANGUAGE OF UNCERTAINTY:
BASIC GRAMMAR

The unpredictability or uncertainty of the outcome of a game of chance such as roulette or bingo is universally recognized. The throw of a coin is accepted without question as a fair means of determining which of two teams should have the choice of batting or fielding. While it is common knowledge that the "laws of chance" apply to such gambling situations, it is not so widely appreciated that this same form of uncertainty pervades many aspects of human endeavor and that the so-called laws can be applied far more extensively and to better purpose.

We shall make frequent use of the word *experiment* in this book. This use will be in the widest possible meaning of the word, as an action or operation aimed at discovering some fact or the taking of an intelligent interest in some aspect of nature. Thus it covers all observational situations from active interference with nature, as in the splitting of atoms or in chemical analyses with twisted arrays of flasks, glass tubing, retorts, and bunsen burners, to the mere observation of our social life as it passes, as in the recording of the number of births in a town in a year or the number of cars arriving at a filling station during a day.

2-1 THE PERVASIVENESS OF UNCERTAINTY

Uncertainty of outcome is an inherent feature of most experimental situations; indeed, if we could correctly predict the outcome there would be little point in experimenting. Consider the experiment of submitting an item from some industrial production process to a test of quality to determine whether it is effective or defective. We cannot predict with any certainty what the outcome of this experiment will be; we are aware from experience that quality of a factory product does vary from item to item. Repetitions of this simple experiment—the testing of successive items—do not necessarily yield the same outcome; some items will turn out to be effective, others defective. Consideration of other simple experiments will soon reinforce this notion that uncertainty pervades the whole of nature. Think about the following experiments: recording the lifetime of an experimental unit (light bulb, insect, government) produced by some process (manufacturing, hatching, election); submitting an experimental unit (animal, insect, household) to a stimulus (drug, insecticide, advertisement) and recording whether the unit responds (reacts, dies, purchases); recording the number of "events" (radioactive particles arriving at a Geiger counter, persons arriving at a supermarket cash desk, incidence of a certain disease, births) in a given interval of time; measuring over some given period the demand for a commodity (transistorized radios, domestic gas, university places). If we imagine repetitions of each of these experiments under as identical conditions as possible, we realize that the same outcome will not necessarily result from each repetition.

We have somewhat facilely used the concept of *repetition* of an experiment. It is clear that no experiment can be repeated in the strict sense of the word; any purported repetition must occur at some other time or in some other place, and there may also be some uncontrollable change in the physical conditions, such as atmospheric pressure, of the experiment. Indeed it would be possible to argue that the uncertainty which is our concern arises only because of the impossibility of realizing the concept of perfect repetition. If we are not to be led into an interminable philosophical discussion at this stage, we must clearly make some assumption. We shall accordingly assume that in a given situation we have been able to agree about what conditions are sufficiently similar to make use of the word *repetition* acceptable. In practice there is seldom any difficulty in arriving at such agreement, though in particular cases careful definition of the term may be called for. If we repeat the experiment of subjecting an animal to a dose of a drug, we must carefully specify whether the same animal is used or whether a different animal must be chosen. What do we mean by repeating the experiment of recording the amount of savings during the week ending September 9? In this context we must be clear whether we mean the recording of the amount of savings for the corresponding period in the following year or whether we envisage some time-machine process which turns the clock back to the start of the week and suppose that people may act differently in their reliving of that week.

To cope with the pervasiveness of uncertainty or variability through all aspects of nature, we must introduce some new language in which we can speak intelligently and quantitatively about uncertainty or variability. In the construction of any language it is necessary to give labels to the relevant real objects or entities of interest and to provide a grammar or syntax for the development of thought about those entities. In the scientific world such language construction is often termed *model-building*.

EXERCISES

If your awareness of the feature of uncertainty or variability and of its importance in real situations is still emerging, perform a few simple experiments or make some simple observations in the following situations or, better still, in situations of your own choice.

1. Keep a record of the times of your daily journey to work over a period. In view of the variability that you observe, have you ever consciously posed the problem of how to arrive at a routine time for leaving home? Presumably you do not want to reach the office too early too often, but also recognize that there are disadvantages in arriving too late too often. You have probably already reached some optimum time by trial and error over a long period. Consider then the problem that would face you in reaching this happy state quickly if you changed your home or your place of work.

2. Record over a period the daily numbers of some common objects you use (matches, paper clips, postage stamps, units of electricity). How would you take account of the variability you observe if you had to contract now for a month's supply?

3. Record the daily frequency of some common experience you undergo (bills received, telephone calls received) over a period. If the variability observed here is a source of annoyance to you, have you considered any ways in which the variability might be controlled?

4. Observe the lifetimes of some components used about the house (electric light bulbs, time to next reservice of a vacuum cleaner). How would you take account of the variability in these times when entering into a contract for replacement or reservicing?

5. Keep weekly records of your personal or household expenditure on food over a period of four weeks. Suppose that you then take as your budget for the following year thirteen times your total expenditure for the four weeks. How reliable would this estimate be in view of the variability in your weekly expenditures? What other uncertain factors should you perhaps make allowance for? For seasonal variation in prices? For increased expenditure during holidays?

6. With the help of friends observe the numbers of vehicles arriving along each of the four roads at a local uncontrolled crossroads over consecutive ten-second intervals. Suppose that it is proposed that traffic lights be put at the junction. How does the variability in the sets of four numbers you have recorded affect your design of the timing sequence of the traffic lights?

2-2 MODEL-BUILDING

A model-building three-year-old may cross, and stick together, two strips of cardboard to produce what is for him a highly satisfactory model airplane.

His more sophisticated ten-year-old brother will expect his plastic construction set to assemble into something tolerably like the real object or photograph that he has seen. The aerodynamicist who wants to determine with reasonable accuracy the forces which will act on a real airplane under certain flying conditions will require an accurate scaling in his model before he can hope to simulate reality in wind-tunnel tests. There are clearly different degrees of simplicity and realism obtainable in the construction of satisfactory models. To be successful a model-builder must have some specific aim. In designing his model he must recognize, and find suitable counterparts in his model for, the particular aspects and relationships in the reality he is attempting to portray; and he must do this in a way which serves his specific aim. Oversimplification at the expense of realism may yield a model which does not serve its specific aim. On the other hand, the loss of simplicity which may attend the search for too much realism can result in a model which is difficult to develop further. The balance between simplicity and realism is always under review by the scientist.

Map-making is another good illustration of model-building; here different aims produce different models for the same region of the earth's surface. An airline company may produce for its customers a rough map of its area of operation, with lines showing its routes and possibly carrying information about the flying times. The motorist requires his model to provide routes and distances, type of road, and information about large towns, bottlenecks, and traffic density. The hill walker or mountaineer will require the detailed representation in, for example, a topographic map put out by the U.S. Department of the Interior, Geological Survey, to meet his specialized needs. The science of map-construction has, of course, led to the theory of (map) projection, with projections which preserve distance or directional relationships.

Model airplanes and maps are examples of fairly direct or simulative model-building by way of scaling and projection, where the entities of the model are obvious counterparts of reality. There are, however, models (mainly mathematical models) which involve a higher degree of abstraction but which are every bit as useful and as simple to comprehend. The reader is certainly familiar with some of these. Arithmetic, with its operations of addition, subtraction, multiplication and division, is a model with a fair degree of sophistication. It allows us to operate with and on symbols (numbers) with ease and skill within the model (for example, $65 \times 144 = 9360$), and so avoid the clumsy alternative of emptying 65 crates, each containing 144 oranges, and enumerating the oranges as first, second, . . . until we reach the final 9360th orange. Elementary algebra is a more sophisticated model which allows us to avoid the necessity of a trial-and-error approach to essentially arithmetic problems. Coordinate or analytical geometry provides a model in which quantitative problems of distance and angle can be discussed, and provides a reasonable approximation

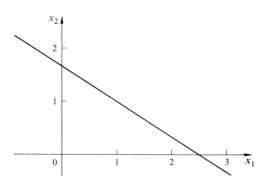

Fig. 2–1 Model for a straight stretch of road: the set of points (x_1, x_2) satisfying $2x_1 + 3x_2 = 5$.

to not-too-large areas of the earth's surface. One aspect of this abstraction is the representation of a straight stretch of road by the set of all points (x_1, x_2) satisfying a linear relationship, for example, $2x_1 + 3x_2 = 5$ (see Fig. 2–1). Even greater abstraction occurs in mathematical physics, where it is common practice to study models which are nothing more than a set of differential equations (i.e., equations involving rates of change of functions) with given initial or boundary conditions.

What then is the degree of abstraction, the balance between simplicity and realism, which produces a satisfactory model for an experiment displaying the feature of uncertainty? It is a remarkable fact that a highly successful model can be formulated in an extremely simple way. To this writer, and I hope soon to the reader, it is the achievement of this combination of simplicity and realism, at a bargain price of minimum abstraction, that is so appealing.

EXERCISES

1. Consider the purpose of, and the balance between simplicity and realism in, models used in the following situations (or preferably in situations of your own choosing):

   a) an artist's impression of, an estate agent's advertisement for, and an architect's plan for a new block of flats;

   b) a colored plate depicting the circulation of blood in the human body, a plastic demonstration model of the main organs and blood vessels with pump-circulated colored fluid to simulate the flow, and a heart-lung machine;

   c) a circuit diagram for an electrical or electronic circuit such as a radio or television set;

   d) a chemical formula for, and a set of colored balls with connecting rods to represent, some complicated molecule.

2. Recall a typical early school problem: "A man invested all his capital until it doubled itself. He then gave $500 to each of his three sons and found he had $2500 capital left. What was his original capital?"

Recall also the use of the model of school algebra, where x is asserted to represent the unknown amount of the original capital. The translation of the informative sentences into the language of the model is the "equation"

$$2x - (3 \times 500) = 2500.$$

The purpose is to discover the original capital and this motivates the bringing into play of mathematical techniques to "solve for x," giving $x = 2000$.

3. Use a coordinate-geometry model to resolve the following topographical problem.

Two roads intersecting at right angles run north–south and east–west. Four towns A, B, C, and D lie on these roads, A being 20 miles east, B 10 miles north, C 18 miles south, and D 12 miles east of the crossroads. Direct straight roads join A to B and C to D. Draw a model of this region by taking the crossroad junction to be the origin O and the roads running due east and due north as the coordinate axes Ox_1 and Ox_2 (or Ox and Oy). Represent the towns by points and the roads by lines. Show that the roads AB and CD are represented by parts of the lines with "equations"

$$x_1 + 2x_2 = 20, \qquad 3x_1 - 2x_2 = 36.$$

It is proposed to extend the road CD until it meets AB. Show that the intersection is 14 miles east and 3 miles north of the crossroad junction.

2–3 THE FEATURE OF STABILITY

Nature would indeed pose a formidable task in model-building if she revealed no redeeming feature to the uncertainty she displays in our confrontation with her. The compensating feature she provides becomes evident when an experiment is repeated a large number of times. Suppose that a roughly cut four-faced piece of plastic with faces colored amber, blue, crimson, and damson is spun in the air repeatedly and a record is kept of which color lands face down for each repetition of this spinning experiment. If a_n, b_n, c_n, d_n denote the number of ambers, blues, crimsons, damsons after n spins, then $rf_n(\text{amber}) = a_n/n$, $rf_n(\text{blue}) = b_n/n, \ldots$ are called the *relative frequencies* of amber, blue, $\ldots$ in the n spins. It is an empirical fact that the relative frequencies of amber, blue, crimson, damson stabilize about some fixed numbers. This is illustrated in Fig. 2–2, where the four relative frequencies (which, of course, sum to 1) are shown after different numbers of spins.

This stability of relative frequency in long runs of repetitions of an experiment can be observed for any repeatable experiment. For example, Fig. 2–3 shows rf_n (lifetime is less than 1000 hours) for various n in a sequence of experiments which recorded the lifetimes of 5120 components produced by a factory process.

We can frame the general definition of relative frequency in the following terms.

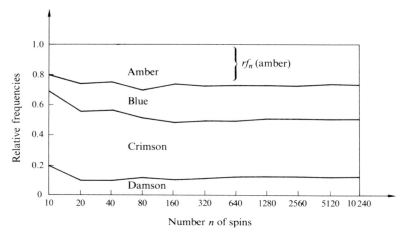

Fig. 2–2 Long-run stability of relative frequencies of the four colors in the spinning experiment. Note that the number *n* of spins is plotted on a scale which doubles at each of ten equal steps.

2–3–1 Definition *Relative frequency.* If an event *E* occurs c_n times in *n* repetitions of an experiment, then the *relative frequency* of *E* in the *n* repetitions is

$$rf_n(E) = \frac{c_n}{n}.$$

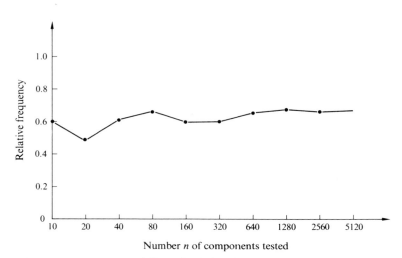

Fig. 2–3 Long-run stability of relative frequency of components with lifetime less than 1000 hours. Note that *n* is plotted on a scale which doubles at each of nine equal steps.

EXERCISES

1. From a glass production line standard sheets are so screened that they have at most four "bubble" defects, but the actual number of bubbles in screened sheets varies from sheet to sheet in an unpredictable way. The table below shows the total number of sheets with different numbers of bubbles at different stages in the production of 5120 sheets. Construct as in Fig. 2–1 a graphic demonstration of the stability of relative frequency of the five possible outcomes of the simple experiment of determining the number of bubbles in a screened sheet.

Number of sheets produced	Number of bubbles				
	0	1	2	3	4
20	8	7	3	0	2
80	26	30	18	4	2
320	90	133	63	26	8
1280	391	490	284	73	42
5120	1592	2000	1112	264	152

A sheet is regarded as acceptable by a customer if it has less than three bubbles. Calculate rf_n(acceptable sheet) at the various stages, and again provide a graphic account of the stability of the relative frequency of this event, as in Fig. 2–2.

2. Can you think of a familiar experiment for which it is possible to carry out repetitions quickly? If so, perform a number of repetitions, record the outcome of each, compute the relative frequency of some event at various stages (say after 10, 20, 30, 40, ... repetitions), and see whether there is any tendency for this relative frequency to stabilize. If not, consider the simple experiment of throwing a drawing pin (thumbtack) on to the floor and recording whether it lands with the point facing up or with the point in contact with the floor. Twenty or even more repetitions of this experiment can be quickly performed by throwing twenty pins at once. The relative frequency rf_{20} (point up) can then easily be recorded and twenty further repetitions carried out.

2–4   RECORD SET

The first aspect of the real world that it is necessary to translate is the experimenter's ability to observe the outcome or result of his experiment. The experimenter uses a measuring or recording instrument suited to the determination of the outcome of his experiment; he does not use a clinical thermometer to record the boiling point of water. We too must be in such a position with our model. We require therefore a representation or symbol for each single logically possible outcome of the experiment. Each such symbol will be called a *simple record* and the set of all such simple records constitutes the *record set*.

Each performance of the experiment yields an outcome which is represented by some one simple record, say x, in the record set X. For an experiment that determines whether or not an individual responds to a stimulus, a suitable record set is $X = \{n, r\}$, where the simple record n represents the outcome "the individual does not respond" and the simple record r represents the outcome "the individual responds." An alternative record set for this experiment, and one more suited as a building unit for more complicated models which count the number of responses in repetitions, is $X = \{0, 1\}$, where the simple record 0 represents no response and 1 represents a (or one) response. For an experiment that determines the number of defective items in a sample of twenty items we can clearly use a record set $X = \{0, 1, 2, \ldots, 20\}$; the symbol or simple record 5, for example, represents the outcome "exactly five items are found to be defective."

We have deliberately chosen the term "record set" to replace the more commonly used "sample space." Our reason for this choice is that "record set" conveys better the intended purpose of this component of our model. A record set is merely a set of symbols that the experimenter can use in a natural way to record the result of his experiment in a notebook. Sample space, on the other hand, carries with it a connotation of sampling of specimens from a population of objects, and there may be no concrete sampling process nor actual population in the practical setting. From what *actual* population is a reading on a thermometer placed in water boiling at atmospheric pressure?

2–4–1 Definition *Record set, simple record.* A *record set* for a model of an experiment is a set of symbols, called *simple records*, each symbol representing a single, logically possible outcome of the experiment, and each such possible outcome being represented by a unique simple record.

EXERCISES

1. Suggest suitable record sets for the following experiments associated with the problems of Chapter 1.

   a) Testing an item and classifying it as effective or defective (Problem 1, Section 1–4).
   b) Recording the value of the output in a trial operation with the new equipment (Problem 2, Section 1–4).
   c) Observing the symptom combination of a machine at time of breakdown (Problem 3, Section 1–5).
   d) Determining the steroid level for a baby (Problem 4, Section 1–5).
   e) Examining every item in the batch and determining the number of defectives in it (Problem 5, Section 1–6).
   f) Counting the number of positive reactions in the three repetitions of the test on an organism (Problem 6, Section 1–7).
   g) Observing the number of successes in n treatment applications (Problem 7, Section 1–8).

2. The proof of a page of a book of tables contains 400 five-digit numbers, arranged in 50 rows of 8 each. Provide suitable record sets for the "experiments" of determining

   a) the number of misprinted digits on the proof,
   b) the number of misprint-free rows on the proof,
   c) the location of the first wrong number (if any) on the page.

3. A psychologist designs two aptitude tests; in the first the subject may score 0, 1, 2, 3, or 4 marks, in the second 0, 1, 2, or 3 marks. Show that a suitable record set for the experiment of examining a subject consists of 20 points on a lattice in the (x_1, x_2)- or (x, y)- plane, the first coordinate representing the score in the first test, the second the score in the second test.

   Identify which of the 20 simple records correspond to
   a) a total score of exactly 4,
   b) a total score of at least 3,
   c) a result with at least one of the scores at least 2.

2–5 EVENTS AND RECORDS

Often we are not so much interested in a particular outcome as in whether it implies some wider event, that is, in whether the outcome belongs to a specific set of outcomes. To a manufacturer who is following the rule "destroy the batch if the sample of 20 items contains more than two (i.e., 3 or 4 or ... or 20) defectives," the event E, "there are more than two defectives," is what matters and the outcome "there are exactly four defectives" is interesting only because it implies this wider event. In terms of our model we thus see that the representation of this event is the subset $R = \{3, 4, \ldots, 20\}$ of X. We call such subsets of X *compound records* or, more briefly, *records*, and say that R is *observed* at a performance of the experiment if the outcome is represented by a simple record belonging to R. The record R is observed if and only if E occurs. The individual subsets $\{0\}, \{1\}, \ldots, \{20\}$ are themselves records consisting of one symbol and have conveniently been distinguished by the term simple records. The record set X itself is a record and is observed at every performance of the experiment.

Two events which are *mutually exclusive*, that is, cannot occur at a single performance of the experiment, must clearly be represented by records having no simple record in common. Such records are called *disjoint*. Thus "there is at most one defective" and "there are at least three defectives" are two mutually exclusive events; the corresponding disjoint records, $R_1 = \{0, 1\}$ and $R_2 = \{3, 4, \ldots, 20\}$, have no simple record in common.

A whole calculus of events and hence of records can be developed by the use of phrases such as "at least one of ...," "both ... and ...," "none of ...," applied to events, and by corresponding operations on their record representations. Only one such operation will be required here, the operation which translates such phrases as "or," "at least one of," "one or other of," applied to mutually exclusive events, say $E_1, E_2, \ldots$. The event "E_1 or E_2 or …" occurs at a performance of an experiment if one or other (at least one) of $E_1, E_2, \ldots$ occurs. If $R_1, R_2, \ldots$ are the corresponding records, then $R_1 + R_2 + \cdots$, the record representation of "E_1 or E_2 or …," is called the *sum* of $R_1, R_2, \ldots$, and consists of every symbol that belongs to one or other of $R_1, R_2, \ldots$. Corresponding to the mutually exclusive events

E_1:   the number of defectives is at most 3,
E_2:   the number of defectives is exactly 4,
E_3:   the number of defectives is between 5 and 7 (both inclusive),

we have

E_1 or E_2 or E_3:   there are at most 7 defectives.

The associated records are

$$R_1 = \{0, 1, 2, 3\}, \qquad R_2 = \{4\}, \qquad R_3 = \{5, 6, 7\},$$

$$R_1 + R_2 + R_3 = \{0, 1, \ldots, 7\}$$

(see Fig. 2–4).

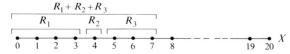

Fig. 2–4   Record set X for the sampling experiment with disjoint records R_1, R_2, R_3 and the record $R_1 + R_2 + R_3$.

We collect here the formal definitions of this section.

2–5–1 Definition   *Record.* A *record* is a subset of the record set and represents an event of the experiment. When the event occurs the record is *observed*.

2–5–2 Definition   *Disjoint records.* Two or more records are *disjoint* when no two of them have any simple records in common. Disjoint records represent mutually exclusive events.

2–5–3 Definition   *Sum of disjoint records.* Let $R_1, R_2, \ldots$ be disjoint records representing mutually exclusive events $E_1, E_2, \ldots$. The record $R_1 + R_2 + \cdots$, called the *sum* of $R_1, R_2, \ldots$, consists of all simple records that belong to one or other of $R_1, R_2, \ldots$, and is observed if one or other of $E_1, E_2, \ldots$ occurs.

EXERCISES

1. Suppose that in the screening of babies (Problem 4, Section 1–5) we regard as normal any baby with steroid level below 3, treat for metabolic disorder any baby with level

above 6, and retest all others by the examination of another specimen. With the record set constructed in Exercise 1(d), Section 2–4, for the screening of a single baby, identify the records $R_1, \ldots, R_4$ corresponding to the following events:

E_1:   the baby is classified as normal,
E_2:   the baby is retested,
E_3:   the baby is treated for the metabolic disorder,
E_4:   the baby is not treated.

Show that

a) R_1, R_2, R_3 are disjoint,
b) $R_1 + R_2 + R_3 = X$.

Would you regard as satisfactory any R_1, R_2, R_3 which did not satisfy these two properties?

Show that $R_4 = R_1 + R_2$.

2. A litter of eight hamsters has been born and it is proposed to examine them to determine how many of them are males. Construct a suitable record set for this experiment and identify the records $R_1, \ldots, R_5$ corresponding to the following events:

E_1:   there are exactly three males,
E_2:   there are at most two males,
E_3:   there are at most three females,
E_4:   no mating is possible within the litter,
E_5:   at least one mating is possible within the litter.

Illustrate these records as in Fig. 2–4.

Show that R_1, R_2 and R_3 are disjoint and that R_4 and R_5 are disjoint. What events correspond to $R_1 + R_2, R_4 + R_5$?

3. Note that the sets of simple records that you identified in Exercise 3, Section 2–4, are records corresponding to the stated events (a), (b), (c). Are any of these three records disjoint? Construct a record which has no simple records in common with any of these three records, and describe in words the associated event.

4. Which, if any, of the three record sets constructed in Exercise 2, Section 2–4, would satisfactorily allow you to represent the following events?

E_1:   the first misprint on the page occurs on the right-hand half of the page,
E_2:   there are at most two digit errors on the page,
E_3:   all the misprints occur in the first row of the page,
E_4:   all the misprints occur in the last column of the page.

5. A computation consists of six additions and five multiplications. Define a suitable record set for the experiment of checking the computation and noting the number of correct additions and the number of correct multiplications. Give a diagrammatic representation of this record set. Identify in your diagram the records $R_1, \ldots, R_5$ representing the following events:

E_1:   exactly three additions are correct,
E_2:   at least two multiplications are wrong,
E_3:   there is at least one correct operation of each type,
E_4:   the total number of correct operations is at most two,
E_5:   the total number of correct operations exceeds 10.

Show that R_4 and R_5 are disjoint, and describe in words the event corresponding to the record $R_4 + R_5$. Are any of the other nine possible pairs of records disjoint?

6. The definition of "E_1 or E_2" can be extended, with a corresponding operation on the associated sets R_1 and R_2, to the case of events E_1, E_2 which are not necessarily mutually exclusive. "E_1 or E_2" occurs at a performance of the experiment if at least one of E_1, E_2 occurs; the corresponding record, denoted by $R_1 \cup R_2$ and called the *union* of R_1 and R_2, consists of all the simple records that belong to either R_1 or R_2 or both. In Exercise 2 show that

$$R_2 \cup R_5 = \{0, 1, 2, \ldots, 7\}$$

and that "E_2 or E_5" can be described as "there are at most seven males."

Identify the records representing the events

a) E_3 or E_5,   b) E_1 or E_5,   c) E_1 or E_2,   d) E_1 or E_2 or E_4,

and describe these events in words.

7. A further operation on events and records can be defined. The event "E_1 and E_2" is said to occur at a performance of the experiment if E_1 and E_2 both occur at that performance. The corresponding record, denoted by $R_1 \cap R_2$ and called the *intersection* of R_1 and R_2, consists of all those simple records that are common to R_1 and R_2. In Exercise 2 show that

$$R_2 \cap R_5 = \{1, 2\}$$

and that "E_2 and E_5" can be described in words as "there are one or two males in the litter."

Identify the records corresponding to the events

a) E_3 and E_5,   b) E_1 and E_5,   c) E_1 and E_2,

and give word descriptions of these events.

2–6 SIMPLE PROPERTIES OF RELATIVE FREQUENCY

If E is some event associated with an experiment and the experiment is repeated n times, E occurring n_0 times, then $rf_n(E) = n_0/n$ is clearly one of the fractions $0/n, 1/n, \ldots, n/n$, and so

1. $rf_n(E)$ is a nonnegative number.

If we consider the uninteresting event "something or other happens" (whose set-representation is the record set X itself), then clearly since this event always occurs its relative frequency is n/n, so that

2. rf_n(something or other happens) $= 1$.

Consider now two mutually exclusive events E_1 and E_2 and suppose that in the n performances E_1 occurs n_1 times and E_2 occurs n_2 times, so that $rf_n(E_1) = n_1/n$, $rf_n(E_2) = n_2/n$. Now the event "E_1 or E_2" occurs $n_1 + n_2$ times (because of the mutually exclusive property), and so $rf_n(E_1$ or $E_2) = (n_1 + n_2)/n = n_1/n + n_2/n$. It follows from the obvious extension of this result to more than two mutually exclusive events that

3. if $E_1, E_2, \ldots$ are *mutually exclusive* events, then $rf_n(E_1$ or E_2 or $\ldots) = rf_n(E_1) + rf_n(E_2) + \cdots$.

EXERCISES

1. Twenty identical boxes, each containing six undamaged eggs, were sent in the mail. The number of damaged eggs in each box was recorded at the end of the journey as follows:

$$0, 0, 3, 2, 2, 0, 6, 1, 1, 1, 4, 5, 6, 0, 0, 1, 3, 3, 0, 0.$$

Calculate the relative frequencies of the following events in these 20 "experiments" of sending a box by post:

E_1: at most one egg is damaged,
E_2: exactly two eggs are damaged,
E_3: more than two, but not all, of the eggs are damaged,
E_4: at least three eggs are damaged,
E_5: an odd number of eggs is damaged.

Also calculate directly from the data the relative frequencies of "E_1 or E_2 or E_3" and of "E_1 or E_2 or E_4." Verify that

a) $rf(E_1$ or E_2 or $E_3) = rf(E_1) + rf(E_2) + rf(E_3)$,
b) $rf(E_1$ or E_2 or $E_4) = rf(E_1) + rf(E_2) + rf(E_4) = 1$,
c) $rf(E_3) < rf(E_4)$.

Explain the reasons for the value of 1 in (b).

2. (This exercise uses the definitions of Exercises 6 and 7, Section 2–5.) In Exercise 1, above, verify that

$$rf(E_3 \text{ or } E_5) < rf(E_3) + rf(E_5),$$

and explain why there is inequality rather than equality. Verify that

$$rf(E_3 \text{ or } E_5) = rf(E_3) + rf(E_5) - rf(E_3 \text{ and } E_5).$$

Do you consider that this last relation will hold for any two events?

3. Perform some experiment, of your own choosing, several times and record the outcomes. Choose a number of interesting events and investigate any relationships in the relative frequencies you compute for them.

2–7 REQUIREMENTS OF A PROBABILITY MODEL

To capitalize on the one stable aspect of nature we require in our model some counterpart of the concept of "number around which the relative frequency stabilizes in a long run of repetitions." It seems reasonable, therefore, to postulate that an appropriate model should contain, corresponding to each event E, some number, say $p(R)$, associated with the corresponding record R. Moreover, these numbers should be interrelated in the same way as the corresponding relative frequencies. Suppose therefore that we boldly adopt the following definition of a probability model.

2–7–1 Definition *Probability model.* We have a possible *probability model* for an experiment whenever we

a) specify a record set X,
b) assign to each record R (subset of X) a number $p(R)$, conveniently called the *probability* of R, such that

1. $p(R) \geq 0$, that is, a nonnegative number, for every R,
2. $p(X) = 1$,
3. for any sequence of *disjoint* records $R_1, R_2, \ldots$, $p(R_1 + R_2 + \cdots) = p(R_1) + p(R_2) + \cdots$.

The reader may at this stage be concerned that these seem slight requirements on the specification of a model, for it is clear that relative frequencies have interesting properties other than those in (1), (2), and (3) of Section 2–6. For example, if $\bar{E}$ is the event *complementary* to E, that is, if $\bar{E}$ occurs whenever E does not, then

$$rf_n(\bar{E}) = (n - n_0)/n = 1 - (n_0/n) = 1 - rf_n(E).$$

We would clearly require that the counterpart,

$$p(\bar{R}) = 1 - p(R), \tag{2–7–1}$$

should hold for the corresponding records R and $\bar{R}$, but we have made no provision for this in (1), (2), and (3) above. It can, however, be readily shown that Eq. (2–7–1) is a necessary *consequence* of (1), (2), and (3); for R and $\bar{R}$ are disjoint and $R + \bar{R} = X$. Hence

$$p(R + \bar{R}) = p(R) + p(\bar{R}) \qquad \text{by (3),}$$

$$p(R + \bar{R}) = p(X) = 1 \qquad \text{by (2),}$$

and the result follows by equating the two expressions for $p(R + \bar{R})$. Indeed, other more involved requirements are equally deducible from (1), (2), and (3), which can be shown to form a minimum requirement.

The instruction or function p that specifies the probabilities attaching to all possible records is called a *probability measure* or *function*. (The reader who is unfamiliar with the general concept of a function should at this stage refer to the short section on this subject in Appendix 1.) Any specification of a record set X and an associated probability function p provides a possible description of the given experiment. Whether or not it is the true description is quite another matter; indeed in most situations there will usually be more than one possible model. The whole object of experimentation may well be simply to narrow down the field of possible models. Note that if we happen to be using the true model, then $p(R)$ corresponds to the relative frequency of its associated event E in the long run.

2–8 SPECIFICATION OF A PROBABILITY MODEL

If a record set X contains a large number of symbols, it would at first glance appear to require some skill to attach probabilities to all the records in such a way that (1), (2), and especially (3) of Definition 2–7–1 are satisfied. Fortunately, we can specify a model simply by attaching to each simple record x its probability $p(x)$ and then specifying, to conform with (3), that

$$p(R) = \sum_R p(x), \qquad (2\text{–}8\text{–}1)$$

the sum of all the $p(x)$ for which x is in R. (The Greek capital letter sigma Σ is a summation instruction. Here it simply instructs the reader to evaluate the formula or function that follows it for each x in the set shown as a suffix to Σ—for example, the set R in Σ_R—and to sum all these values. Further details are given in Appendix 2.) Instead of having to worry about (3) for all selections of disjoint records, we must ensure only the two simple requirements:

$$p(x) \geq 0 \quad \text{for every } x \text{ in } X, \qquad (2\text{–}8\text{–}2)$$

$$\sum_X p(x) = 1, \qquad (2\text{–}8\text{–}3)$$

the first ensuring that (1) is satisfied and the second that (2) is satisfied. A useful way of viewing this specification is to suppose that we have available, because of (2), a unit of probability plasticine and we attach to x an amount $p(x)$. To discover what we have specified to the record R, we then collect together and measure all the probability plasticine that has been placed on the symbols in R.

EXERCISES

1. a) Describe in words the events $\bar{E}_1, \bar{E}_3, \bar{E}_5$ of Exercise 1, Section 2–6, and verify in each case that the relationship

$$rf(\bar{E}) = 1 - rf(E)$$

holds.

b) Verify also that in Exercise 1, Section 2–6,

$$rf(E_4 \text{ and } E_5) = rf(E_4) - rf(E_4 \text{ and } E_5).$$

The model counterpart of this last relationship for any two records R_1, R_2 is

$$p(R_1 \cap \bar{R}_2) = p(R_1) - p(R_1 \cap R_2).$$

Can you deduce this property from properties (1), (2) and (3) of Definition 2–7–1(b)?

c) Find the records corresponding to $\overline{E_1 \text{ or } E_2}$ and to "$\bar{E}_1$ and $\bar{E}_2$" in Exercise 2, Section 2–5, and deduce that these are different ways of expressing the same event, and so

$$rf(E_1 \text{ or } E_2) = 1 - rf(\bar{E}_1 \text{ and } \bar{E}_2).$$

Is this a general relationship? If so, deduce its probability counterpart from properties (1), (2) and (3) of Definition 2–7–1(b).

2. The relationship of Exercise 2, Section 2–6, suggests that the property

$$p(R_1 \cup R_2) = p(R_1) + p(R_2) - p(R_1 \cap R_2)$$

should hold for any records R_1, R_2. By expressing R_1 as the sum of the disjoint records $R_1 \cap R_2$ and $R_1 \cap \bar{R}_2$, or otherwise, deduce it from properties (1), (2) and (3) of Definition 2–7–1(b).

2–9 EXAMPLES OF PROBABILITY MODELS

Let us consider how we may specify a probability model for the experiment of recording whether or not a subject responds to a stimulus. To each simple record 0 (no response) and 1 (response), we must attach nonnegative numbers $p(0)$ and $p(1)$ such that $p(0) + p(1) = 1$. Thus we can easily specify a number of possible models as in Table 2–1. We emphasize that all of these models are possible. Which, if any, is the correct one will depend on how nature is actually operating. The object of experimenting—for example, of applying insecticide to an insect—will almost certainly be to attempt to determine which model is the most reasonable. Indeed, there is obviously here a whole class of possible models; for we clearly obtain a possible model if we take any number s in the interval $0 \leq s \leq 1$, which we shall denote briefly by S, and assign probability s

TABLE 2–1

Possible models for stimulus experiment

Model	Probability function	x	
		0	1
1	$p_1(x)$	0.5	0.5
2	$p_2(x)$	1	0
3	$p_3(x)$	0.246	0.754

to the simple record 1 and $1 - s$ to the simple record 0. There are as many possible models as there are numbers s in S. In the present example the symbol s acts as an *index* for the labeling of the models of the class, and the complete set of indexes may be called the *index set S*.

Since we shall often have to consider such classes, it is important to be able to identify which particular model is being referred to at any stage of our analysis. It is therefore sensible to introduce the indexing into the notation to show clearly the particular model referred to. It is possible to use a suffix notation such as p_s to achieve this, but a more convenient way, from the viewpoint of later developments, is to display the index within the parentheses containing the simple record, separating the simple record and the index by a vertical bar. Thus the model corresponding to the index s specifies probabilities for the simple records of its record set $X = \{0, 1\}$ by

$$p(0 \mid s) = 1 - s, \qquad p(1 \mid s) = s.$$

The vertical bar may be read as "for given." Thus $p(1 \mid s)$ is read "the probability of observing 1 (response) for given s." The probability functions for models 1, 2, 3 of the table are then written as $p(\cdot \mid 0.5)$, $p(\cdot \mid 0)$, $p(\cdot \mid 0.754)$, where the dot indicates that we can substitute either 0 or 1 into the function.

Another useful descriptive term for s is "state of nature"; for example, in the insecticide experiment the probability s of a kill is a property of the insect–insecticide confrontation, a state of nature. Instead of asking the question, "Which of a class of possible models is the true one, the one with which nature operates?" we can equivalently ask, "Which is the correct index or state of nature?"

We now recognize that we may regard the two rows in Table 1–4 as the specifications of the two possible probability models for the experiment of determining the steroid level of a baby. Here we may take as record set $X = \{1, 2, \ldots, 8\}$, the eight simple records representing the eight possible steroid levels. There are just two possible indexes, say s_1 and s_2 corresponding to the states of nature "the baby is normal" and "the baby is abnormal," and so the index set is $S = \{s_1, s_2\}$. The first row of the table then gives the probability function $p(\cdot \mid s_1)$—for example, $p(1 \mid s_1) = 0.05$, $p(2 \mid s_1) = 0.35$, $p(3 \mid s_1) = 0.45$— and the second row the probability function $p(\cdot \mid s_2)$—for example, $p(4 \mid s_2) = 0.07$. If we are asked for the probability that a normal baby has steroid level 3 or less, our attention is immediately directed toward the record $R = \{1, 2, 3\}$ and the index s_1 (since a normal baby is under consideration). We thus compute the required probability as

$$p(R \mid s_1) = \sum_R p(x \mid s_1)$$
$$= p(1 \mid s_1) + p(2 \mid s_1) + p(3 \mid s_1)$$
$$= 0.05 + 0.35 + 0.45$$
$$= 0.85.$$

EXERCISES

1. An experiment has record set $X = \{0, 1, 2, 3\}$. Which of the following specifications are possible probability models?

Probability function	x			
	0	1	2	3
$p_1(x)$	0.16	0.35	0.42	0.07
$p_2(x)$	0.21	0.27	0.31	0.15
$p_3(x)$	0.46	−0.23	0.41	0.36
$p(x\mid s)$ $(0 \le s \le 1)$	s^2	$\frac{1}{2}s(1-s)$	$\frac{3}{2}s(1-s)$	$(1-s)^2$

2. An ornithologist, after long and extensive study of nests of a certain species of bird, has suggested that the following is a suitable model to describe the variable number of nestlings per nest:

x	0	1	2	3	4	5	6	7
$p(x)$	0.02	0.05	0.10	0.23	0.32	0.19	0.08	0.01

Verify that this is a possible model for the experiment of determining the number of nestlings in a nest. What probabilities does it assign to the records R_1, R_2, R_3 representing the following events?

E_1: there are no nestlings,
E_2: there are at least two nestlings,
E_3: there are at least two and at most 5 nestlings.

A second ornithologist claims that a more appropriate model is the following:

x	0	1	2	3	4	5	6	7
$p(x)$	0.03	0.07	0.12	0.14	0.29	0.23	0.11	0.01

Which ornithologist assigns the higher probability to (a) R_2, (b) R_3?

3. A genetic theory suggests that a suitable model to describe the variability in the number of males in a litter of eight hamsters is the following:

x	0	1	2	3	4	5	6	7	8
$p(x)$	0.008	0.049	0.131	0.247	0.256	0.191	0.091	0.024	0.003

What are the probabilities associated with the five events of Exercise 2, Section 2–5?

A second theory based on the assumption that males and females are equally likely provides the following model:

x	0	1	2	3	4	5	6	7	8
p(x)	0.004	0.031	0.109	0.219	0.274	0.219	0.109	0.031	0.004

Which theory assigns the greater probability to the possibility of achieving a mating within the litter?

4. A company is trying to develop a satisfactory multicell battery and its investigations have involved determining the number x of active cells which remain at the end of six months of intensive use for each of a large number of batteries. These investigations suggest that for their eight-cell battery a suitable model is:

x	0	1	2	3	4	5	6	7	8
$p_1(x)$	0.01	0.03	0.04	0.06	0.11	0.17	0.22	0.30	0.06

and for their six-cell battery:

x	0	1	2	3	4	5	6
$p_2(x)$	0.08	0.09	0.10	0.16	0.23	0.19	0.15

The characteristics of these batteries are such that the eight-cell battery can be regarded as satisfactory only if at least five of its batteries remain active after this period, whereas only three are required to provide satisfaction with the six-cell battery. On these criteria of satisfactoriness, which battery ought the company to develop?

5. Organisms of two different types A and B are difficult to classify without extensive and expensive analysis. A quick and cheap test gives some hope of achieving at least a preliminary classification. It has been noted that organisms of type A have a greater tendency to give a positive reaction to the test than organisms of type B. It is decided to base the preliminary classification on the results of six such tests, and the models for the variability in the total number of positive reactions in the six tests for a type A and a type B organism are shown below.

Type of organism		x					
		0	1	2	3	4	5	6
A	$p_A(x)$	0.00	0.01	0.01	0.04	0.13	0.29	0.52
B	$p_B(x)$	0.62	0.18	0.10	0.05	0.03	0.01	0.01

What are the probabilities

a) that a type A organism gives at most three positive reactions?

b) that a type B organism gives more than three positive reactions?

A suggested rule for preliminary classification is to label as type *A* any organism which has more than three positive reactions, and otherwise to label it as *B*. What are the probabilities that such a rule

a) misclassifies a type *A* organism as *B*?
b) misclassifies a type *B* organism as *A*?

Find a rule which reduces this first probability of misclassification to 0.02. What is the consequent probability of misclassifying a type *B* organism as *A*?

6. Identify a class of probability models in Problem 3, Section 1–5. Introduce a suitable notation to specify these models clearly. Express and calculate in terms of this notation the "probabilities" that

a) an engine fault does not cause overheating,
b) only one symptom is displayed when a gearbox fault occurs.

CHAPTER 3

THE LANGUAGE OF UNCERTAINTY: TOWARDS FLUENCY

In Chapter 2 we saw that the basic syntax of the language of probability is exceedingly simple. Only three basic rules (Definition 2–7–1) are required, and of these the first two are almost trivial. In the present chapter we move towards greater fluency by learning how simple it is to piece together the basic elements to form more interesting constructions.

3–1 MODELS FOR COMPOUND EXPERIMENTS

The construction of the chemical formula of a complex compound by the linking together, according to simple combinatorial rules, of smaller molecular groupings is one very good example of the compounding of models. This facility of constructing a model of a complex situation by a suitable combination of models for component parts also plays a central role in the development of probability models.

We saw in Sections 2–8 and 2–9 that it is possible to limit the specification of probabilities to a subclass (namely the simple records) rather than use the whole class of records, and then to extend the specification to the whole class of records by way of property (3) of Definition 2–7–1. This method of model-building—specifying the probabilities of relatively few records and then extending to all other records directly by property (3), or by the consistency implications of property (3)—is extremely common. In fact, it might be said to pervade the whole art of probability model-building. How can we keep a grasp on a situation by specifying in some suitable form probabilities of records associated with only those aspects whose mechanism we feel we understand?

This feature of model-building is discussed in the next three sections, where we investigate the possibility of constructing a model for a compound experiment—that is, an experiment which can conveniently be regarded as some type of combination of more basic component experiments—in terms of the models associated with the component experiments.

3-2 UNRELATED OR INDEPENDENT EXPERIMENTS

An Illustrative Example Suppose that we have two experiments e_1 and e_2 unrelated in the sense that the outcome of one in no way affects the description of the other. For example, if e_1 is the determination of the number of defective fuses in a box of three from factory 1 and e_2 is the determination of the number of defective fuses in a box of two from some quite independent factory 2, we have two such independent experiments. Let us further suppose that we have already adopted or suggested the following models: for e_1 record set $X_1 = \{0, 1, 2, 3\}$ and probability function p_1, and for e_2 record set $X_2 = \{0, 1, 2\}$ and probability function p_2, as shown in Table 3–1. How then should we describe the compound experiment $e = (e_1, e_2)$ which determines the numbers of defectives in a pair of boxes, one from factory 1 and one from factory 2?

TABLE 3–1

	Model for e_1					Model for e_2		
x_1	0	1	2	3	x_2	0	1	2
$p_1(x_1)$	0.1	0.3	0.4	0.2	$p_2(x_2)$	0.2	0.5	0.3

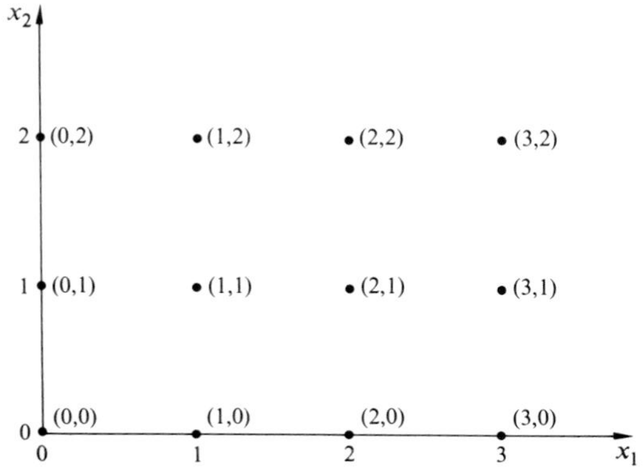

Fig. 3–1 The two-dimensional record set X of the compound experiment with components having record sets X_1 and X_2.

Record Set It is clear enough what the record set X for e must be if we wish to preserve the information about the quality of production in each factory. To record the outcome of e we must note the symbols representing the outcomes of e_1 and e_2 separately and in order. Thus a record set for e consists of all ordered pairs (x_1, x_2), where x_1 is a simple record from X_1 and x_2 is a simple record from X_2. This record set X for e can then be represented in the two-dimensional form of Fig. 3–1.

Probability Function The next question is: What is the appropriate way to spread the available unit of probability plasticine over the record set X? Here again we have to relate our postulate to the facts of experience.

Let us suppose that the compound experiment has been performed 20 times, each performance determining the quality of a pair of boxes, and that the simple records are

$$(0, 1), (3, 1), (1, 2), (1, 2), (2, 2), (2, 1), (0, 2), (2, 1), (1, 2), (1, 0),$$
$$(2, 1), (1, 1), (0, 1), (1, 1), (1, 0), (2, 1), (1, 0), (1, 1), (2, 1), (1, 2).$$

The first simple record, $(0, 1)$, indicates that in the first pair of boxes, that from factory 1 had no defective fuses and that from factory 2 had exactly one defective fuse. We can immediately calculate the relative frequency of any event associated with this compound experiment. For example,

rf_e(factory 1 box contains no defectives,

factory 2 box contains exactly one defective) $= \frac{2}{20}$,

since $(0, 1)$ appears twice in the 20 pairs. (Note that we have used the suffix e to make clear that the relative frequency refers to repetitions of the experiment e. Also, to avoid too cumbersome a notation, we have suppressed the dependence of relative frequency on n, the number of repetitions performed.)

The 20 performances of the compound experiment contain 20 performances of e_1 with simple records

$$0, 3, 1, 1, 2, 2, 0, 2, 1, 1, 2, 1, 0, 1, 1, 2, 1, 1, 2, 1,$$

the first symbols in each of the above pairs. We can therefore compute the relative frequency of any event associated with e_1 alone. For example,

rf_{e_1}(factory 1 box contains no defectives) $= \frac{3}{20}$.

Similarly, from the 20 induced performances of e_2 we have

rf_{e_2}(factory 2 box contains exactly one defective) $= \frac{11}{20}$.

Since the event "factory 1 box contains no defectives, factory 2 box contains exactly one defective" occurs at a performance of e when and only when the event "factory 1 box contains no defectives" occurs at the associated performance of e_1 and the event "factory 2 box contains exactly one defective" occurs at the associated performance of e_2, we might hope to find some connection between the three relative frequencies we have calculated. We note that the first relative frequency ($\frac{2}{20} = 0.1$) is roughly the same as the product ($\frac{3}{20} \times \frac{11}{20} = 0.0825$) of the other two relative frequencies. This prompts us to enquire whether this rough relationship tends to an equality as the number of repetitions increases.

It is an empirical fact that if we were to repeat the compound experiment n times—and so perform e_1 n times and e_2 n times, calculating rf_e (observing x_1, x_2 defectives) in the n performances of e, rf_{e_1} (observing x_1 defectives) in the n performances of e_1, and rf_{e_2} (observing x_2 defectives) in the n performances of e_2—then we would find that, for large n, rf_e (observing x_1, x_2 defectives) is close to

$$rf_{e_1}(\text{observing } x_1 \text{ defectives}) \times rf_{e_2}(\text{observing } x_2 \text{ defectives}).$$

(See Exercise 1, Section 3–2, for such evidence.) Since in our model-building probabilities are playing the counterparts of relative frequencies in long runs, we then obtain our probability function p for e by setting

$$p(x_1, x_2) = p_1(x_1)p_2(x_2) \tag{3-2-1}$$

as the probability attaching to the simple record (x_1, x_2) of the compound experiment. Then property (3) of Definition 2–7–1 ensures that we can calculate the probability attaching to any other record R through the summation

$$p(R) = \sum_R p(x_1, x_2); \tag{3-2-2}$$

that is, we add together the $p(x_1, x_2)$'s associated with all (x_1, x_2) belonging to R. For example, if interest is in the event "the total number of defective fuses is exactly 2," then the associated record is $R = \{(2, 0), (1, 1), (0, 2)\}$ and

$$p(R) = p(2, 0) + p(1, 1) + p(0, 2) \qquad \text{by (3–2–2)},$$

$$= p_1(2)p_2(0) + p_1(1)p_2(1) + p_1(0)p_2(2) \qquad \text{by (3–2–1)},$$

$$= (0.4 \times 0.2) + (0.3 \times 0.5) + (0.1 \times 0.3) \qquad \text{from Table 3–1},$$

$$= 0.26.$$

3–2–1 Definition *Product probability model.* Let e_1, e_2 be independent experiments, their models having record sets X_1, X_2 and probability functions p_1, p_2. The compound experiment which determines the outcomes of both experiments has the following *probability model*:

1. a record set X consisting of all (x_1, x_2) with x_1 in X_1 and x_2 in X_2 (this set is often called the *product set* $X_1 \times X_2$ of X_1 and X_2),
2. a probability p, formed as the *product function* of p_1 and p_2:

$$p(x_1, x_2) = p_1(x_1)p_2(x_2), \qquad (x_1 \text{ in } X_1, x_2 \text{ in } X_2).$$

The extension of Eq. (3–2–1) to the compounding of more than two independent experiments is obvious; for example,

$$p(x_1, x_2, x_3) = p_1(x_1)p_2(x_2)p_3(x_3) \qquad (3\text{–}2\text{–}3)$$

for three independent experiments. When the independent experiments are *n* repetitions of the same basic experiment, we use the term *n replicates* of the basic experiment.

Example The probabilities that a letter posted locally by first-class mail arrives by the first, second, third delivery the next day are 0.7, 0.2, 0.1, whereas the corresponding probabilities for a letter sent by second-class mail are 0.3, 0.5, 0.2. Two letters are posted independently, one by first-, and one by second-class mail. What are the probabilities that

1. the first-class letter arrives before the second-class letter,
2. at least one of the letters does not arrive by the first delivery?

Three letters are posted independently by second-class mail. What is the probability that all three letters arrive by the same delivery?

Solution. The experiments e_1 and e_2, which separately determine the deliveries of the first- and second-class letters, have the models shown in Table 3–2.

TABLE 3-2

Model for e_1				Model for e_2			
x_1 (no. of delivery)	1	2	3	x_2 (no. of delivery)	1	2	3
$p_1(x_1)$	0.7	0.2	0.1	$p_2(x_2)$	0·3	0·5	0.2

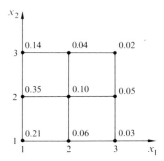

Fig. 3–2 Record set for the deliveries of a first- and second-class letter, with probabilities shown beside each simple record. Check that the sum of these probabilities is 1.

The record set X for $e = (e_1, e_2)$ is shown in Fig. 3–2, and the probabilities calculated by (3–2–1) are attached to the points (x_1, x_2). For example, $p(1, 2) = p_1(1)p_2(2) = 0.7 \times 0.5 = 0.35$.

1. The event of interest here has associated record

$$R_1 = \{(1, 2), (1, 3), (2, 3)\}$$

and the probability attached to this record is easily computed from Fig. 3–2 to be

$$p(R_1) = 0.35 + 0.14 + 0.04 = 0.53.$$

2. Let R_2 denote the record associated with this second event. Since the complementary event (Section 2–7) is "both letters arrive by the first delivery," we have $\bar{R}_2 = \{(1, 1)\}$. Then, by (2–7–1), we have

$$p(R_2) = 1 - p(\bar{R}_2) = 1 - 0.21 = 0.79.$$

For the three-letter problem we have three replicates of the basic experiment e_2. The simple records are then triplets of numbers, recording the deliveries of the first, second and third letters; for example, $(2, 2, 1)$ represents the outcome "the first and second letters both arrive by the second delivery and the third letter by the first delivery." The record representing the event "all three letters arrive by the same delivery" consists of the simple records $(1, 1, 1)$, $(2, 2, 2)$, $(3, 3, 3)$. The probability assigned to each of these simple records can then be found by (3–2–3) as products of associated probabilities of the basic experiment:

$$p(1, 1, 1) = p_2(1)p_2(1)p_2(1)$$
$$= 0.3 \times 0.3 \times 0.3 = 0.027,$$
$$p(2, 2, 2) = 0.5 \times 0.5 \times 0.5 = 0.125,$$
$$p(3, 3, 3) = 0.2 \times 0.2 \times 0.2 = 0.008.$$

The probability associated with the compound event is then obtained by addition analogous to (3–2–2):

$$0.027 + 0.125 + 0.008 = 0.160.$$

EXERCISES

1. Left-hand and right-hand gloves are mass-produced by independent operations of independent machines and are paired as they are produced. From records of 6400 such pairs, the total numbers of defective left-hand gloves, of defective right-hand gloves, and of pairs with both hands defective were determined at various stages as follows:

Number of pairs produced	100	200	400	800	1600	3200	6400
Number with defective left-hand glove	7	20	61	102	210	429	860
Number with defective right-hand glove	9	14	42	96	166	339	681
Number with both gloves defective	2	5	8	15	29	49	92

Compute rf(left-hand defective), rf(right-hand defective), and rf(both hands defective) at each stage, and investigate the closeness of

$$rf\text{(both hands defective)}$$

and

$$rf\text{(left-hand defective)} \times rf\text{(right-hand defective)}.$$

2. Two experiments e_1 and e_2 are independent and have models as specified in the following table:

Model for e_1					Model for e_2						
x_1	0	1	2	3	x_2	0	1	2	3	4	5
$p_1(x_1)$	0.4	0.3	0.2	0.1	$p_2(x_2)$	0.16	0.25	0.34	0.13	0.08	0.04

Represent the record set of the compound experiment (e_1, e_2) in diagrammatic form as in Fig. 3–1, attaching to each simple record its appropriate probability as assigned by (3–2–1). Identify the records of the compound experiment representing the following events and compute by (3–2–2) their probabilities:

E_1: the sum of the two results is exactly 4,
E_2: the sum of the two results is at most 7,
E_3: the result of e_1 is 1,
E_4: the difference in the two results is at least 1,
E_5: neither result exceeds 2,
E_6: at least one result is under 2.

3. One factory process produces packs of four nuts and a second unrelated process packs of four bolts. The number of defective bolts and of defective nuts varies from pack to pack, and past experience has established that reasonable models for the description of these variable numbers are as follows:

Nuts					Bolts				
x_1	0	1	2	3	4	x_2	0	1	2	3	4
$p_1(x_1)$	0.77	0.13	0.06	0.03	0.01	$p_2(x_2)$	0.82	0.08	0.05	0.03	0.02

A pack of nuts and a pack of bolts are taken from the two processes. What are the probabilities

a) that there are more defective nuts than bolts?
b) that two, and only two, satisfactory nut-bolt combinations can be effected?
c) that the number of uncombinable items is at most 1?

4. A married couple makes a proposal for a policy to an insurance company. From the company's life tables the actuary derives the following probability models to describe the variability in the duration of life of men and women of the ages of the proposers.

Year of policy	Probability that death occurs	
	Husband	Wife
First	0.05	0.02
Second	0.07	0.04
Third	0.08	0.04
Subsequent	0.80	0.90

For the quotation of suitable premiums for suggested policies the actuary is interested in the following eventualities:
a) both husband and wife survive three years of the policy;
b) the husband predeceases his wife within three years of the policy;
c) at least one dies within two years of the policy.

Settlement is made where necessary at the end of the year, and the actuary assumes that husband and wife mortalities are independent. What probabilities does he assign?

5. In a model for the spread of a certain disease an epidemiologist supposes that a carrier has probability s of infecting any one contact, and that contacts react independently of each other. Show that the total number of infections among two contacts of a single carrier is 0, 1, 2 with probabilities $(1 - s)^2, 2s(1 - s), s^2$, and that the total among three contacts of a single carrier is 0, 1, 2, 3 with probabilities $(1 - s)^3, 3s(1 - s)^2, 3s^2(1 - s), s^3$.

6. The first ornithologist of Exercise 2, Section 2–9, sets out one morning with the intention of finding at least ten nestlings. What probability does he assign to the achievement of this objective with two nestfuls?

The second ornithologist hopes that in two nestfuls he will be able to find not only at least ten nestlings altogether but also at least four from each nest. What probability does he attach to this hope?

7. Organisms of two types A and B behave differently in their reaction (positive or negative) to a test, A having probability 0.7 and B probability 0.2 of showing a positive reaction. For a second independent test these probabilities are 0.8 and 0.4.

a) For a type A organism subjected to both tests, what is the probability of at least one positive reaction?

b) For a type *B* organism submitted to both tests, what is the probability of no positive reaction?

c) If a type *A* organism is subjected to the first test only and a type *B* organism to the second test only, what is the probability that they both show the same reaction?

3–3 SEQUENTIAL EXPERIMENTS

Consider now two experiments performed in sequence to form a compound experiment, where the experiment performed at the second stage depends on the outcome of the first stage. For example, the first-stage experiment may be the setting up of a page of type and the making of x_1 unmarked errors, and the second experiment the reading of the page and the detecting of x_2 of these unmarked errors. Another example is found in a view of the natural propagation of seeding plants as a two-stage process. The formation of x_1 seeds by a plant constitutes the first stage; the second stage then consists of observing how many (x_2 say) of these x_1 seeds find suitable conditions and germinate. Any description of the second-stage experiment depends crucially on how many seeds are formed at the first stage.

An Illustrative Example We shall use a simple illustrative example to make concrete some of the concepts of model-building for such two-stage experiments. Suppose that a factory process produces boxes of two items, the number of effective items in a box being 0, 1, 2 with probabilities 0.1, 0.3, 0.6; the production of a box forms the first stage of our two-stage experiment. If we take as record set $X_1 = \{0, 1, 2\}$, we have the model shown in Table 3–3, where the subscript 1 in the probability function p_1 indicates its association with the first-stage experiment.

TABLE 3–3

Model for first-stage experiment: $p_1(x_1)$

x_1 (no. of effectives)	0	1	2
$p_1(x_1)$	0.1	0.3	0.6

At the second stage one item is chosen at random from the box produced and a test is performed to determine whether or not the item is effective. There are thus three possibilities at this second stage. The first stage may have produced a box with

1. no effectives ($x_1 = 0$), in which case the outcome of the second-stage experiment will certainly be a defective;

2. one effective ($x_1 = 1$), and then the second stage yields a defective or effective with probabilities $\frac{1}{2}$ and $\frac{1}{2}$;
3. two effectives ($x_1 = 2$), the only possible outcome of the second-stage experiment then being an effective item.

There is thus for the second-stage experiment a class of possible models. Since the actual model operating at the second stage is completely determined by the x_1 observed at the first stage, we can use x_1 as an index (recall Section 2–9) for this class of second-stage models. Following the indexing notation of Section 2–9 and its use of the vertical bar, we can denote the probability function for the second-stage experiment, following x_1 at the first stage, by $p_2(\cdot \mid x_1)$. The subscript 2 attached to p_2 is a reminder that we are dealing with the second-stage experiment. If we use the symbol 0 to represent a defective (no effectives) and 1 to represent an effective at this second stage, we can take $X_2 = \{0, 1\}$ as the record set for each of the possible second-stage models. At first sight this may seem nonsensical, since a first-stage production of a box with no effectives rules out the possibility of observing 1 at the second stage. This can be accommodated, however, by the simple device of attaching zero probability to the second-stage simple record 1 when the index $x_1 = 0$. Thus we can conveniently use the same record set for all second-stage models.

The models for the second-stage experiment can then be arranged formally as in Table 3–4, each row providing one of the three possible models.

TABLE 3–4

Models for second-stage experiment:
$p_2(x_2 \mid x_1)$

x_1	x_2		Row sums
	0	1	
0	1	0	1
1	$\frac{1}{2}$	$\frac{1}{2}$	1
2	0	1	1

For this sampling experiment it has been very natural to build up a description in terms of two stages that take place in sequence, and in terms of models appropriate to the separate stages. Our subsequent interest may direct attention to some other aspect; for example, we may wish to obtain only an effective item at the second stage, regardless of how it has arisen.

The Compound Experiment As a step in this direction we first study what model should be used to describe the two-stage experiment as a whole, that is, as a compound experiment determining the number of effectives in the box and then the nature of the item selected. To record this information we would merely set down (x_1, x_2), and so the record set is formed from X_1 and X_2 as in the product model of Section 3–2.

What probability function p should be used to assign probabilities $p(x_1, x_2)$ to the simple records (x_1, x_2) of the compound experiment in a meaningful way? For guidance we again examine the properties of relative frequencies in repetitions of the compound experiment. Suppose that the two-stage experiment has been performed 12 times and that the resulting simple records are

$$(1, 0), (2, 1), (2, 1), (2, 1), (1, 1), (1, 0),$$

$$(0, 0), (2, 0), (0, 0), (2, 1), (1, 0), (2, 1).$$

Since $(1, 0)$ appears three times in these 12 repetitions we have

$$rf \text{(box contains one effective, sampling gives defective)} = \tfrac{3}{12}. \qquad (3\text{–}3\text{–}1)$$

In these 12 repetitions the first-stage experiment is performed 12 times with simple records

$$1, 2, 2, 2, 1, 1, 0, 2, 0, 2, 1, 2,$$

and the first-stage event "box contains one effective" has thus relative frequency $\tfrac{4}{12}$. We write

$$rf_1 \text{(box contains one effective)} = \tfrac{4}{12}, \qquad (3\text{–}3\text{–}2)$$

the subscript 1 again emphasizing that only the first-stage experiment is involved. Also in the 12 repetitions of the compound experiment the second-stage experiment which follows $x_1 = 1$ is performed four times with simple records

$$0, 1, 0, 0,$$

and so the relative frequency of a defective in those four experiments is $\tfrac{3}{4}$. We can express this in the form

$$rf_2 \text{(sampling gives defective} \mid \text{box contains one effective)} = \tfrac{3}{4}, \qquad (3\text{–}3\text{–}3)$$

where the subscript 2 indicates that we are referring to the second stage and the condition after the vertical bar that we are considering only performances of the second stage indexed by $x_1 = 1$.

The relative frequency (3–3–1) associated with the compound experiment is equal to the product of the other two relative frequencies (3–3–2) and (3–3–3). The reader should have no difficulty in seeing that this is a general result for events related in the above way. Since probabilities play the counterpart of relative frequencies in our models, and, in particular, $p_1(1)$ corresponds to

(3–3–2), $p_2(0 \mid 1)$ to (3–3–3), and $p(1, 0)$ to (3–3–1), we can set

$$p(1, 0) = p_1(1)p_2(0 \mid 1).$$

The generalization of this relationship suggests the following definition.

3–3–1 Definition *Two-stage model.* Let the model for the first stage of a two-stage experiment have record set X_1 and probability function p_1; and let the model for the second-stage experiment following x_1 have record set X_2 and probability function $p_2(\cdot \mid x_1)$. Then the *two-stage model* of the compound experiment which records (x_1, x_2) has the same "product" record set as in Definition 3–2–1 and a probability function p specifying probabilities of simple records (x_1, x_2) by

$$p(x_1, x_2) = p_1(x_1)p_2(x_2 \mid x_1) \qquad (x_1 \text{ in } X_1, x_2 \text{ in } X_2). \qquad (3\text{–}3\text{–}4)$$

Here again we have simply specified the probabilities associated with the simple records; it is then an easy problem in probability calculus to determine the probability of any record of the compound experiment by summing $p(x_1, x_2)$ over the simple records constituting the record of interest. Interest is often centered on the second-stage experiment, for example, in the second-stage event "the sampled item is effective (regardless of the composition of the box)." The associated record of the compound experiment is then

$$\{(0, 1), (1, 1), (2, 1)\},$$

and so has probability

$$p(0, 1) + p(1, 1) + p(2, 1) = p_1(0)p_2(1 \mid 0) + p_1(1)p_2(1 \mid 1) + p_1(2)p_2(1 \mid 2)$$

$$= (0.1 \times 0) + (0.3 \times \tfrac{1}{2}) + (0.6 \times 1) = 0.75 \qquad (3\text{–}3\text{–}5)$$

from Tables 3–3, 3–4.

Second-Stage Marginal Experiment Our understanding of the mechanism of the experiments is often such that it is natural to think of the sequential description, the compound description or the "marginal" second-stage description being derived from this. In particular, we see that the derivation (3–3–5) generalizes to give the "marginal" probability $p_2(x_2)$ of observing x_2 at the second stage (regardless of what has taken place in the first-stage experiment):

$$p_2(x_2) = \sum_{X_1} p_1(x_1)p_2(x_2 \mid x_1), \qquad (3\text{–}3\text{–}6)$$

where the summation instruction is to compute the product that follows for each x_1 in X_1 (for the given x_2) and then to add these products.

Probability Trees The whole two-stage process can be illustrated by a probability-tree diagram (see Fig. 3–3), with the $p_1(x_1)$ probabilities placed on the

First-stage experiment   Second-stage experiment

$p_1(x_1)$ x_1 $p_2(x_2|x_1)$ x_2

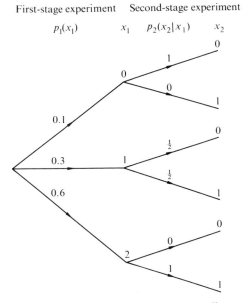

Fig. 3–3 Probability tree for the two-stage sampling experiment.

appropriate branches spreading from the first node on the left. From each node in the second position emanates one branch for each simple record of the second-stage experiment, and the probabilities placed on these branches are the probabilities associated with the appropriate second-stage model. The advantages of this visual display are that the logical relationships are seen at a glance, and that the summation instruction (3–3–6) has a simple verbal expression: To compute $p_2(x_2)$, take each route leading to x_2 at the second stage, multiply together the probabilities associated with each route, and then add these products. The reader should verify the particular result (3–3–5) by this graphic method.

Example Suppose that the first-stage experiment is the observing of the division of a cell, which has probabilities 0.2, 0.3, 0.5 of producing 0, 1, or 2 cells of the first generation. Suppose that then cells of the first generation are independently subjected to a dose of radiation, each cell having probability 0.4 of surviving. What are the probabilities that from one parent cell, the number of first-generation cells surviving radiation is 0, 1, or 2?

Solution. Here $X_1 = \{0, 1, 2\}$ with $p_1(0) = 0.2$, $p_1(1) = 0.3$, $p_1(2) = 0.5$: We can arrange the three probability-density functions $p_2(\cdot | 0)$, $p_2(\cdot | 1)$, $p_2(\cdot | 2)$ for the second-stage experiment in tabular form, as shown in Table 3–5. Equivalently, we can represent the two stages by a probability tree (Fig. 3–4).

TABLE 3–5

$p_1(x_1)$ and $p_2(x_2 \mid x_1)$

x_1	$p_1(x_1)$	$p_2(x_2 \mid x_1)$ x_2		
		0	1	2
0	0.2	1	0	0
1	0.3	0.6	0.4	0
2	0.5	0.36	0.48	0.16

The first two rows of Table 3–5 have an obvious derivation. The final row requires some explanation. If there are two cells of the first generation ($x_1 = 2$) then the second-stage radiation experiment may be regarded as two replicates of the more basic experiment: submit a cell to radiation and record whether

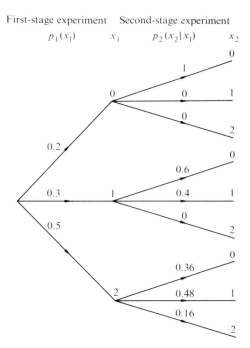

Fig. 3–4 Probability tree for the two-stage cell-division experiment.

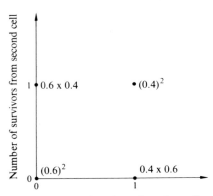

Fig. 3–5 Product model for description of survivors from two cells submitted to radiation. The probabilities attaching to the four simple records (0, 0), (1, 0), (0, 1), (1, 1) are shown.

it survives (success) or dies (failure). The product model for independent experiments considered in the preceding section then applies (see Fig. 3–5) and we have for the probabilities of a total of 0, 1, 2 successes in this second-stage experiment

$$p_2(0 \mid 2) = (0.6)^2, \qquad p_2(1 \mid 2) = 2(0.4)(0.6), \qquad p_2(2 \mid 2) = (0.4)^2.$$

Hence, from either (3–3–6) or the probability-tree rule,

$$p_2(0) = (0.2 \times 1) + (0.3 \times 0.6) + \{0.5 \times (0.6)^2\} = 0.56,$$

$$p_2(1) = (0.2 \times 0) + (0.3 \times 0.4) + \{0.5 \times 2(0.6)(0.4)\} = 0.36,$$

$$p_2(2) = (0.2 \times 0) + (0.3 \times 0) + \{0.5 \times (0.4)^2\} = 0.08.$$

EXERCISES

1. The first stage of a two-stage experiment consisted in recording the number of eggs laid at one nesting by a blackbird, and the second stage in recording the number of these eggs that hatched. The following are the records in the form (eggs laid, eggs hatched) for 20 nesting pairs:

$$(4, 3), (4, 4), (5, 2), (3, 2), (6, 4),$$
$$(6, 3), (4, 3), (4, 4), (4, 2), (4, 3),$$
$$(5, 3), (4, 4), (4, 1), (3, 3), (2, 2),$$
$$(5, 3), (4, 3), (4, 3), (6, 5), (4, 3).$$

Following the notation of this section, evaluate $rf(4$ eggs, 3 nestlings), $rf_1(4$ eggs), $rf_2(3$ nestlings $\mid 4$ eggs), and verify that these satisfy a relation similar to that of this section.

Verify also the following relative frequency counterpart of (3–3–6):

$$rf(3 \text{ nestlings}) = \sum_{x_1 = 3}^{6} rf_1(x_1 \text{ eggs})rf_2(3 \text{ nestlings} \mid x_1 \text{ eggs}).$$

2. The first stage of a two-stage experiment has model

x_1	0	1	2
$p_1(x_1)$	0.2	0.7	0.1

and the three possible second-stage experiments have the following models:

	$p_2(x_2 \mid x_1)$			
x_1	x_2			
	0	1	2	3
0	0.1	0.2	0.3	0.4
1	0.5	0.1	0.2	0.2
2	0.3	0.3	0.3	0.1

Construct the appropriate model for the compound experiment.

a) What is the probability that x_2 exceeds x_1?

b) What is the probability that $x_2 = 0$?

Construct the probability tree as in Fig. 3–3, and use it to confirm the value already obtained in (b) for the probability that $x_2 = 0$.

3. The proportion of males in a large island population is 0.48. Recent investigations suggest that the probability that a male will develop a certain eye defect is 0.2, whereas for a female the probability is 0.1. What proportion of the island population as a whole will develop the eye defect?

4. A load of raw material for a batch process can be of two qualities, Q_1 and Q_2, with probabilities 0.3 and 0.7. It has been realized that a batch processed from a load of quality Q_1 may be of grade 1 or 2 with probabilities 0.6 and 0.4, whereas a load of quality Q_2 leads to a batch of grade 1, 2, or 3 with probabilities 0.2, 0.3, 0.5. A load of unknown quality has just arrived.

a) What is the probability that it produces a batch of at least grade 2?

b) What is the probability that the load is of quality Q_1 and produces a batch of at least grade 2?

5. A physicist reckons that the probabilities associated with the emission of no, one, or two particles in an accelerator experiment are $\frac{1}{2}, \frac{1}{3}, \frac{1}{6}$. Any particles emitted behave independently after emission but are ephemeral, there being a probability of $\frac{3}{5}$ that

a particle will disin‘·grate before it can be observed. What are the probabilities that, in a single accelerator experiment,

a) two particles will be emitted but only one observed?

b) at least one particle will be observed?

6. A student reckons that the probability of passing an examination at the first attempt is 0.6. If he fails he is allowed to retake the examination six months later, and he estimates that, because of the extra time for study, his chance of passing the reexamination is 0.7. What probability does he assign to his passing the examination by the end of the second try?

   If he fails the second time, he is allowed a third attempt in another six months; in this he assesses his chance of success as again 0.7. What is the probability that he will have passed before or on the third attempt?

7. To guard against losses by evaporation a packer of cartons of nominal weight 100 gm ensures that each packet contains 103 gm at the time of packaging. An extensive study of the losses involved by the time a packet is sold suggests that the probabilities associated with losses of 0, 1, 2, 3, 4, 5, 6 gm are 0.10, 0.15, 0.25, 0.30, 0.10, 0.05, 0.05. On the assumption that the probabilities are 0.3, 0.2, 0.1 that a customer will check the weight of an underweight pack containing 97, 98, 99 gm, respectively, and that the corresponding probability for a pack of 100 gm or over is 0.05, what are the probabilities

   a) that an underweight pack will be detected?

   b) that a pack of satisfactory weight will be unnecessarily weighed?

   c) that a pack will be weighed whether unnecessarily or not?

   A new packaging process with probabilities 0.10, 0.15, 0.25, 0.32, 0.06, 0.06, 0.06 associated with losses of 0, 1, 2, 3, 4, 5, 6 gm is developed. How are the probabilities (a) through (c) affected?

3-4 EXPERIMENTS WITH TWO-DIMENSIONAL RECORDS

The information we wish to record from an experiment often cannot be represented by a single number but can be represented by, say, a pair of numbers (x_1, x_2); yet there is no obvious way to regard this experiment as a compound experiment, either with independent components or as two experiments carried out in sequence. For example, the experiment may determine the length and weight of some insect. This can certainly not be regarded as the compound experiment with independent component experiments e_1 and e_2 recording separately the length and weight, for clearly long insects will tend to be heavy insects. Nor is there any obvious reason why we should describe the recording of the two quantities in any sequential way.

For such experiments the reasonable way to set up a model is to specify a probability function on the two-dimensional record set X, that is, to specify for each simple record (x_1, x_2) the associated probability $p(x_1, x_2)$ in such a way that

$$\sum_X p(x_1, x_2) = 1.$$

Having constructed a model in this natural two-dimensional way, we may wish, because of the demands of applications, to seek an equivalent sequential version of the same model. To bring out the structure of this reformulation, let us study a simple illustrative example.

An Illustrative Example A survey of antique armchairs acquired by a firm of dealers has provided information on the proportions with x_1 undamaged arms and x_2 undamaged legs. Since the survey was large, we assume that the proportions essentially specify a probability function p on the obvious two-dimensional record set (see Table 3–6). One of the firm's carpenters, who

TABLE 3–6

Probability model for condition of antique armchairs

Number x_1 of undamaged arms	$p(x_1, x_2)$ Number x_2 of undamaged legs					Row sums, $p_1(x_1)$
	0	1	2	3	4	
0	0.01	0.02	0.03	0.07	0.10	0.23
1	0.02	0.03	0.08	0.14	0.13	0.40
2	0.03	0.05	0.10	0.12	0.07	0.37
Column sums, $p_2(x_2)$	0.06	0.10	0.21	0.33	0.30	1.00

undertakes the complete repair of all one-armed chairs (that is, chairs with exactly one undamaged arm and possibly damaged legs), asks the following two questions.

1. What proportion of the chairs acquired by the firm come my way?
2. What proportion of the chairs assigned to me have two undamaged legs?

The Marginal First-Stage Experiment Since the event "a chair is one-armed" is represented by the set of simple records $(1, 0)$, $(1, 1)$, $(1, 2)$, $(1, 3)$ $(1, 4)$, the answer to question 1 is immediate: We must sum the entries in the row $x_1 = 1$. We denote this probability by $p_1(1)$, the subscript 1 indicating that we are dealing only with the first of the two aspects, arms and legs. The three marginal row sums 0.23, 0.40, 0.37 add up to 1, so the function p_1 defined by this process is a probability function. If instead of recording the detail of (x_1, x_2) we perform the "marginal" experiment of recording only x_1, then this marginal experiment has model with record set $X_1 = \{0, 1, 2\}$ and probability function p_1.

3–4–1 Definition *Marginal experiment model.* If a model with two-dimensional records (x_1, x_2) is specified by a probability function p, then the *marginal experiment* which records x_1 only has probability function p_1 assigned by

$$p_1(x_1) = \sum_{x_2 \text{ in } X_2} p(x_1, x_2). \tag{3–4–1}$$

The Conditional Second-Stage Experiment The answer to question 2 is easily obtained if we imagine a large number N of chairs acquired by the firm. Of these, $0.40N$ will be one-armed and $0.08N$ will be one-armed and two-legged. Hence the required proportion is

$$\frac{0.08N}{0.40N} = \frac{0.08}{0.40}.$$

In terms of probabilities already specified, this ratio is $p(1, 2)/p_1(1)$ and if we set

$$p_2(2 \mid 1) = \frac{p(1, 2)}{p_1(1)} \tag{3–4–2}$$

we have essentially the relationship (3–3–4). The reason for this is that question 2 only arises if the marginal first-stage experiment yields a simple record $x_1 = 1$, and this automatically directs us to the concept of a "conditional" second-stage experiment following $x_1 = 1$. This explains our choice of notation, and (3–4–2) shows how the probability function $p_2(\cdot \mid 1)$ for the second-stage model can be computed. These ideas can be formalized in the following way.

3–4–2 Definition *Equivalent sequential two-stage model.* A model with two-dimensional records and probability function p can be regarded in a *sequential two-stage* way, the first stage experiment being as specified in Definition 3–4–1. The *conditional* second-stage experiment following x_1 then has the model with typical record x_2 and probability function $p_2(\cdot \mid x_1)$ given by

$$p_2(x_2 \mid x_1) = \frac{p(x_1, x_2)}{p_1(x_1)}. \tag{3–4–3}$$

For our example we can display the equivalent two-stage model in a table similar to Table 3–5 (see Table 3–7).

A Second Sequential Formulation We can also envisage applications in which the reorganization into a sequential model more naturally takes the recording of x_2 first. A carpenter who undertakes the repair of all three-legged chairs could pose the following questions.

1. What proportion of chairs acquired by the firm are assigned to me?
2. What proportion of the chairs assigned to me have two undamaged arms?

Following the earlier argument, and switching the roles of rows and columns

TABLE 3-7

$p_1(x_1)$ and $p_2(x_2 \mid x_1)$ for equivalent sequential two-stage model

x_1	$p_1(x_1)$	$p_2(x_2 \mid x_1)$ x_2				
		0	1	2	3	4
0	0.23	$\frac{1}{23}$	$\frac{2}{23}$	$\frac{3}{23}$	$\frac{7}{23}$	$\frac{10}{23}$
1	0.40	$\frac{2}{40}$	$\frac{3}{40}$	$\frac{8}{40}$	$\frac{14}{40}$	$\frac{13}{40}$
2	0.37	$\frac{3}{37}$	$\frac{5}{37}$	$\frac{10}{37}$	$\frac{12}{37}$	$\frac{7}{37}$

and subscripts 1 and 2, we answer the first question by computing

$$p_2(3) = \sum_{x_1 \text{ in } X_1} p(x_1, 3)$$

$$= \text{sum of the entries in column } x_2 = 3 \text{ in Table 3–6}$$

$$= 0.33,$$

and the second question by computing

$$p_1(2 \mid 3) = \frac{p(2, 3)}{p_2(3)} = \frac{0.12}{0.33} = \frac{4}{11}.$$

Formally we can express this sequential model in terms of the following definition.

3-4-3 Definition *Alternative equivalent two-stage model.* A model with two-dimensional record (x_1, x_2) and probability function p can be regarded as a sequential experiment with two stages defined in the following way:

1. a marginal (first-stage) experiment recording x_2 and with probability function p_2 given by

$$p_2(x_2) = \sum_{x_1 \text{ in } X_1} p(x_1, x_2), \tag{3-4-4}$$

2. a conditional (second-stage) experiment with typical simple record x_1 and probability function $p_1(\cdot \mid x_2)$ given by

$$p_1(x_1 \mid x_2) = \frac{p(x_1, x_2)}{p_2(x_2)}. \tag{3-4-5}$$

For our example the complete table for the marginal model and the conditional models corresponding to this sequential viewpoint can again be easily constructed (see Table 3–8).

TABLE 3–8

$p_2(x_2)$ and $p_1(x_1 \mid x_2)$ for alternative equivalent two-stage model

x_2	$p_2(x_2)$	$p_1(x_1 \mid x_2)$ x_1		
		0	1	2
0	0.06	$\frac{1}{6}$	$\frac{2}{6}$	$\frac{3}{6}$
1	0.10	$\frac{2}{10}$	$\frac{3}{10}$	$\frac{5}{10}$
2	0.21	$\frac{3}{21}$	$\frac{8}{21}$	$\frac{10}{21}$
3	0.33	$\frac{7}{33}$	$\frac{14}{33}$	$\frac{12}{33}$
4	0.30	$\frac{10}{30}$	$\frac{13}{30}$	$\frac{7}{30}$

An Important Relationship   Finally in this section we point out a relationship between the three tables that will play an important role in later chapters. We have seen that the sequential tables may be constructed from the original table. It is also true that the original table can be constructed from either of the sequential tables; this is merely an application of the compound model-building of Section 3–3. It follows that if we are given only one sequential table we can derive the other sequential table from it. Let us indicate briefly how this may be done. Suppose that only Table 3–7 is given. Then we can construct Table 3–6 by (3–4–3) or (3–3–4):

$$p(x_1, x_2) = p_1(x_1)p_2(x_2 \mid x_1);$$

for example,

$$p(1, 2) = p_1(1)p_2(2 \mid 1)$$

$$= 0.40 \times \tfrac{8}{40} = 0.08.$$

Then we obtain the sequential Table 3–8 from Table 3–6, as before.

EXERCISES

1. A library which allows its adult readers a maximum of three books at any one time has established from its records a model to describe the variability in the borrowing habits of married couples. The table below shows the probabilities associated with the possible pairs of numbers of books borrowed for weekend reading.
   What are the probabilities
   a) that a wife will borrow exactly three books?
   b) that at least one of the couple will have more than one book out?
   c) that the husband of a wife who has borrowed three books will have borrowed at least one book?

Number of books borrowed by husband	Number of books borrowed by wife			
	0	1	2	3
0	0.09	0.05	0.03	0.02
1	0.04	0.05	0.07	0.05
2	0.01	0.09	0.11	0.10
3	0.01	0.06	0.09	0.13

2. A psychologist classifies new entrants at age 20 into government service as potentially *clerical, executive,* or *administrative* material. From records of such forecasts and the eventual grade achieved by age 45, the following probability model for the (forecast, achievement) pattern is obtained.

Forecast	Achievement by age 45		
	Clerical	Executive	Administrative
Clerical	0.46	0.10	0.02
Executive	0.13	0.15	0.04
Administrative	0.05	0.03	0.02

What are the probabilities

a) that a new entrant will reach the administrative grade?

b) that a new entrant labeled as clerical material will reach the administrative grade?

c) that an employee now in the administrative grade was originally labeled as clerical or executive material?

3. The admissions office of a certain college wished to find a suitable indicator of students' overall performance in college. Using data on the scores students obtained in an exam given to all entering freshmen and on their cumulative averages at graduation, the college statistician found that the following model described the probabilities associated with various (entrance score, final cumulative average) combinations. (A student who does not have a C average or better at the end of his senior year does not receive a degree.)

Entrance score	Final cumulative average			
	A	B	C	Below C
5	0.07	0.13	0.02	0.01
4	0.06	0.11	0.02	0.01
3	0.05	0.10	0.03	0.02
2	0.04	0.09	0.05	0.03
1	0.02	0.05	0.05	0.04

What are the probabilities

a) that a student will have entrance score less than 3 and yet will obtain a degree?

b) that a student with entrance score 4 will do no better than obtain a C average?

c) that a student will obtain a B average?

d) that a student will have entrance score at least 3?

It is anticipated that, because of some excellent research work done within the college, the quality of applicants will improve, and that in the future new students will have scores 5, 4, 3, 2, 1 with probabilities 0.25, 0.35, 0.25, 0.10, 0.05. It is hoped that the standard of examination will remain as before, so that a student with a given entrance score will have the same opportunity of obtaining a certain average. Considering this anticipation and hope, can you measure in some suitable way the change in the structure of overall performance for the college?

4. Patients referred to a certain clinic have been classified according to age and whether or not they must immediately be admitted to the hospital, and the following probabilistic pattern describing the variability (in age, hospital requirement) has emerged.

Age in years	Hospital-bed requirement	
	Yes	No
≤ 70	0.16	0.34
> 70	0.24	0.26

What are the probabilities that a patient referred to the clinic

a) requires a hospital bed?

b) is over 70 years old?

What are the probabilities

c) that a patient over 70 requires a hospital bed?

d) that a patient just admitted to a hospital bed is over 70?

A new auxiliary clinic is to be opened for patients over 70, and it is anticipated that this will divert about one-half of the patients over 70 from the present clinic, though it will not alter the pattern of requirement for hospitalization of those still referred to it. What is the new probability that a patient referred to the old clinic will require a hospital bed?

5. For each of the following sequential models construct the alternative sequential model.

a)

x_1	$p_1(x_1)$	$p_2(x_2 \mid x_1)$	
		x_2	
		0	1
0	0.7	0.6	0.4
1	0.3	0.2	0.8

b)

x_2	$p_2(x_2)$	$p_1(x_1 \mid x_2)$			
		x_1			
		0	1	2	3
0	0.2	0.1	0.2	0.3	0.4
1	0.3	0.2	0.3	0.4	0.1
2	0.5	0.3	0.4	0.1	0.2

3–5 INDUCED EXPERIMENTS

For the purposes of model-building it may be natural and convenient to construct a full model of a compound experiment from component models, but often it is some particular aspect which is of interest rather than the detail we have built up in the compounding process.

An Illustrative Example Suppose that we have made an intensive study of the functioning of a certain type of component and have formed a picture of the variability in the lifetimes of specimens of such a component in the form of a probability model. (For simplicity, we assume that components do not fail in the middle of a day.)

TABLE 3–9

Probability model for lifetime of component

Lifetime (days)	0	1	2	3
Probability	0.1	0.2	0.4	0.3

To give a boost to the lifetime of a machine which uses this type of component, we may design the machine so that it has two independently produced components and that it uses only the first component until it fails (after lifetime x_1 say) and then automatically switches to the second component. If this second component has lifetime x_2, then the machine has lifetime $x_1 + x_2$. Our customers want information about the lifetime of the machine, not about the lifetimes of its individual components. Our problem is then the following: From our knowledge of the variability of the lifetimes of components, can we construct a model to describe the distribution of the lifetimes of the machines?

The Induced Experiment The model describing the variability of the two component lifetimes, the "basic" experiment which records (x_1, x_2), is simply the product model based on Table 3–9, (recall Section 3–2). This is presented diagrammatically in Fig. 3–6, which shows the probabilities attaching to the simple records. If instead of recording this detail (x_1, x_2) we imagine an "induced" experiment which records $x_1 + x_2$ only, what is the appropriate model for this induced experiment? What record set Y should be used and what probability function q introduced to assign bits of the available unit of probability plasticine to the simple records y in Y?

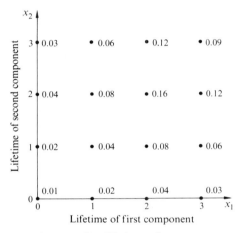

Fig. 3–6 Record set for recording lifetimes of two components of machine, with the probabilities associated with the simple records.

The Induced Experiment Record Set A suitable record set is easily determined. The possible lifetimes of the machine are 0, 1, 2, 3, 4, 5, 6 days, so we take $Y = \{0, 1, \ldots, 6\}$. Note that these simple records are the possible values of $x_1 + x_2$ as (x_1, x_2) varies through the basic record set X.

The Induced Experiment Probability Function It is just as easy to specify the probability function q. Consider the particular simple record $y = 2$ of the induced experiment. The machine has lifetime 2 days if and only if the component lifetimes (x_1, x_2) are $(2, 0)$, $(1, 1)$, or $(0, 2)$. Thus corresponding to the simple record $y = 2$ of the induced experiment, we have an associated record $R_2 = \{(2, 0), (1, 1), (0, 2)\}$ of the basic experiment. A simple record of the induced experiment is observed when and only when the associated record of the basic experiment is observed. Thus in repetitions of the basic experiment (and so of the induced experiment) the relative frequencies of associated record and corresponding simple record are equal, and so we set

$$q(2) = p(R_2) = p(2, 0) + p(1, 1) + p(0, 2)$$
$$= 0.04 + 0.04 + 0.04 = 0.12.$$

A similar argument can be adopted for the other simple records of Y. The steps can be set out in tabular form, as in Table 3–10. Beside each simple record y we can set its associated record R_y; then we obtain $q(y)$ by calculating the probability of the associated record in the basic model.

TABLE 3–10

Construction of model for lifetime of machine

y	Associated record R_y	$q(y)$
0	(0, 0)	0.01
1	(1, 0), (0, 1)	0.04
2	(2, 0), (1, 1), (0, 2)	0.12
3	(3, 0), (2, 1), (1, 2), (0, 3)	0.22
4	(3, 1), (2, 2), (1, 3)	0.28
5	(3, 2), (2, 3)	0.24
6	(3, 3)	0.09
		————
		1.00

We can visualize a physical channeling of the unit of probability plasticine from the record set X of the basic experiment to the record set Y of the induced experiment as follows. Suppose the plane of the page containing Fig. 3–7 is tilted until the plasticine on X slides down the guide lines, and accumulates on the appropriate simple records of Y. The quantity of plasticine so placed on a simple record y is the correct amount of $q(y)$.

We have met the idea of an induced experiment earlier. In our example on defective fuses (Section 3–2) we can think of the induced experiment which records the total number $x_1 + x_2$ of defective fuses in the two boxes rather than the detailed composition (x_1, x_2) of the two boxes. The record R discussed there is the associated record of the simple record 2 (the total number of defective fuses) of the induced experiment. In the illustrative example of Section 3–3 the recording of the number of effectives (0 or 1) arising from the combined process of production and sampling is another example. Instead of dealing with the detail (x_1, x_2) of the compound sequential experiment we are interested only in the aspect x_2. Indeed, we used there the term "associated record" in a natural way in our construction of $p_2(x_2)$, which can now be interpreted as the probability function of the induced marginal experiment.

The aspect of (x_1, x_2) that we examine should be relevant to the practical problem. In general, it will be some construct $t(x_1, x_2)$ of x_1 and x_2. Some involved aspect may be of interest. For instance, if (x_1, x_2) denotes the position of a particle moving on a plane surface, then we would let $t(x_1, x_2) = \sqrt{x_1^2 + x_2^2}$ to study the distance of the particle from the origin. If (x_1, x_2) denotes the lifetimes of two vital components of a machine and the machine fails as soon

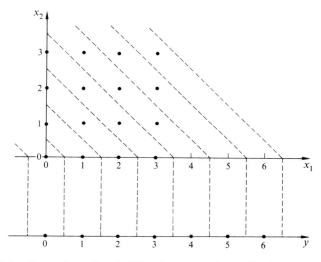

Fig. 3–7. Channeling of probability from record set of basic experiment, the (x_1, x_2) lattice, to the record set of the induced experiment. Guide lines $----$.

as one or other of the components fails, then setting $t(x_1, x_2) = \min(x_1, x_2)$, the smaller of x_1 and x_2, would direct our attention toward the study of the lifetime of the machine. (For a discussion of min see Appendix 3.) We state this formal problem of distribution calculus in a definition as follows.

3–5–1 Definition *Induced experiment.* Suppose that we are given a model with typical record (x_1, x_2) and probability function p. The "experiment" that records $t(x_1, x_2)$ rather than the detail (x_1, x_2) is called an *induced experiment* and has the following model:

1. a record set Y consisting of all the values taken by $t(x_1, x_2)$ as (x_1, x_2) varies through the basic experiment record set,

2. a probability function q determined as follows: For each y in Y construct the associated record R_y, consisting of all simple records (x_1, x_2) of the basic experiment which lead to y in the sense that $t(x_1, x_2) = y$. Set $q(y) = p(R_y)$.

There is no reason why the concept should be confined to records of the form (x_1, x_2). For example, if x_1, x_2, x_3 refer to three blood-pressure readings on a person, we may wish to study the variability of the average $t(x_1, x_2, x_3) = \frac{1}{3}(x_1 + x_2 + x_3)$. Again, instead of a simple record x (representing, say, the diameter of a ball bearing) we may ask questions about $\frac{1}{6}\pi x^3$ (its volume).

Example. The distribution of sex in litters consisting of six rats has been studied and the model in Table 3–11 arrived at to describe the variable number x of male rats in one such litter. A biologist hopes to breed from a litter of six rats. Describe the variability in the maximum number of matings possible at any given time.

TABLE 3–11

Sex distribution in six-rat litters

x (no. of males)	0	1	2	3	4	5	6
$p(x)$	0.05	0.18	0.30	0.24	0.15	0.07	0.01

Solution. The possible number of matings is 0, 1, 2, 3, so we take $Y = \{0, 1, 2, 3\}$. We then have the associated records of Table 3–12. For example, exactly one mating is possible ($y = 1$) if there is exactly one male or exactly five males (exactly one female), so that $R_1 = \{1, 5\}$ is the associated record of the basic

TABLE 3–12

Construction of model for maximum number of matings

y	Associated record R_y	$q(y)$
0	0, 6	0.06
1	1, 5	0.25
2	2, 4	0.45
3	3, 3	0.24
		1.00

experiment. Then

$$q(1) = p(1) + p(5) = 0.18 + 0.07 = 0.25.$$

The reader may wish to verify that the aspect $t(x)$ of x considered here can be expressed as $t(x) = \min \{x, 6 - x\}$, the smaller of x and $6 - x$.

EXERCISES

1. The following model describes the joint variability of (x_1, x_2).

	x_2			
x_1	-1	0	1	2
-1	0.20	0.16	0.04	0.00
1	0.37	0.15	0.06	0.02

Deduce appropriate models to describe the variability of

a) $x_1 + x_2$,   b) x_1,   c) x_2/x_1.

2. An electrician wants one half-mΩ resistor and one mΩ resistor. He picks two resistors from a large box containing 2000 half-mΩ and 1000 mΩ resistors so carelessly that his two choices are effectively independent; a half-mΩ resistor has probability $\frac{2}{3}$ of being selected at each choice. He connects the chosen resistors in series (so that the total resistance is $R_1 + R_2$ if the two resistors have resistances R_1 and R_2). Write down the appropriate model to describe the uncertainty about (R_1, R_2) and then obtain the appropriate model to describe the induced experiment which records total resistance.

If the two resistors are connected in parallel, their overall resistance is $R_1 R_2/(R_1 + R_2)$. Obtain the model to describe total resistance in this case.

3. The standard cost of production and the standard selling price of an item are respectively 10 and 15. It has been found, however, that there are variable adjustments to cost of 0, 1, 2 per item with probabilities 0.5, 0.3, 0.2 and independent variable adjustments to selling price of $-1, 0, 1$ with probabilities 0.2, 0.7, 0.1. Obtain an appropriate model to describe the variability in profit per item.

4. I must prepare a number of different mazes with which I wish to investigate the competitive learning capabilities of rats. For each maze I would like to use two young rats which must be from different litters. The probability pattern for different sizes of litter is as follows:

Size	1	2	3	4	5	6
Probability	0.05	0.08	0.22	0.33	0.21	0.11

I have requisitioned the rats from two unrelated prospective litters. I am wondering how many mazes I am likely to use. Provide me with as much information as you can that is relevant to my query.

I am anxious to avoid having unused pairs of rats left over and I would like to keep the probability of this undesirable eventuality down to 0.1. How many mazes should I prepare?

5. A simple theory of cell division suggests that the probabilities of a cell of any generation producing 0, 1, 2 cells of the next generation are $\frac{1}{6}, \frac{1}{3}, \frac{1}{2}$, and that cells behave independently of each other. What are the appropriate models to describe

a) the number of second-generation cells arising from one cell of the zeroth generation?
b) the total number of first- and second-generation cells arising from one cell of the zeroth generation?
c) the size of the smaller of the first and second generations arising from one cell of the zeroth generation?

6. Standard sheets of canvas board may have flaws of two types, knots and holes, but automatic optical screening ensures that no board is issued with more than three of each kind of flaw. The random characteristics of the production process are expressed in the following probability model:

Number of knots	Number of holes			
	0	1	2	3
0	0.30	0.14	0.06	0.02
1	0.13	0.07	0.02	0.01
2	0.06	0.04	0.03	0.02
3	0.05	0.03	0.01	0.01

How would you describe the variability in the total number of flaws, of either type, in sheets?

A second process is characterized by the following table:

Number of knots	Number of holes			
	0	1	2	3
0	0.30	0.09	0.04	0.04
1	0.18	0.06	0.04	0.02
2	0.09	0.03	0.04	0.01
3	0.02	0.01	0.02	0.01

Show that the variability in the total number of flaws is exactly the same as for the first process.

3–6 BINOMIAL TRIALS

One induced experiment of great importance relates to binomial trials.

3–6–1 Definition *Binomial trial.* A *binomial trial* is an experiment with only two possible outcomes.

The adjective "binomial" expresses the need for only *two names* to describe the outcomes, failure and success in an examination, defective and effective components in sampling, survival and death in an insecticide trial, and so on; the choice of names depends on the applied setting. Let us use the names "failure" and "success." Then a suitable model for this binomial trial is a record set $X = \{0, 1\}$, where 0 represents a failure and 1 a success. To state that the success probability in a trial is s is to specify a probability function p by

$$p(0) = 1 - s, \qquad p(1) = s.$$

(We shall not be considering classes of possible models in this section, so we do not adopt the indexing notation of Section 2–9.)

Usually a binomial trial is repeated many times; for example, an insecticide may be tried on 100 houseflies. In such circumstances we are interested not in the fate of individual houseflies but in the total number killed, the total number of successes with the insecticide, out of the 100 trials.

3–6–2 Definition *Binomial counting experiment.* If n independent repetitions of a binomial trial are performed, we refer to the compound experiment which records the outcomes of all these replicates as n binomial *trials.* The induced experiment which records only the total count of successes in these n binomial trials is a *binomial counting experiment.*

Binomial Counting Experiments Let us make plausible a general result which we state later by demonstrating its truth for two particular cases, $n = 2, 3$.

Two binomial trials with success probability s are performed and yield simple records x_1 and x_2 (remember that 0 means failure and 1 means success). The total number of successes in the two trials is then $x_1 + x_2$, so the binomial counting experiment is simply the induced experiment which records $x_1 + x_2$ instead of the detail (x_1, x_2). Figure 3–8 shows the compound product model (Section 3–2) for the two binomial trials and the derivation of the model for the binomial counting experiment by the channeling process of Fig. 3–7.

If the application of an insecticide to a housefly has probability s of killing the housefly, then the probabilities that out of two houseflies subjected to the insecticide a total of 0, 1, 2 will be killed are $(1 - s)^2, 2s(1 - s), (1 - s)^2$.

We can obtain the total count from three binomial trials by adding to the total count y (0, 1, or 2) of the first two trials the count x_3 (0 or 1) of the third binomial trial. The compound product experiment which records y and x_3

can again be put in diagrammatic form, as in Fig. 3–9, and the probability channeled into the correct simple records of the record set $Z = \{0, 1, 2, 3\}$ of the binomial counting experiment.

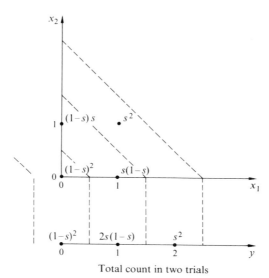

Fig. 3–8 Model for two binomial trials with simple record (x_1, x_2) and for the binomial counting experiment which records $y = x_1 + x_2$.

If three houseflies are separately subjected to the insecticide, the probability that exactly two are killed is $3s^2(1 - s)$.

We can build up to larger experiments by this trial-by-trial approach. We state here the general result.

Binomial Distribution If n binomial trials are conducted and in each there is a probability s of success, then the probability that the total number of successes is y is given by $q(y)$ in Table 3–13. The distribution of probabilities by the function q describes the binomial counting experiment.

TABLE 3–13

Model for binomial counting experiment: general n

y	0	1	2	3	$\cdots$	n
$q(y)$	$(1 - s)^n$	$ns(1 - s)^{n-1}$	$\dfrac{n(n-1)}{1 \cdot 2}s^2(1 - s)^{n-2}$	$\dfrac{n(n-1)(n-2)}{1 \cdot 2 \cdot 3}s^3(1 - s)^{n-3}$	$\cdots$	s^n

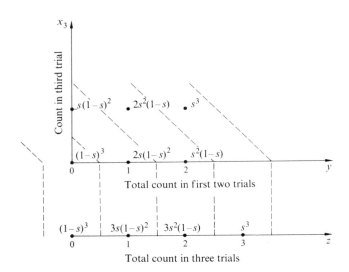

Fig. 3–9   Model for binomial counting experiment based on three binomial trials.

For $n = 4$ we have the table of probabilities given in Table 3–14. If four houseflies are submitted to the insecticide the probability that at least two are killed is

$$6s^2(1 - s)^2 + 4s^3(1 - s) + s^4.$$

TABLE 3–14

Model for binomial counting experiment: $n = 4$

y	0	1	2	3	4
$q(y)$	$(1 - s)^4$	$4s(1 - s)^3$	$6s^2(1 - s)^2$	$4s^3(1 - s)$	s^4

Example An insecticide manufacturer claims that the probability of causing death with his insecticide is 0.9 per housefly. There are four houseflies in my room. What is the probability that at least two of them will survive an application of the insecticide?

Solution. Here the model is as in Table 3–14, with y representing the number killed and $s = 0.9$. "At least two survive" has corresponding record $\{0, 1, 2\}$

with probability

$$q(0) + q(1) + q(2) = (0.1)^4 + 4 \times 0.9 \times (0.1)^3 + 6 \times (0.9)^2 \times (0.1)^2$$
$$= 0.0523.$$

There is roughly a one-in-twenty chance that at least two flies will survive.

Example In a parapsychology experiment a blue card, a red card, and a yellow card are shuffled, and one drawn at random is shown to a "transmitter." The "receiver" in another room is asked to record the color. This process is repeated seven times. On the assumption that the receiver has no telepathic powers and merely guesses the color of each card, what is the probability of his making at least five correct guesses?

Solution. Here we have seven binomial trials, success at any trial being the correct guess of the color of the card. Since each of the three colors is equally likely to be chosen by the receiver, the success probability is clearly $\frac{1}{3}$. Our binomial counting experiment which determines the total number y of correct choices has a model of the type in Table 3–13 with $n = 7$ and $s = \frac{1}{3}$ (see Table 3–15). "At least five correct choices" is represented by the record $\{5, 6, 7\}$ and has probability

$$q(5) + q(6) + q(7) = \frac{99}{2187} = 0.045.$$

TABLE 3–15

y	0	1	2	3	4	5	6	7
$q(y)$	$\frac{128}{2187}$	$\frac{448}{2187}$	$\frac{672}{2187}$	$\frac{560}{2187}$	$\frac{280}{2187}$	$\frac{84}{2187}$	$\frac{14}{2187}$	$\frac{1}{2187}$

Thus if we adopt 5 as a qualifying score for further experiments, the probability that we would mistakenly accept a receiver with no telepathic powers for further consideration is 0.045.

EXERCISES

1. For the particular case $n = 4$, $s = 0.3$, compute $q(y)$ for $y = 0, 1, \ldots, 4$, and thus verify that Table 3–14 specifies a probability model.

2. The famous eighteenth-century French mathematician d'Alembert argued that if an unbiased coin (that is, one with probability $\frac{1}{2}$ associated with the outcome "heads" in a single throw) is thrown twice, then the possible numbers of heads recorded— 0, 1, or 2—all have probabilities $\frac{1}{3}$. What are your views on this argument?

3. A pharmaceutical firm claims that a new preparation has been found to effect a cure in 90 percent of cases of a certain skin disease. A physician has five patients with this

skin disease and he proposes to try the new preparation on each. On the basis of the firm's claim, what probabilities can he assign to the following outcomes:

a) all five patients will be cured?
b) at least three patients will be cured?
c) at least one of his five patients will remain uncured?

4. A catering firm is trying to develop a satisfactory model to describe the lifetime of its china. After some discussion it has been suggested that a suitable model for cup breakage is to suppose that at each serving there is a constant probability s of breakage and that servings are independent. Once broken, a cup is scrapped. As statistical adviser you are asked to supply the probabilities of the following events:

a) a cup will survive its first serving,
b) a cup will survive its sixth serving,
c) a cup will break on the sixth serving,
d) a cup will break before the sixth serving.

What is the probability that of five cups independently used at least one will break before the sixth serving?

5. An *experiment* consists of four binomial trials in each of which there is a probability s of success. What are the probabilities that in such an experiment

a) there are exactly two successes?
b) there are fewer successes than failures?
c) there is at least one success?

A *series* consists of three such independent experiments, an experiment being deemed *satisfactory* if it contains at least one successful trial. What are the probabilities that in a series

d) all experiments are satisfactory?
e) at most one experiment is satisfactory?

Two independent series of experiments are to be conducted. What is the probability that one and only one of the series will consist entirely of satisfactory experiments?

6. An educator is investigating the effectiveness of multiple-choice questions in examinations. He is particularly interested in preventing a "guesser"—that is, someone who chooses one of the offered answers at random (all answers having thus an equal chance of selection)—from too easily obtaining a passing mark. In an examination of eight questions, each offering two answers, and with a pass grade of six or more correct answers, show that the probability that a guesser passes is $\frac{37}{256}$. The educator would like to reduce this probability to below 0.01 by retaining the same number of questions and the same passing grade but increasing the number of answers offered per question. Show that he must offer four choices per question to achieve this.

3–7 AVERAGE AND EXPECTATION

The concept of average is well known in everyday life. We now introduce, by way of a concrete example, the model counterpart of the average over a long run of replicates of an experiment.

An Illustrative Example The numbers of male rats in 20 six-rat litters of the type in Table 3–11 have been recorded as

$$2, 2, 5, 3, 4, 2, 1, 0, 3, 2, 4, 6, 2, 2, 3, 2, 3, 0, 4, 2.$$

From these observations we can calculate that the average number of male rats per litter is

$$\tfrac{1}{20}(2 + 2 + 5 + 3 + \cdots + 4 + 2) = 2.6,$$

and we can reexpress this averaging process as

$$\tfrac{1}{20}\{(0 \times 2) + (1 \times 1) + (2 \times 8) + (3 \times 4) + (4 \times 3) + (5 \times 1) + (6 \times 1)\}$$

$$= (0 \times \tfrac{2}{20}) + (1 \times \tfrac{1}{20}) + (2 \times \tfrac{8}{20}) + \cdots + (6 \times \tfrac{1}{20})$$

$$= 0 \times rf(0) + 1 \times rf(1) + 2 \times rf(2) + \cdots + 6 \times rf(6), \qquad (3\text{–}7\text{–}1)$$

where $rf(x)$ is the relative frequency with which we observe x males in a litter. For example, 8 out of 20 litters have exactly 2 males, so $rf(2) = \tfrac{8}{20}$.

The long-run relative frequency of an outcome has as its model counterpart the probability of the corresponding simple record. Therefore, the form of (3–7–1) suggests that in our model it will be useful to define, and give a suitable name and notation to, the quantity

$$0 \times p(0) + 1 \times p(1) + 2 \times p(2) + \cdots + 6 \times p(6),$$

where $p(0), \ldots, p(6)$ are the probabilities in Table 3–11. Directions for the computation of this quantity—the expectation of x or the mean of x—can be given compactly by the summation instruction $\Sigma_x \, xp(x)$. So that we can refer to the expectation even more briefly, we denote it by $\mathscr{E}(x)$. Thus $\mathscr{E}$ is an "operator" which gives the instruction: compute the expectation of x, by forming the product of each simple record with its probability, and then summing these products.

3–7–1 Definition *Expectation of x.* For a model with record set X and probability function p the *expectation* or *mean* of x is defined as

$$\mathscr{E}(x) = \sum_X xp(x). \qquad (3\text{–}7\text{–}2)$$

For the model of Table 3–11,

$$\mathscr{E}(x) = 0 \times 0.05 + 1 \times 0.18 + 2 \times 0.30 + \cdots + 6 \times 0.01$$

$$= 2.51,$$

so the mean number of male rats per litter is 2.51. We must not be disappointed that this does not coincide with the average value 2.60 obtained from the 20 litters. Remember that we must interpret $\mathscr{E}(x)$ as the average that we would obtain in a large number of six-rat litters (provided, of course, we have constructed the true model that nature is actually using to produce male rats). If we had a larger number N, say, of litters, it would be reasonable to hope that the average number of male rats per litter would correspond more closely to $\mathscr{E}(x)$, or equivalently, the total number of male rats to $N\mathscr{E}(x)$.

Continuation of Example Suppose that we are not so much interested in the number x of male rats as in the maximum number $t(x)$, say, of matings possible at a given time; review the construction of Table 3–12. For the 20 observed litters the average number of matings is

$$\tfrac{1}{20}\{t(2) + t(2) + t(5) + t(3) + \cdots + t(4) + t(2)\}$$
$$= t(0)rf(0) + t(1)rf(1) + \cdots + t(6)rf(6) = 1.8,$$

by the same process of rearrangement as in (3–7–1). This leads by the argument used earlier to a generalization of Definition 3–7–1.

3–7–2 Definition *Expectation of* $t(x)$. For a model with record set X and probability function p the *expectation* or *mean* of $t(x)$ is defined as

$$\mathscr{E}\{t(x)\} = \sum_X t(x)p(x). \qquad (3\text{–}7\text{–}3)$$

To compute this expectation we take every simple record x, form the product of $t(x)$ and $p(x)$, and sum these products.

In our example the mean number of matings per six-rat litter is

$$t(0)p(0) + t(1)p(1) + t(2)p(2) + \cdots + t(5)p(5) + t(6)p(6)$$
$$= 0 \times 0.05 + 1 \times 0.18 + 2 \times 0.30 + \cdots + 1 \times 0.07 + 0 \times 0.01$$
$$= 1.87.$$

Hence if our model is correct and we take a large number N of six-rat litters and form as many matings as we can within litters, then we can expect to obtain about $1.87N$ matings.

An alternative way to obtain the mean number of matings per litter is first to construct the induced model (Table 3–12) which describes the variability in the number of matings possible, and then to find the mean of y:

$$\mathscr{E}(y) = \sum_Y yq(y). \qquad (3\text{–}7\text{–}4)$$

From Table 3–12 we have

$$\mathscr{E}(y) = 0 \times q(0) + 1 \times q(1) + 2 \times q(2) + 3 \times q(3)$$
$$= 0 \times 0.06 + 1 \times 0.25 + 2 \times 0.45 + 3 \times 0.24$$
$$= 1.87,$$

as before. The equivalence of (3–7–3) and (3–7–4) as methods of calculating the expectation of $t(x)$, verified for this example, can be shown to hold generally. We can use either the basic model and (3–7–3) or the induced model and (3–7–4), whichever is more convenient.

Mean Number of Successes in n Binomial Trials Suppose that we were to apply the insecticide (with kill probability s) of Section 3–6 to 200 rooms each containing 4 houseflies. Can we obtain any idea of the average number of flies per room that we would kill? The model supplies an answer to this question in the form of $\mathscr{E}(y)$, where y has the distribution of Table 3–14. Then

$$\mathscr{E}(y) = 0 \times (1 - s)^4 + 1 \times 4s(1 - s)^3 + 2 \times 6s^2(1 - s)^2$$
$$+ 3 \times 4s^3(1 - s) + 4 \times s^4$$
$$= 4s\{(1 - s)^3 + 3s(1 - s)^2 + 3s^2(1 - s) + s^3\}$$
$$= 4s.$$

The sum in the braces is equal to 1, since it is the sum of the probabilities on the complete record set Z of Fig. 3–9.

3–7–1 Theorem *Binomial mean.* The mean number of successes in n binomial trials, each having success probability s, is ns.

A formal proof of this can be given by the mathematical evaluation of $\mathscr{E}(y)$ from Table 3–13 along the lines of the above evaluation for the case $n = 4$. We shall content ourselves with making the general result plausible by the insecticide example. Suppose that the insecticide manufacturer puts n flies into each of a large number b of bottles. Since the mean number of kills per bottle evaluated from the model represents the long-run average number of kills per bottle, we attempt to evaluate the latter. Now the manufacturer is effectively subjecting bn houseflies to the insecticide, so the relative frequency of success (kill) in these bn trials is

$$rf(\text{success}) = \frac{\text{total number killed}}{bn}.$$

Since this long-run relative frequency will be roughly the kill probability s, we have

$$\text{total number killed} = bns.$$

Thus there are altogether bns houseflies killed in the b bottles, so the average number of houseflies killed per bottle is

$$\frac{bns}{b} = ns,$$

which is in accord with the general result quoted.

It is a straightforward arithmetical property of an average that it is never smaller than its smallest component nor larger than its largest component. For example, the average number of male rats in the 20 litters is 2.6, which is greater than 0 (the smallest number of males) and smaller than 6 (the largest number of males). A similar property is true of "weighted averages" such as the mean of x:

$$\text{minimum } x \text{ in } X \leq \mathscr{E}(x) \leq \text{maximum } x \text{ in } X$$

(see Appendix 4). For instance, in our rat model this takes the form $0 \leq 2.51 \leq 6$, which is true. If we compute $\mathscr{E}(x)$ and find that its value does not lie in the range of values of x in the record set X, we can be sure that we have made a computational error. Also $\mathscr{E}\{t(x)\}$ must fall somewhere in the range of values in the record set Y of the induced experiment or a mistake in calculation is indicated. Thus in our example $\mathscr{E}\{t(x)\} = 1.87$, which lies between 0 and 3.

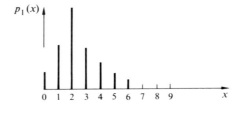

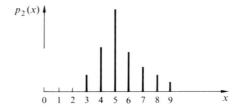

Fig. 3-10   Diagrammatic representation of the two models of Table 3-16.

The mean $\mathscr{E}(x)$ thus provides some indication of where the unit of probability is located within the record set X. For example, the two probability models of Table 3-16, while having the same pattern (see Fig. 3-10) are located differently within the record set; the second model is displaced three units to the right of the first model. This is brought out by the fact that the means for models 1 and 2 are 2.43 and 5.43 = 2.43 + 3. The mean therefore is useful as a measure of the location of a distribution within the record set.

TABLE 3–16

Two probability models

x	0	1	2	3	4	5	6	7	8	9
$p_1(x)$	0.07	0.19	0.35	0.17	0.11	0.07	0.04	0.00	0.00	0.00
$p_2(x)$	0.00	0.00	0.00	0.07	0.19	0.35	0.17	0.11	0.07	0.04

EXERCISES

1. For the basic probability model

x	0	1	2	3
$p(x)$	0.29	0.47	0.19	0.05

evaluate $\mathcal{E}(x)$.

Obtain the appropriate model for the induced experiment which records $t(x)$ as defined below, rather than x.

x	0	1	2	3
$t(x)$	1	3	5	7

Find the mean associated with this induced model. Verify that you obtain the same answer if you apply (3–7–3) to the basic probability model.

Note that $t(x) = 2x + 1$. Verify that

$$\mathcal{E}(2x + 1) = 2\mathcal{E}(x) + 1.$$

Do you think that this result would hold for any basic probability model?

2. The number x of bacteria colonies which develop on a small dish of nutrient in an infected environment is described by the following model:

x	0	1	2	3	4
$p(x)$	0.02	0.11	0.31	0.42	0.14

When the nutrient is sprayed with a mild antibiotic the distribution is assessed to be:

x	0	1	2	3	4
$p(x)$	0.21	0.43	0.21	0.12	0.03

What reduction in the mean number of colonies per dish has resulted from the use of the antibiotic?

The "infectiveness" of x colonies has been defined as x^2. What reduction in the mean infectiveness per dish has the antibiotic achieved?

3. A multiple-choice vocabulary test presents six words and offers five different meanings for each. What is the mean number of correct answers obtained by a guesser who chooses his answers at random?

   If a grade "excellent" is awarded in the test only when all six correct answers are given, what is the probability that a guesser will obtain the grade "excellent"? What is the expected number of "excellent" guessers in a group of 50 guessers?

4. I propose to contract with a cab-hire firm for a daily journey of 3 miles. The contract offered me by one firm involves a charge of 1 per mile and 0.3 per minute of the journey. Study of the traffic conditions has suggested to me that the variable time of the journey is reasonably well described by the following probability model:

Number of minutes	5	6	7	8	9	10
Probability	0.08	0.13	0.33	0.25	0.14	0.07

   What is the average cost per journey?

   A second firm offers a contract of 1.5 per mile and 0.1 per minute. Which contract will be more advantageous to me in the long run?

5. A desk-calculator servicing firm offers to carry out any repair within three days for a standard charge of 5 and to make a penalty repayment of 3 for each day beyond the stated three. A retrospective study suggests the following model for the variability in time for repair:

No. of days for repair	1	2	3	4	5	6
Probability	0.52	0.26	0.12	0.05	0.03	0.02

   What is the mean net payment of the firm per repair?

   Because of increased costs it is proposed to increase the standard charge by 2 and to adjust the penalty repayment so that the mean net payment is increased by 1.5. What should the new penalty payment be?

3–8 A MEASURE OF SPREAD

We saw in the preceding section that the mean can act as a useful indicator of the location of probability within the record set. Very seldom, however, will it convey anything like a full description of the distribution of probability over the record set. Does it, for example, tell us how concentrated or how spread out around the mean the distribution is?

An Illustrative Example Suppose that a packaging machine is being developed which will weigh and package as accurately as possible 500 gm of detergent. Three prototypes of different design have been produced; the probability models constructed to describe the variability in their weighings are shown in the rows of Table 3–17. All three models have the same mean, 500 gm, but obviously

the three prototypes are not equally effective. Prototype 1 is more precise—
that is, less variable—in the weights of its packets than prototype 2, which
itself concentrates the weights of its packets more closely around 500 gm than
does prototype 3. The question we must pose is: Can we find for a probability
model some summarizing measure of spread, which is large if the unit of
probability plasticine is widely spread about the mean and is smaller the more
concentrated the distribution is?

TABLE 3–17

Three probability models with different "spreads"

x	495	496	497	498	499	500	501	502	503	504	505
$p_1(x)$	0.01	0.01	0.03	0.05	0.11	0.56	0.11	0.06	0.03	0.01	0.01
$p_2(x)$	0.02	0.04	0.05	0.07	0.14	0.36	0.14	0.07	0.05	0.04	0.02
$p_3(x)$	0.04	0.06	0.08	0.11	0.13	0.16	0.13	0.11	0.08	0.06	0.04

Now with prototype 3, values of x some distance from the mean 500 occur
relatively frequently (for example, $x = 505$ with probability 0.04) compared
with prototype 1, where values of x far from the mean are relatively infrequent
(for example, $x = 505$ with probability 0.01). Thus if we were to compute the
long-run average of distances or departures of actual packet weights from the
mean, we would find this to be larger for prototype 3 than for prototype 1,
and that the long-run average for prototype 2 would lie between those for
prototypes 1 and 3. The long-run average of any measurement which increases
with distance will also show such a feature and will form the basis of a measure
of spread. It is usual to take as a measurement of departure from the mean
one which will be easy to handle mathematically in subsequent statistical
development, and this is the square of the departure, $(x - m)^2$, where m is the
mean; in our present example $m = 500$. The model counterpart of this long-run
average is the expectation of $(x - m)^2$. This is called the *variance* and is the
measure of spread that we will use.

3–8–1 Definition *Variance.* For a model with record set X, probability
function p, and mean $m = \mathscr{E}(x)$, the *variance of x* is denoted $\mathscr{V}(x)$ and defined by

$$\mathscr{V}(x) = \mathscr{E}\{(x - m)^2\} = \sum_X (x - m)^2 p(x).$$

Therefore, to compute the variance we must first compute the mean m,
then run through every x in the record set X, form the products $(x - m)^2 p(x)$,
and sum these products.

Let us see whether this measure of spread fulfills our hopes in relation to our example. For model 1,

$$\mathscr{V}(x) = (495 - 500)^2 \times 0.01 + (496 - 500)^2 \times 0.01 + (497 - 500)^2 \times 0.03$$
$$+ \cdots + (504 - 500)^2 \times 0.01 + (505 - 500)^2 \times 0.01$$
$$= 2.06.$$

For model 3,

$$\mathscr{V}(x) = (495 - 500)^2 \times 0.04 + (496 - 500)^2 \times 0.06 + (497 - 500)^2 \times 0.08$$
$$+ \cdots + (504 - 500)^2 \times 0.06 + (505 - 500)^2 \times 0.04$$
$$= 6.50.$$

The variance for model 2 can be obtained similarly. Table 3–18 summarizes the finding that the more spread out the distribution of probability about the mean, the greater the variance.

TABLE 3–18

Variances for the three models

Model	p_1	p_2	p_3
Variance	2.06	4.02	6.50

EXERCISES

1. By inspection of the following three probability models—for example, by drawing the counterpart of Fig. 3–10—suggest which has the largest and which the smallest variance.

x	0	1	2	3	4	5	6
$p_1(x)$	0.08	0.11	0.18	0.26	0.18	0.11	0.08
$p_2(x)$	0.03	0.07	0.19	0.42	0.19	0.07	0.03
$p_3(x)$	0.05	0.09	0.15	0.42	0.15	0.09	0.05

Confirm your intuitive conclusion by computing the variances for the three models.

2. A manufacturer has a choice of two cutting tools for the production of components of a standard length. The variability of cut lengths has been described in terms of the probability models below, where x denotes the departure in mm from the standard length.

x	-0.4	-0.3	-0.2	-0.1	0	0.1	0.2	0.3	0.4
$p_1(x)$	0.03	0.06	0.11	0.17	0.26	0.17	0.11	0.06	0.03
$p_2(x)$	0.02	0.05	0.11	0.18	0.28	0.18	0.11	0.05	0.02

Which cutting tool do you suggest that the manufacturer use, assuming that costs are the same for each?

3–9 PROPERTIES OF MEAN AND VARIANCE

There are a number of simple properties of mean and variance which we will need in later chapters (Sections 5–10, 7–3, 7–9). While it is convenient to collect these in this section, the reader may, if he wishes, defer the study of them and return to this section only when the need arises. All the properties provide methods of reducing the computational labor of evaluating means and variances and are especially useful when we are less concerned with the basic measurement or simple record x or (x_1, x_2) than with some other aspect. For example, if x refers to temperature in degrees Fahrenheit and we wish to convert to the centigrade scale, our attention is focussed on $\frac{5}{9}x - \frac{160}{9}$. Similarly, given x_1, x_2 as the lifetimes of two components, we may wish to study their total lifetime $x_1 + x_2$, as in Section 3–5. In fact, our attention is directed toward induced experiments (Section 3–5) and possibly toward the means and variances associated with the induced models. The question that we now address ourselves to is: Are there any induced models for which the means and variances can be readily expressed in terms of the means and variances of the basic models?

Linear Properties Suppose that we know the mean and variance of x and wish to calculate the mean and variance of $bx + c$, where b and c are given constants. By Definition 3–7–2 we have

$$\mathscr{E}(bx + c) = \sum_x (bx + c)p(x).$$

Since

$$(bx + c)p(x) = bxp(x) + cp(x),$$

we have, summing each side over all x in X,

$$\sum_x (bx + c)p(x) = b\sum_x xp(x) + c\sum_x p(x)$$

$$= b\mathscr{E}(x) + c,$$

by Definition 3–7–1 and Eq. (2–8–3). Hence we have the following theorem.

3–9–1 Theorem   *Mean of a linear function.* If b and c are given constants, then

$$\mathscr{E}(bx + c) = b\mathscr{E}(x) + c.$$

A special case of this result has already appeared in Exercise 1, Section 3–7.

The corresponding result for the variance is also easily obtained. Write $m = \mathscr{E}(x)$. Then, from Theorem 3–9–1 and the definition of variance, the variance of $bx + c$ is the expectation of

$$\{(bx + c) - (bm + c)\}^2 = b^2(x - m)^2,$$

and, by Definition 3–8–1,

$$\mathscr{E}\{b^2(x - m)^2\} = \sum_X b^2(x - m)^2 p(x)$$

$$= b^2 \sum_X (x - m)^2 p(x)$$

$$= b^2 \mathscr{V}(x),$$

We then have the following result.

3–9–2 Theorem   *Variance of a linear function.* If b and c are given constants, then

$$\mathscr{V}(bx + c) = b^2 \mathscr{V}(x).$$

The following example illustrates the use of Theorems 3–9–1 and 3–9–2.

Example   A model to describe the variability in the temperature x (in degrees Fahrenheit) of the freezing point of standard "antifreeze" solutions is as shown in Table 3–19. The manufacturer wishes to quote the mean and variance of the freezing temperature on the centigrade scale.

TABLE 3–19

Model for freezing point distribution

x	18	19	20	21	22	23	24
$p(x)$	0.09	0.29	0.34	0.15	0.08	0.04	0.01

Solution. We have, by Definition 3–7–1,

$$\mathscr{E}(x) = 18 \times 0.09 + 19 \times 0.29 + \cdots + 24 \times 0.01$$

$$= 20 \text{ (degrees Fahrenheit)},$$

and, by Definition 3–8–1,

$$\mathcal{V}(x) = (18 - 20)^2 \times 0.09 + (19 - 20)^2 \times 0.29 + \cdots + (24 - 20)^2 \times 0.01$$

$$= 1.64. \tag{3-8-1}$$

Then the mean and variance in terms of the centigrade scale are given as

$$\mathcal{E}(\tfrac{5}{9}x - \tfrac{160}{9}) = \tfrac{5}{9}\mathcal{E}(x) - \tfrac{160}{9} \qquad \text{by Theorem 3–9–1}$$

$$= -\tfrac{60}{9} \text{ (degrees centigrade)};$$

and

$$\mathcal{V}(\tfrac{5}{9}x - \tfrac{160}{9}) = (\tfrac{5}{9})^2 \mathcal{V}(x) \qquad \text{by Theorem 3–9–2}$$

$$= 0.506.$$

The reader may wish to construct the induced model associated with $\tfrac{5}{9}x - \tfrac{160}{9}$ and compute the mean and variance for this induced model.

Mean-Square Property The variance of x is the expectation of $(x - m)^2$, where $m = \mathcal{E}(x)$. Can we relate the expectation or mean of $(x - c)^2$, where c is a given constant, to $\mathcal{V}(x)$? The answer is contained in the following theorem.

3–9–3 Theorem *Mean-square property.* If c is a given constant, then

$$\mathcal{E}\{(x - c)^2\} = \mathcal{V}(x) + (m - c)^2.$$

To obtain the mean of the square $(x - c)^2$ we must add to the variance the square of the difference between m and c.

The proof is by straightforward algebra. We have

$$(x - c)^2 = \{(x - m) + (m - c)\}^2$$

$$= (x - m)^2 + (m - c)^2 + 2(m - c)x - 2(m - c)m.$$

Hence, multiplying each side by $p(x)$ and summing over all x in X, we have

$$\sum_X (x - c)^2 p(x) = \sum_X (x - m)^2 p(x) + (m - c)^2 \sum_X p(x)$$

$$+ 2(m - c) \sum_X xp(x) - 2(m - c)m \sum_X p(x)$$

$$= \mathcal{V}(x) + (m - c)^2$$

by Definition 3–8–1, Eq. (2–8–3), and Definition 3–7–1.

To illustrate the truth of this relationship let us compute $\mathcal{E}\{(x - 22)^2\}$ for the model of Table 3–19. We have by direct computation, using Definition

3–7–2,

$$\mathscr{E}\{(x - 22)^2\} = (18 - 22)^2 \times 0.09 + (19 - 22)^2 \times 0.29$$
$$+ \cdots + (24 - 22)^2 \times 0.01$$
$$= 5.64.$$

Theorem 3–9–3, with $m = 20$, $c = 22$, and $\mathscr{V}(x)$ from (3–8–1), gives

$$\mathscr{E}\{(x - 22)^2\} = 1.64 + (20 - 22)^2$$
$$= 5.64,$$

as above.

Sum Properties As indicated earlier, we are often interested in sums, especially the sum $x_1 + \cdots + x_n$ of the simple records $x_1, \cdots, x_n$ from n replicates (recall Section 3–5). The following theorem shows the simple relationship between the mean and variance of the sum and the mean and variance associated with a single replicate.

3–9–4 Theorem *Mean and variance of a sum.* If $x_1, \cdots, x_n$ are simple records associated with n replicates of an experiment, then

$$\mathscr{E}(x_1 + \cdots + x_n) = n\mathscr{E}(x_1),$$
$$\mathscr{V}(x_1 + \cdots + x_n) = n\mathscr{V}(x_1).$$

We shall not attempt to prove this theorem, since a proof—though simple—involves ideas of multiple summation which are beyond the scope of this book. We shall content ourselves with a demonstration of its truth in a particular example, the example on machine lifetimes in Section 3–5. From Table 3–9, with x_1, x_2 denoting the lifetimes of the two components, we have

$$\mathscr{E}(x_1) = \mathscr{E}(x_2) = 0 \times 0.1 + 1 \times 0.2 + 2 \times 0.4 + 3 \times 0.3 = 1.9,$$
$$\mathscr{V}(x_1) = \mathscr{V}(x_2) = (0 - 1.9)^2 \times 0.1 + (1 - 1.9)^2 \times 0.2$$
$$+ (2 - 1.9)^2 \times 0.4 + (3 - 1.9)^2 \times 0.3$$
$$= 0.890,$$

so that, from Theorem 3–9–4, we have

$$\mathscr{E}(x_1 + x_2) = 2\mathscr{E}(x_1) = 2 \times 1.9 = 3.8,$$
$$\mathscr{V}(x_1 + x_2) = 2\mathscr{V}(x_1) = 2 \times 0.890 = 1.780.$$

Are these the mean and variance for the induced model which describes $x_1 + x_2$ instead of (x_1, x_2)? We can easily verify that they are by evaluating $\mathscr{E}(y)$, $\mathscr{V}(y)$

from the induced model in Table 3–10, for, by the definitions of mean and variance,

$$\mathscr{E}(y) = 0 \times 0.01 + 1 \times 0.04 + 2 \times 0.12 + \cdots + 6 \times 0.09$$

$$= 3.8,$$

$$\mathscr{V}(y) = (0 - 3.8)^2 \times 0.01 + (1 - 3.8)^2 \times 0.04 + \cdots + (6 - 3.8)^2 \times 0.09$$

$$= 1.780,$$

in agreement with the easier computation from the basic component model.

Mean and Variance of a Binomial Count   One particular application of Theorem 3–9–4 is to a binomial counting experiment. If $x_1, \ldots, x_n$ are the simple records (each a 0 or a 1) associated with n binomial trials, each with success probability s, then the corresponding binomial counting experiment has simple record $x_1 + \cdots + x_n$. The theorem allows us to find the mean and variance of the total count by evaluating only $\mathscr{E}(x_1)$ and $\mathscr{V}(x_1)$. Since the model for x_1 is

x_1	0	1
$p_1(x_1)$	$1 - s$	s

we have

$$\mathscr{E}(x_1) = 0 \times (1 - s) + 1 \times s = s,$$

$$\mathscr{V}(x_1) = (0 - s)^2 \times (1 - s) + (1 - s)^2 \times s$$

$$= s(1 - s).$$

Hence

$$\mathscr{E}(x_1 + \cdots + x_n) = ns,$$

$$\mathscr{V}(x_1 + \cdots + x_n) = ns(1 - s).$$

3–9–5 Theorem   *Mean and variance of a binomial count.*   The mean and variance of the total binomial count in n binomial trials, each with success probability s, are ns and $ns(1 - s)$.

The first part of this theorem is already familiar as Theorem 3–7–1.

EXERCISES

1. The numbers of defects (x) in sweaters from a knitting machine are distributed as follows:

x	0	1	2	3	4
$p(x)$	0.45	0.31	0.15	0.07	0.02

The production cost of a sweater is 40 and the cost of removing each defect is 3. What is the mean cost of producing a defect-free sweater? Provide a measure of the variability in the costs of producing defect-free sweaters from the knitting machine.

What are the mean and variance of the total cost of producing three defect-free sweaters?

2. Consider two replicates of an experiment with probability model

x	0	1	2	3
$p(x)$	0.1	0.3	0.4	0.2

with simple records x_1 and x_2. Compute the mean and variance of $x_1 + x_2$ using Theorem 3–9–4.

Obtain the induced probability model for $x_1 + x_2$ and verify that its mean and variance are in agreement with those already obtained.

3. The weights (mg) of small individual organisms are distributed according to the model

x (mg)	7	8	9	10	11	12	13
$p(x)$	0.10	0.29	0.32	0.15	0.09	0.04	0.01

What can be said about the mean and variance of the total weight of a colony of 100 independent organisms?

4. The distribution of a certain characteristic of electrical components has mean 120 and variance 30.5. A transmitter requires such a component with characteristic 117 to obtain full power, and the loss of power from the use of a component with a different characteristic is equal to the square of the difference. What is the mean loss of power of transmitters using the given components?

3–10 A PROBABILITY GLOSSARY

A useful way to sum up the considerations of this chapter and the preceding one is to draw up a short glossary showing the counterpart, in the language of probability, of various features of the real world.

Real world	Probability language
Experiment	Probability model
Experimenter's ability to observe	Record set X
Outcome	Simple record
Event E	Record R
$E_1, E_2, \ldots$ mutually exclusive	$R_1, R_2, \ldots$ disjoint
E_1 or E_2 or $\ldots$, where $E_1, E_2, \ldots$ are mutually exclusive	$R_1 + R_2 + \cdots$

E occurs	R is observed
E does not occur	$\bar{R}$ is observed
Something or other happens	X is observed
Stability of relative frequency	Existence of probability
Relative frequency of E: $rf(E)$	Probability of R: $p(R)$
How likely is E?	What is the value of $p(R) = \Sigma_R \, p(x)$?
Unrelated experiments	Probability function specified by $p(x_1, x_2) = p_1(x_1)p_2(x_2)$
Sequential experiments	Probability function specified by $p(x_1, x_2) = p_1(x_1)p_2(x_2 \mid x_1)$
Consider $t(x)$ rather than x	Consider an induced experiment
Long-run average of x	Expectation $\mathscr{E}(x)$
Independent repetitions of an experiment	Replicates
Experiment with only two outcomes	Binomial trial

CHAPTER 4

MODELS FOR
COMPETITIVE BEHAVIOR

Competition is a natural preoccupation of human beings. When we are not competing against other schoolboys in examinations, against other candidates in elections, against other businessmen in commerce, we find relaxation in competitive sport, be it against another golfer on a golf course or another fisherman for a fish. In Chapters 2 and 3 we saw how to construct models to describe uncertainty. In the present chapter we study the building of models to describe competition.

4–1 AN ILLUSTRATIVE GAME

To discover the essential structure of a game, let us invent and investigate the simple game of One-two-three. To describe any game we must specify how it may be played; we have to set out the *rules*.

Rules of One-two-three

1. One-two-three is a game for two contestants of different ages, the younger to be called the *player* and the older the *opponent*.
2. The opponent selects two different digits from the set 1, 2, 3 and writes them down on a piece of paper without disclosing his choice to the player.
3. The aim of the player is to guess the parity (evenness or oddness) of the sum of the two numbers selected by the opponent and also the larger of the two selected numbers. He writes down his guesses on a piece of paper.
4. The two pieces of paper are then displayed, and scores assigned in the following way.

92

a) If the player guesses the parity of the sum, he is awarded a score equal to the sum ; if the player fails to guess the parity, these points go to the opponent.

b) If the player, having correctly guessed the parity of the sum, also guesses the identity of the larger digit selected by the opponent, a bonus of two points is added to his score. The player pays no penalty if he fails to guess the larger digit selected.

These rules describe a well-defined game. It is convenient to distinguish between the generic term or concept—the *game* of One-two-three—and an application of the rules on a particular occasion in a confrontation between two specific persons. We shall call the operation of the rules on a particular occasion a *play* of the game. It is then possible to speak of two confrontations as two plays of the game, and so on. The rules of the game describe what constitutes a play of the game.

Let us analyze this game of One-two-three more closely.

Rule 1 merely specifies the number of participants and assigns to each a convenient name. One-two-three is a *two-person* game. There are, of course, *n*-person games where *n* is more than two; Bingo, Monopoly, and Poker are examples of games best suited to more than two participants. However, it will be sufficient for our purposes to confine our attention to two-person games.

While rules 2 and 3 prescribe the conduct of a play, they still leave some choice to the player and to the opponent. From these rules we can determine the various opportunities which are open to the two participants. Rule 2 shows that the opponent can choose one of three *strategies* available to him, namely $1 + 2$, $1 + 3$, $2 + 3$. Rule 3 allows the player to choose even or odd for the parity; and 2 or 3 for the larger digit. Note that since 1 cannot be the larger digit, the player can exclude this possibility. Actually no difficulty in our analysis would arise if the player stupidly included this possibility. We see therefore that the player has to choose from four strategies : (even, 2), (even, 3), (odd, 2), (odd, 3).

The Payoff Structure When the participants have chosen their strategies, acted according to them (in this case committed them to paper), and so brought the play to an end (by showing their commitments), rule 4 provides instructions for the settlement or *payoff*. For example, if the opponent chooses his strategy $1 + 2$ and the player his strategy (odd, 2) then the player gains, by (a), $3 (= 1 + 2)$ points for guessing the parity "odd," and by (b), a bonus of 2 points for guessing correctly the larger digit selected. The total gain to the player from the play is thus 5. Again if the opponent selects $1 + 3$ and the player guesses (odd, 3) then, by (a), the opponent scores $4 (= 1 + 3)$ points. The correct guess of the higher digit by the player does not entitle him to a bonus since he failed to guess the parity. Instead of expressing the payoff as a gain of 4 points to the opponent we can present it as a negative gain of -4 points to the player.

This approach enables us to present a complete picture of the game in the form of a table in which the gains (possibly negative) *to the player* for each of the 12 (= 3 × 4) possible pairings of strategies are given (see Table 4–1). For example, the entry in the fourth row and second column is −4, telling us as before that the player loses 4 points to his opponent if he guesses odd parity and larger digit 3 when the opponent chooses 1 + 3.

TABLE 4-1

Payoff matrix for One-two-three

Player's strategy	Opponent's strategy		
	1 + 2	1 + 3	2 + 3
(even, 2)	−3	4	−5
(even, 3)	−3	6	−5
(odd, 2)	5	−4	5
(odd, 3)	3	−4	7

EXERCISES

1. In the game of Fingers, when the referee shouts "Display," you and your opponent simultaneously bring your right hands from behind your backs with a certain number of fingers displayed. You may display one, two, or three fingers; your opponent may display only one or two fingers. If you display more fingers than your opponent, and if the total number of fingers displayed is odd, you receive points equal to the difference; if the total number of fingers displayed is even, you lose two points to your opponent. If your opponent displays more fingers than you, then he receives the difference regardless of the parity of the total. If you and your opponent display the same number of fingers, no points are awarded to either player.

   Arrange the rules for Fingers in the form given in this section, specifying the sets of strategies and the table of payoffs.

2. A change in the game of Fingers (Exercise 1) has been proposed along the following lines. Both you and your opponent can now display one, two, or three fingers. If you both display the same number or if the total is odd, then your opponent receives one point. Otherwise the player with the greater number of fingers displayed gains points equal to the difference. Rewrite the rules in the form of this section, identifying the sets of strategies and the payoff structure. Do you regard the proposals as satisfactory? Give reasons for your answer.

3. In the game of Society the two contestants must simultaneously declare their chosen status, plutocrat, bourgeois, or proletarian. If both contestants declare the same status,

there is no advantage to either; otherwise the settlement prescribed by the rules is as follows. A plutocrat has an advantage of 2 over a bourgeois because of his superior wealth; a bourgeois is regarded as one up on a proletarian; but a proletarian has an advantage of 1 over a plutocrat because of his right to withold his labor. Express the rules of this game in the terms of this section, and identify the payoff structure of Society.

4–2 STRUCTURE OF A TWO-PERSON GAME

We have seen that a game consists of a set of rules which describe how a play of the game is to be conducted. First, the rules name one of the two contestants as the player and the other as the opponent. Study of the rules enables us to determine the set of all strategies open to the player and also the set of all possible strategies for the opponent. The claim that these sets of strategies can be determined seems an oversimplification even for simple games such as Tick-tacktoe and Poker. The fact that the players take turns to move and that chance in the shuffle of a pack of cards may intervene seem at first glance to impose insuperable obstacles on the labeling of strategies. However, if the reader recognizes that games terminate and that a sequence of moves (and this includes the role of chance) can be represented as a branching tree, he will soon be convinced of the plausibility of this claim. For some games such as Chess, the determination of the sets of strategies may involve a formidable enumeration problem, but in principle this can be achieved. In this book the playing of pas-time games, however intellectually stimulating, is not our immediate interest, and there is no need to elaborate this point. We shall be concerned mainly with cases in which there is only a finite number of mutually exclusive strategies available to each player. Such games are called *finite games.*

Let us suppose that the player has just m possible strategies, conveniently labeled $a_1, \ldots, a_m$, so that at a play he must choose some strategy a from the set $A = \{a_1, \ldots, a_m\}$. Thus in One-two-three we may call (even, 2) strategy a_1, (even, 3) strategy a_2, (odd, 2) strategy a_3, and (odd, 3) strategy a_4. Similarly, we assume that the opponent has just n possible strategies, conveniently labeled $s_1, \ldots, s_n$; at each play he must choose some strategy s from the set $S = \{s_1, \ldots, s_n\}$. Our choice of notation is obviously preemptive; we shall soon identify the player with a decision-maker, his strategies then being the possible courses of action, and the opponent with nature, his strategies then being the possible states of nature.

After the player and opponent have chosen their strategies, say a and s, the play concludes by a calculation, according to the rules, of the *utility* (points scored, gain, payoff) of the play to the player. We denote this by $U(a, s)$ to show its dependence on the strategies chosen, and recall that a negative utility signifies a loss to the player. Since any loss to the player is essentially a gain to the opponent, such games are often referred to as *zero-sum* games.

To sum up we have the following definition.

4–2–1 Definition *Two-person, zero-sum, finite game.* The rules of a *two-person, zero-sum, finite game* fulfill the following four functions.

1. Define the player and the opponent.
2. Specify the set $A = \{a_1, \ldots, a_m\}$ of the player's possible strategies.
3. Specify the set $S = \{s_1, \ldots, s_n\}$ of the opponent's possible strategies.
4. Specify for each a in A and each s in S the utility $U(a, s)$ to the player of a play in which he chooses a from A and the opponent chooses s from S.

EXERCISES

Translate the following situations into a model in the form of a competitive game, identifying the player and opponent, together with their sets A and S of strategies, and constructing an appropriate utility or payoff structure $U(a, s)$.

1. I hope to market a revolutionary perpetual pen-and-pencil set. If I go into production I intend to sell each set at a profit of p. If I sell a set that is defective in any way, then my replacement costs amount to $r > p$. If I wish I may test the sets before selling them at a cost t per set. Any defective pen or pencil so detected has to be scrapped and brings no return, so I lose the cost c of its production; if only one item in a set passes the test, it can be sold separately at a profit of s.

2. My dentist informs me that I have a root infection in my upper left canine and that at present he cannot say with any certainty whether or not the tooth is amenable to root treatment and subsequent root-post crowning. He explains that the alternative is to have the tooth extracted and replaced by a false one. If root treatment fails, this will be necessary. After these explanations he leaves the decision between treatment and extraction to me. To help me in my decision-making, I decide to try to quantify my dissatisfaction or satisfaction with the various eventualities. I estimate that there is a positive gain of 4 utiles (units of usefulness) to me from successful root treatment, that unsuccessful root treatment is annoying and involves a loss of 7 utiles, that the relief from a *necessary* extraction is worth 6 utiles, but that an unnecessary extraction is annoying to the tune of 2 utiles.

4–3 INTRODUCTION OF A NEW PRODUCT FORMULATED AS A GAME

We have already hinted at the possibility of formulating as games situations other than recreational games. Let us consider our first decision problem about the introduction of a new product (Problem 1, Section 1–4) and try to formulate it as a game, called Introprod for brevity. We can best achieve this by treating a play of our game as the confrontation of the industrialist or decision-maker with a single item. Since the problem concerns mass production, we shall clearly have to consider long sequences of plays of the game in analyzing the decision process.

Rules of Introprod

1. There are two contestants, the decision-maker (previously the player) and nature (previously the opponent).
2. Nature may choose to confront the decision-maker with either a defective item or an effective item. She has thus two possible strategies or states in her set S of strategies:

   s_1:   present a defective item,
   s_2:   present an effective item.

3. The decision-maker has the option of ignoring the item, in which case nature withdraws it and the next play commences. Note that this corresponds to the industrialist's option not to introduce the product. If he decides to introduce the product he may sell or scrap an item without testing it, or he may first perform a test which positively identifies the item as defective or effective and then choose between selling or scrapping. We can thus list all the distinct strategies or actions of the decision-maker which make up the set A:

   a_1:   do not introduce,
   a_2:   introduce and sell without testing,
   a_3:   introduce and test: if item is defective, scrap;
           if item is effective, sell,
   a_4:   introduce and scrap without testing,
   a_5:   introduce and test: if item is defective, sell;
           if item is effective, scrap,
   a_6:   introduce, test, and sell, whatever the result of the test,
   a_7:   introduce, test, and scrap, whatever the result of the test.

   Note that we have introduced some obviously mad actions, such as a_5, a_6, and a_7. These, although possible actions, could immediately be excluded; we have included them here simply to illustrate how they are readily eliminated by the decision-making process.
4. The table of utilities to the decision-maker is given in Table 4–2.

   The utilities given in the table have been derived from the information provided in Problem 1 of Section 1–4. For instance, it is clear that if action a_1 is taken and the product is not introduced, there is neither a gain nor a loss (regardless of what nature has in store). Again suppose that the decision-maker adopts action a_5. If nature has presented a defective item (state s_1), then the decision-maker, by selling a defective item, has a selling profit of 3, but pays out 1 for testing and 7 for replacement, a net gain of $3 - 1 - 7 = -5$. If nature has presented an effective item (state s_2), then the decision-maker scraps an effective item, making a scrap loss of 1 and paying out 1 for testing and so obtaining a utility of $-1 - 1 = -2$. Entries in other positions in the table are similarly calculated.

TABLE 4–2

Utilities $U(a, s)$ for Introprod

Decision-maker's action	State of nature	
	s_1	s_2
a_1	0	0
a_2	-4	3
a_3	-2	2
a_4	-1	-1
a_5	-5	-2
a_6	-5	2
a_7	-2	-2

The fact that we have managed to formulate the problem of introducing a new product as a game suggests that a study of games may have some bearing on decision-making under uncertainty.

4–4 SIMPLE AND RANDOMIZED STRATEGIES

In the translation of the problem of introducing a new product into the game of Introprod we said that decision-making would require consideration of a sequence of plays of the game. Now it is most unlikely that the production process is sufficiently under control to force nature to present an effective item at every play or is so far out of control as to allow her to present a defective item at every play. We are aware that items coming from the production line will be variable in quality, some being defective and some being effective, but we cannot predict which. It is obviously an advantage to clear thinking to introduce this feature of uncertainty explicitly into our game model. This will be achieved if we allow nature to select her strategy or state by conducting a previous random experiment. Suppose that the overall proportion of defectives among the items produced is $\frac{1}{4}$. We can simulate the uncertain way in which production takes place by supposing that nature tosses two coins and chooses strategy s_1 (defective) if both coins show heads and chooses strategy s_2 (effective) otherwise. Production of successive items then proceeds as if by replicates of such an experiment, effectively with record set $S = \{s_1, s_2\}$ and probability function π specified by

$$\pi(s_1) = \tfrac{1}{4}, \qquad \pi(s_2) = \tfrac{3}{4}.$$

We use the lower-case Greek letter pi (π) instead of the previously used p to denote the probability function to emphasize that this experiment by nature is a convenient figment of our imagination; also, we wish to reserve the symbol p mainly for probability functions of less imaginary experiments.

Another way to simulate uncertainty is to visualize nature spinning a roulette wheel of unit circumference divided into two unequal segments, the first black segment of length 0.07 and the second white segment of length 0.93. If she then produces a defective on any spin in which black comes up, and an effective on any spin in which white comes up, she is effectively operating a model with record set $S = \{s_1, s_2\}$ and $\pi(s_1) = 0.07, \pi(s_2) = 0.93$. In a sequence of plays this will have the effect of ensuring in the long run a proportion 0.07 of defective items, but also of preventing us from knowing what the next play or operation will yield.

To distinguish this more general type of strategy from the two direct strategies s_1 and s_2 originally introduced, we shall use the terms *randomized strategy* for the general form and *simple strategy* for the basic ones. The terms *mixed* and *pure* are also frequently used. Note that although nature has only two simple strategies, namely s_1 and s_2, there are an infinite number of randomized strategies, one corresponding to each number in the interval [0, 1]. Note also that the set of randomized strategies includes as special cases the two simple strategies, s_1 corresponding to $\pi(s_1) = 1$, and s_2 corresponding to $\pi(s_2) = 1$ or equivalently $\pi(s_1) = 0$.

More generally, we can extend the opponent's set $S = \{s_1, \ldots, s_n\}$ of simple strategies to a set of randomized strategies. For example, in the game of One-two-three (Section 4-1) we can label the opponent's strategies $1 + 2$, $1 + 3$, $2 + 3$ as s_1, s_2, s_3. The opponent may try to confound the player by throwing two coins and choosing s_1, s_2, s_3 according to whether "no head," "one head," or "two heads" is observed. He is then operating a randomized strategy, or probability function, π on S, with

$$\pi(s_1) = \tfrac{1}{4}, \qquad \pi(s_2) = \tfrac{1}{2}, \qquad \pi(s_3) = \tfrac{1}{4}.$$

In games there is no reason why the opponent should have the sole prerogative of using a randomized strategy. We can obviously allow the player with set $A = \{a_1, \ldots, a_m\}$ of simple strategies to choose his simple strategy for a play by performing an ancillary experiment with record set A and probability function $p(a)$ on A. This would constitute a randomized strategy p for the player. For example, the player in One-two-three can take his $A = \{a_1, a_2, a_3, a_4\}$, these four simple strategies corresponding to (even, 2), (even 3), (odd, 2), (odd, 3). If he tosses three coins and chooses a_1, a_2, a_3, a_4, according to whether "no heads," "one head," "two heads," or "three heads" is obtained, then he can be said to operate the randomized strategy p on A, with

$$p(a_1) = \tfrac{1}{8}, \qquad p(a_2) = \tfrac{3}{8}, \qquad p(a_3) = \tfrac{3}{8}, \qquad p(a_4) = \tfrac{1}{8}.$$

For the computation of these probabilities consider three binomial trials (tosses), with success (head) probability $\tfrac{1}{2}$ for an unbiased coin (see Section 3–6).

We can readily formulate the general definition.

4-4-1 Definition *Randomized strategy of opponent.* If an experiment, whose model has record set $S = \{s_1, \cdots, s_n\}$ and probability function π, is performed to select a strategy for the play of a game, the *randomized strategy π* is said to be used.

EXERCISE

1. Play the game with the following payoff with a friend as opponent.

Player's strategy	Opponent's strategy	
	s_1	s_2
a_1	0	2
a_2	2	0
a_3	3	1

After a few trial plays, ask your friend to determine his choice of strategy at each play by first tossing a coin, choosing strategy s_1 if it comes down heads and choosing strategy s_2 otherwise. Which do you consider your best simple strategy to oppose this randomized strategy?

Now ask your friend to toss two coins before choosing, and to choose strategy s_1 if and only if both show heads. Try to determine what your best simple strategy is to take advantage of your knowledge about the mechanism of this randomized strategy.

Now you use the following two-coin randomized strategy (without disclosing its nature to your friend). If both coins are heads, choose strategy a_1, if both are tails, choose strategy a_2; otherwise choose strategy a_3. Invite your friend to discover his best way of dealing with you. Is there any way in which you can be even more subtle?

4-5 RANDOMIZED STRATEGY OF OPPONENT KNOWN TO PLAYER: BAYESIAN STRATEGIES

Although the payoff at a play of a game has been shown as the net gain to the player, no real distinction in status can be drawn between the two contestants.

It is a simple matter, involving only a transposition—a switching of columns and rows—and a change of sign of the elements of the payoff table to present the game more positively from the opponent's point of view. We have seen, however, in Introprod, that to exploit the theory of games for decision-making we need only to help the player choose his strategy, and it is toward this end that our further study of games will be directed.

There are two distinct, though related, cases which we must consider.

1. The randomized strategy π used by the opponent is known to the player; that is, the values of $\pi(s_1), \ldots, \pi(s_n)$ are known to him.
2. The randomized strategy used by the opponent is not known to the player.

The analysis of case 1 is the subject of this section, and we use Introprod to illustrate the argument. When, as in Introprod, the opponent has only two simple strategies, s_1 (present a defective item) and s_2 (present an effective item), the player will know which randomized strategy the opponent is using if he knows $k = \pi(s_1)$; for then he also knows $\pi(s_2) = 1 - k$. We can then refer to the opponent's randomized strategy k.

Opponent's Randomized Strategy $k = \frac{1}{4}$ If the player knows that the opponent is using randomized strategy $k = \frac{1}{4}$, how should he react? First, suppose that he restricts his choice to his simple strategies. Suppose, moreover, that there is to be repeated confrontation between the player and the opponent (as is the case in Introprod) over a long run of plays of the game. Consider what happens if the player uses strategy a_2, say, at each play. The advantage to him can then be measured by the total utility, or, equivalently, by the average utility per play, over a long run of plays. At any play against the opponent's given randomized

TABLE 4–3

Utilities $U(a, s)$ and values $V(a, k)$ for Introprod

Decision-maker's action	State of nature		Values $V(a, k)$ for		
	s_1	s_2	$k = \frac{1}{4}$	$k = \frac{3}{4}$	general k
a_1	0	0	0	0	0
a_2	-4	3	$\frac{5}{4}$	$-\frac{9}{4}$	$3 - 7k$
a_3	-2	2	1	-1	$2 - 4k$
a_4	-1	-1	-1	-1	-1
a_5	-5	-2	$-\frac{11}{4}$	$-\frac{17}{4}$	$-2 - 3k$
a_6	-5	2	$\frac{1}{4}$	$-\frac{13}{4}$	$2 - 7k$
a_7	-2	-2	-2	-2	-2

strategy he gains -4 with probability $\frac{1}{4}$ and 3 with probability $\frac{3}{4}$, and his long-run average utility per play is represented by the expected utility

$$-4 \times \tfrac{1}{4} + 3 \times \tfrac{3}{4} = \tfrac{5}{4}.$$

We denote this by $V(a_2, \frac{1}{4})$; inclusion of a_2 and $\frac{1}{4}$ in the notation is to show the dependence on the strategy a_2 chosen by the player and the particular randomized strategy $k = \frac{1}{4}$ of the opponent. We may call $V(a_2, \frac{1}{4})$ the *value* to the player of simple strategy a_2 against the opponent's randomized strategy $k = \frac{1}{4}$.

The definition of value can easily be presented in a general way.

4-5-1 Definition *Value of a simple strategy.* The *value* to the player of using *simple* strategy a against the opponent's known randomized strategy π on $S = \{s_1, \ldots, s_n\}$ is defined as

$$V(a, \pi) = U(a, s_1)\pi(s_1) + \cdots + U(a, s_n)\pi(s_n)$$

$$= \sum_S U(a, s)\pi(s). \qquad (4\text{-}5\text{-}1)$$

If we apply this to strategy a_3 in our game of Introprod, we have

$$V(a_3, \tfrac{1}{4}) = U(a_3, s_1) \times \tfrac{1}{4} + U(a_3, s_2) \times \tfrac{3}{4}$$

$$= -2 \times \tfrac{1}{4} + 2 \times \tfrac{3}{4} = 1.$$

The values of the strategies $a_1, \ldots, a_7$ are shown in the column headed $k = \frac{1}{4}$ in Table 4-3.

We can describe this process of selecting the player's best simple strategy in terms of the maximizing instruction max:

$$V(a_2, \tfrac{1}{4}) = \tfrac{5}{4} = \max \{0, \tfrac{5}{4}, 1, -1, -\tfrac{11}{4}, \tfrac{1}{4}, -2\}$$

$$= \max_A V(a, \tfrac{1}{4}),$$

this last form being an instruction to compute $V(a, \frac{1}{4})$ for each a in A and to choose the largest. (See Appendix 3 for further details on max instructions.)

The player must clearly choose a simple strategy which gives the greatest value for the known randomized strategy of the opponent. Against the opponent's randomized strategy $k = \frac{1}{4}$ the player maximizes the value if he chooses strategy a_2, and the value is $\frac{5}{4}$ per play. The interpretation of this is, of course, that if we know that there is a one-in-four chance that an item will turn out to be defective, our best policy is simply to introduce the new product and sell without testing. Our long-term net return per item will then be $\frac{5}{4}$.

We can now see that the player or decision-maker is quite right in the present circumstances to restrict attention to his simple strategies, for he cannot improve his position by choosing a randomized strategy. Suppose, in fact, that he does employ a randomized strategy p to counter the opponent's or nature's known randomized strategy π. Since the randomized strategies are operated independently, the probability that at one play his simple strategy a and the opponent's simple strategy s will be operated is, by (3–2–1), $p(a)\pi(s)$, in which case the utility is $U(a, s)$. The value (or expected utility) per play is thus the sum of all products of the form $U(a, s)p(a)\pi(s)$ over the possible pairs (a, s). For a p that allocates

$$p(a_1) = \tfrac{3}{10}, \qquad p(a_2) = \tfrac{2}{10}, \qquad p(a_3) = p(a_4) = p(a_5) = p(a_6) = p(a_7) = \tfrac{1}{10},$$

we can present these products in tabular form (Table 4–4). For example, the entry in row a_2 and column s_1 is

$$U(a_2, s_1)p(a_2)\pi(s_1) = -4 \times \tfrac{2}{10} \times \tfrac{1}{4} = -\tfrac{8}{40}.$$

TABLE 4-4

Computation of value of player's randomized strategy

Decision-maker's action	State of nature		Row sums
	s_1	s_2	$V(a, \tfrac{1}{4})p(a)$
a_1	0	0	0
a_2	$-\tfrac{8}{40}$	$\tfrac{18}{40}$	$\tfrac{10}{40}$
a_3	$-\tfrac{2}{40}$	$\tfrac{6}{40}$	$\tfrac{4}{40}$
a_4	$-\tfrac{1}{40}$	$-\tfrac{3}{40}$	$-\tfrac{4}{40}$
a_5	$-\tfrac{5}{40}$	$-\tfrac{6}{40}$	$-\tfrac{11}{40}$
a_6	$-\tfrac{5}{40}$	$\tfrac{6}{40}$	$\tfrac{1}{40}$
a_7	$-\tfrac{2}{40}$	$\tfrac{6}{40}$	$\tfrac{4}{40}$
		Total	$\tfrac{4}{40}$

We can now sum all these entries in two stages, first finding the row sums and then adding these row sums to get the overall total. These row sums take the form

$$V(a, \tfrac{1}{4})p(a).$$

For example, the row sum opposite a_2 is

$$U(a_2, s_1)p(a_2)\pi(s_1) + U(a_2, s_2)p(a_2)\pi(s_2)$$
$$= \{U(a_2, s_1)\pi(s_1) + U(a_2, s_2)\pi(s_2)\}p(a_2)$$
$$= V(a_2, \tfrac{1}{4})p(a_2).$$

The addition of these row sums is therefore the forming of a weighted average (see Appendix 4) of the seven values $V(a, \tfrac{1}{4})$, the weights being the $p(a)$. Since this weighted average $(\frac{4}{40})$ of values cannot exceed the greatest $(\frac{5}{4})$ of the values, there can thus be no advantage to the player in adopting a randomized strategy.

4–5–2 Definition *Value of a randomized strategy.* The *value* to the player of using *randomized* strategy p on $A = \{a_1, \ldots, a_m\}$ against the opponent's known randomized strategy π on $S = \{s_1, \ldots, s_n\}$ is defined as

$$V(p, \pi) = \sum_A V(a, p)p(a), \qquad (4\text{–}5\text{–}2)$$

where $V(a, \pi)$ is the value of the simple strategy a, as in Definition 4–5–1.

The general problem has been reduced to the calculation of the m values $V(a, \pi)$ with the subsequent selection of the largest—a very straightforward procedure. Indeed, as we shall soon see, we may be able to avoid the evaluation of all the m values. The instructions for determining the player's optimum strategy for the general case are now easily formulated.

Player's Optimum Strategy If the player knows the randomized strategy π on $S = \{s_1, \ldots, s_n\}$ used by the opponent, then he must compute all the values $V(a, \pi)$ as in Definition 4–5–1, and then choose as optimum strategy a simple strategy a^* which has the largest value; that is, a^* is obtained by the instruction

$$V(a^*, \pi) = \max_A V(a, \pi). \qquad (4\text{–}5\text{–}3)$$

Note that the player's optimum strategy depends crucially on the randomized strategy of the opponent. To illustrate this point, we show the values corresponding to the opponent's randomized strategy $k = \frac{3}{4}$ in the column headed $k = \frac{3}{4}$ in Table 4–3; the reader should compute for himself these values for Introprod. The player must now turn to a_1 as his optimum strategy. In other words, if we know that three out of four items will turn out to be defective, our best policy is not to go ahead with production.

EXERCISES

1. For the opponent's first randomized strategy in the game of Exercise 1, Section 4–4, $\pi(s_1) = \frac{1}{2}$, $\pi(s_2) = \frac{1}{2}$. For this case, draw up a table of values as in Table 4–3. Which of the three actions (strategies) would you choose? Does this agree with the strategy you chose earlier when actually playing the game? If not, repeat the game and see whether you are better off.

   Compute $V(p, \pi)$ for $p(a_1) = \frac{1}{2}$, $p(a_2) = \frac{1}{2}$, $p(a_3) = 0$. Is it worth your while to try this strategy? Put it into operation against your opponent and see what happens.

   Now consider your opponent's second randomized strategy, namely, $\pi(s_1) = \frac{1}{4}$, $\pi(s_2) = \frac{3}{4}$, and answer the above questions.

2. My dentist (the same one as in Exercise 2, Section 4–4) tells me that over the past year he has had the policy of root-treating the many root infections that have come his way,

and that 70 percent of them were successful. Analyze my decision problem as a game with the randomized strategy of the opponent known, and tell me what my decision should be.

3. Suppose that in Exercise 1 of Section 4–2

$$p = 7, \qquad r = 12, \qquad c = s = 3, \qquad t = 1.$$

What is my appropriate action if I can be sure that 70 percent of sets are perfect, 20 percent contain only one defective item, and 10 percent have both pen and pencil defective?

Invent examples of this kind of information about the quality of production which lead to different kinds of action.

4. The daily demand for a perishable commodity is variable but never exceeds 3 units, and the variability has been found to be accurately described by the following probability model.

Number of units demanded	0	1	2	3
Probability	0.3	0.1	0.2	0.4

A decision on the quantity to produce on a particular day has to be made at the start of the day before the actual demand is known. The profit from a sold item is 1 and the loss from an unsold item is 1. What production policy should be adopted?

4–6 GRAPHIC REPRESENTATION OF THE ANALYSIS

In the game of Introprod the formula we have obtained for the values applies for any randomized strategy k of the opponent. For example,

$$V(a_2, k) = U(a_2, s_1) \times k + U(a_2, s_2) \times (1 - k)$$
$$= -4 \times k + 3 \times (1 - k)$$
$$= 3 - 7k.$$

The values corresponding to the other simple strategies of the player are shown in the column headed "general k" in Table 4–3. This allows us to obtain a broader view of the problem through a very useful graphic representation, which for each a shows the variation in $V(a, k)$ with k. For example, Fig. 4–1 shows the plot of $V(a_2, k)$ against k; this is of course simply the straight line with equation

$$V(a_2, k) = 3 - 7k.$$

Similarly, we can show the straight lines corresponding to the other strategies. To determine the best strategy corresponding to a particular k we then need simply to look at Fig. 4–2 and find which of the lines gives the highest value at the appropriate k. The heavy line in Fig. 4–2 traces this highest value and forms an

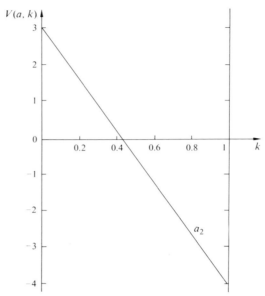

Fig. 4-1 Value graph for decision-maker's action a_2 in the game of Introprod.

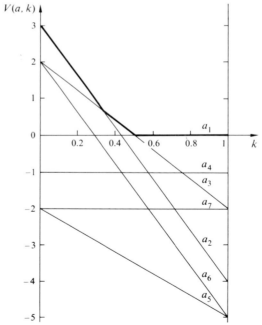

Fig. 4-2 Value graphs for the game of Introprod.

upper boundary. For example, corresponding to the opponent's randomized strategy with $k = \frac{1}{4}$ we see that the line corresponding to a_2 gives the highest value, in accordance with our previous result; for the opponent's randomized strategy with $k = \frac{2}{5}$ we would choose a_3; for the opponent's randomized strategy with $k = \frac{3}{4}$, strategy a_1.

The graphic representation emphasizes that corresponding to different randomized strategies for the opponent we may obtain different best simple strategies for the player. It is convenient to have a suitable terminology.

4-6-1 Definition *Bayesian strategy.* An optimum strategy for the player as determined by Eq. (4–5–2) is called a *Bayesian strategy relative to* π.

EXERCISES

1. Draw the value graphs associated with the following game.

Player's strategy	Opponent's strategy	
	s_1	s_2
a_1	0	1
a_2	2	-1
a_3	1	-2
a_4	3	-3

By interpreting these graphs, or otherwise, establish that

a) against the opponent's randomized strategy $k = \pi(s_1) = 0.8$ the player's best strategy is a_4 with value 1.8,

b) against any opponent's randomized strategy $k < \frac{1}{2}$ the player's strategy a_1 is always best with value never falling below $\frac{1}{2}$;

c) action a_3 is never best.

2. Draw the value graphs for the games or situations of Exercises 1 of Section 4–1, 2 of Section 4–2, 1 of Section 4–4, and reconsider the solution of the problems raised in these exercises by interpretation of the value graphs.

3. A call for assistance from a delivery van has been phoned from a public call box but unfortunately the message recorded is ambiguous and the breakdown could be either at A or B, which are at distances of 30 and 50 minutes away and 60 minutes from each other. The alternatives open to the recovery team are to go to A first, to go to B first, or to wait at the depot for a second call from the delivery van. This second call, if necessary, can be assumed to come ten minutes after the recovery team should have arrived on the scene. Express the problem facing the recovery team as a game with

payoff the loss (and therefore negative) of time involved in not knowing the correct location.

Draw the value graphs for this game. If the recovery team figures that odds in favor of the location's being *B* are 5 to 3, what is the best course of action. Under what circumstances, if any, is it best to wait at the depot?

4–7 ADMISSIBLE AND INADMISSIBLE STRATEGIES

In formulating Introprod we reluctantly admitted for consideration the clearly absurd simple strategies or actions a_5, a_6, and a_7. If we can discover the formal expression of this absurdity, we shall have found a useful means of eliminating certain strategies, possibly without the need to compute their values. It is a marked feature of Fig. 4–2 that the heavy line is formed from parts of lines associated with only three of the strategies, namely a_1, a_2, and a_3. The lines for strategies a_4, a_5, a_6, and a_7 all lie below the heavy line and so are not contenders for the title of best strategy. An even stronger feature about the undesirability of these strategies is that their lines lie completely under one of the other lines; for example, a_4 lies under a_1, a_5 under a_2, a_6 under a_2, and a_7 under a_1. Analytically, this means that, for all π (or equivalently for all k),

$$V(a_4, \pi) < V(a_1, \pi), \qquad V(a_5, \pi) < V(a_2, \pi),$$
$$V(a_6, \pi) < V(a_2, \pi), \qquad V(a_7, \pi) < V(a_1, \pi).$$

The strict inequality need not apply for all π; so long as $\leq$ applies for all π and $<$ for some π, we shall dismiss the inferior strategy. We can formalize this into a definition.

4–7–1 Definition *Admissible and inadmissible simple strategies.* A strategy a is *inadmissible* if there is some other strategy a', say, such that

$$V(a, \pi) \leq V(a', \pi) \qquad \text{for all } \pi,$$

and such that the strict inequality $<$ holds for some π. If no such a' exists, then the strategy a is called *admissible*. Graphically speaking, the lines associated with any two admissible strategies intersect.

Inadmissible strategies can clearly be dismissed from consideration. The question then arises: Can we recognize inadmissible strategies more immediately without having to resort to drawing value graphs? The answer is that we can do so very easily because we can find an equivalent simpler property of the utility function.

4–7–2 Definition *Dominated strategy.* A simple strategy a is said to be *dominated* by the simple strategy a' if $U(a, s) \leq U(a', s)$ for every s in S with strict inequality for some s.

The equivalence of the definitions of inadmissible and dominated is set out in the following theorem; a formal proof is given in Appendix 4.

4–7–1 Theorem *Equivalence of inadmissible and dominated.* A simple strategy is inadmissible if and only if it is dominated by some other simple strategy.

It is very easy to scan the table of utilities and discard any of the player's strategies which are so dominated. For example, the -5 and -2 of strategy a_5 are less than the corresponding -4 and 3 of strategy a_2. Thus strategy a_5 is dominated by strategy a_2, and so is inadmissible.

The concept of admissibility and inadmissibility can be extended to randomized strategies of the player.

4–7–3 Definition *Admissible and inadmissible randomized strategies.* The player's randomized strategy p is *inadmissible* if there is some other strategy (possibly randomized) q such that

$$V(p, \pi) \leq V(q, \pi) \qquad \text{for all } \pi,$$

with the strict inequality $<$ applying for some π. Otherwise p is said to be *admissible*.

A question of interest for future analysis is the following. Having arrived at the class of admissible simple strategies, how do we extend it to incorporate all admissible randomized strategies? The answer is simple. The class of admissible randomized strategies is the class formed by randomizing the set of all simple admissible strategies. For example, in Introprod, the class of admissible strategies consists of

$a_1:$ do not introduce,
$a_2:$ introduce and sell without testing,
$a_3:$ introduce and test: if item is defective, scrap;
        if item is effective, sell,

and all randomized strategies based on these, that is with

$$p(a_4) = \cdots = p(a_7) = 0.$$

Thus if the player tosses two coins and takes action a_1 when the outcome is two heads, a_2 when one head and one tail, a_3 when two tails, he is operating a randomized strategy p with

$$p(a_1) = \tfrac{1}{4}, \qquad p(a_2) = \tfrac{1}{2}, \qquad p(a_3) = \tfrac{1}{4}, \qquad p(a_4) = \cdots = p(a_7) = 0;$$

and this randomized strategy is admissible.

EXERCISES

1. By inspection of the following payoff table determine which of the player's strategies are inadmissible.

Player's strategy	Opponent's strategy	
	s_1	s_2
a_1	4	-1
a_2	2	2
a_3	3	-2
a_4	0	1
a_5	1	3
a_6	2	1

Verify that the value graph of an inadmissible strategy never rises above the value graph of some admissible strategy. Verify also that the value graphs associated with each pair of admissible strategies intersect.

2. Review Exercises 1 of Section 4–1, 2 of Section 4–2, and 1 of Section 4–4, and identify which of the strategies of the player or actions of the decision-maker are inadmissible.

4–8 ADMISSIBILITY OF BAYESIAN STRATEGIES

It would be alarming if we found that the Bayesian strategies which we had been advocating turned out to be inadmissible. Fortunately this is not so. Suppose that a is a Bayesian strategy relative to π, where $\pi(s) > 0$ for every s in S. The method of establishing the admissibility of a will be to show that the alternative conclusion that a is inadmissible leads to a contradiction. Suppose then that a is inadmissible. We have seen that there is then an a' such that

$$U(a, s) \leq U(a', s) \qquad \text{for every } s \text{ in } S,$$

with strict inequality for some s. If $\pi(s) > 0$ for all s in S, then

$$U(a, s)\pi(s) \leq U(a', s)\pi(s) \qquad \text{for every } s \text{ in } S,$$

with strict inequality for some s. The sum of left-hand sides over S must then be less than the corresponding sum of the right-hand side. It follows immediately from Definition 4–5–1 that

$$V(a, \pi) < V(a', \pi),$$

so that a is not a Bayesian strategy relative to π, a contradiction. Hence we conclude that a is admissible.

The restriction to $\pi(s) > 0$ for every s in S is clearly necessary. Consider the game with the utility matrix as in Table 4–5. Both a_1 and a_2 are Bayesian strategies relative to $\pi(s_1) = 1$, $\pi(s_2) = 0$, but a_1 is inadmissible since it is dominated by a_2.

TABLE 4–5

Table of $U(a, s)$

Player's strategy	Opponent's strategy	
	s_1	s_2
a_1	1	0
a_2	1	2

The restriction that $\pi(s)$ be positive for all states of nature is not a source of worry in our context, since if we admit a state of nature as possible, we must surely consider only randomized strategies that have a positive chance of selecting that state.

EXERCISES

1. For the game with payoff table

Player's strategy	Opponent's strategy	
	s_1	s_2
a_1	3	-1
a_2	4	-2
a_3	2	-1

show that a_2 is the Bayesian strategy relative to $\pi(s_1) = 0.6$, $\pi(s_2) = 0.4$. Verify that a_2 is admissible.

Show that a_3 is a Bayesian strategy relative to $\pi(s_1) = 0$, $\pi(s_2) = 1$, but that it is inadmissible. Why is this possible?

2. Review Exercises 1 of Section 4–1, 2 of Section 4–2, and 1 of Section 4–4, and verify that each of the Bayesian strategies you found is admissible.

4–9 RANDOMIZED STRATEGY OF OPPONENT UNKNOWN TO PLAYER

The player's first step must clearly be to rid himself of any inadmissible strategies. The concept of inadmissibility is thus simply a means of weeding out obviously inferior strategies. It seldom leads to the choice of a unique strategy. If it does, then the unique admissible strategy must be a simple strategy, for the upper boundary of the value graphs of the simple strategies (recall Fig. 4–2) must coincide with the value graph of a single simple strategy, which will of course be admissible. If this were not so, the upper boundary would contain parts of the *intersecting* value graphs of two simple strategies and these two strategies would both be admissible, contrary to our supposition of uniqueness.

For the case in which the exclusion of all inadmissible strategies leads to a unique admissible simple strategy a^*, there is no problem. This is clearly the best strategy regardless of the randomized strategy used by the opponent, and

$$V(a^*, \pi) \geq V(p, \pi) \qquad \text{for all } \pi \text{ and all } p.$$

The strategy a^* is clearly a Bayesian strategy relative to every π. Such an overwhelmingly good strategy is called a *uniformly best strategy*. Note that the value graph of a uniformly best strategy lies above the value graph of all other strategies. As an example of a uniformly best strategy, consider Introprod with selling loss 1, replacement cost 3, scrapping loss 2, and testing cost 1, per item. Then the matrix of utilities (omitting the obviously ridiculous strategies a_5, a_6, a_7) is given in Table 4–6, and strategies a_2, a_3, and a_4 are each dominated by strategy a_1. This is thus the uniformly best strategy. Since there is in this problem a loss involved in selling and in scrapping, it is rather obvious that the best policy is not to go into production. A uniformly best strategy very seldom exists in a problem of any substance.

TABLE 4-6

Table of $U(a, s)$

Decision-maker's action	State of nature	
	s_1	s_2
a_1	0	0
a_2	-4	-1
a_3	-3	-2
a_4	-2	-2

Some decision-makers feel satisfied when they have reduced the problem to a statement of the admissible strategies. They would argue that this is as much as can be achieved under the circumstances. There is nothing in the formulation which allows us to choose one admissible strategy rather than another. A decision-maker cannot be accused of malpractice so long as he uses an admissible strategy.

While this is a defensible position, it seems to the author that it is a peculiarly negative and artificial attitude to adopt. In practice, as we shall see, the class of admissible strategies may vary extremely widely, so widely as to range over the courses of action which are intuitively obvious. This is certainly the case in Introprod, where strategies a_1, a_2, and a_3 are all admissible. The concept of admissibility may exclude only the obvious nonstarter and still leave essentially a very wide choice.

What then can be done? Three of the possibilities open to us are as follows:

1. We may return to the previous case by making some working assumption about π in as reasonable a way as possible.
2. We may try to restrict further the class of admissible strategies by excluding some on a criterion other than admissibility. This involves the introduction of some *principle of exclusion.*
3. We may adopt a pessimistic viewpoint and attempt to prepare for the worst that nature or the opponent can bestow on us.

Our problems are such that opportunity 2 is seldom open to us. We therefore now concentrate attention on 3. This leads us to the max-min principle.

4–10 THE CASE OF THE PESSIMISTIC PLAYER (MAX-MIN)

To illustrate the argument underlying the present analysis, we shall examine an even simpler game than Introprod. Consider the game defined by the matrix of utilities of Table 4–7, and with the opponent's strategy completely

TABLE 4–7

Table of $U(a, s)$

Player's strategy	Opponent's strategy	
	s_1	s_2
a_1	3	-2
a_2	-1	2

unknown to the player. The player's thoughts will run along the following lines : "Suppose that I operate a randomized strategy p, with $p(a_1) = c$, $p(a_2) = 1 - c$. Then if my opponent uses his simple strategy s_1, the value to me is

$$V(p, s_1) = 3c - 1(1 - c) = -1 + 4c,$$

and if he uses his simple strategy s_2, the value to me is

$$V(p, s_2) = -2c + 2(1 - c) = 2 - 4c.$$

I can show the variation in these values graphically (Fig. 4–3). Since I am very pessimistic, I must imagine my opponent to be omniscient and red in tooth and claw. I must therefore assume that he knows my p or c and, on the supposition that he confines himself to the choice of one of his simple strategies, he will choose the simple strategy which minimizes the value to me. If $c < \frac{3}{8}$ (the point where the value graphs cross) this is his strategy s_1 ; for $c > \frac{3}{8}$ this is his strategy s_2 ; for $c = \frac{3}{8}$ either strategy will do. I now notice that I have been quite right to assume that my opponent chooses one of his simple strategies, for $V(p, \pi)$, being a weighted average of the $V(p, s)$, would be to my advantage. What then must I do? I must clearly choose the value of c so that I make this minimum value as large as possible. I will achieve this if I move my c to $\frac{3}{8}$, when the value to me is $\frac{1}{2}$. If I move c to the left of $\frac{3}{8}$, my opponent will choose his simple

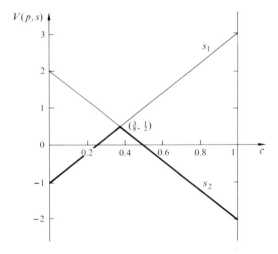

Fig. 4–3 Value graphs for a randomized strategy of the player and for the two simple strategies of the opponent. The heavy line picks out $\min \{V(p, s_1), V(p, s_2)\}$.

strategy s_1 and will lower the value to me; if I move my c to the right, he will choose strategy s_2 and again lower the value to me. Yes, I must play randomized strategy $p(a_1) = \frac{3}{8}$, $p(a_2) = \frac{5}{8}$, and content myself with the value $\frac{1}{2}$ per play."

A comparison of the analyses of Figs. 4-2 and 4-3 shows that whereas in the first the heavy line of interest is the *upper* boundary of the value graph diagram, in the latter we are interested in the *lower* boundary. The underlying reason for this extreme difference in approach lies in the information that is available. When the player knows the opponent's randomized strategy he can act boldly, take the positive step of searching for a maximum, and so is led to the upper boundary. When he does not have this information he is necessarily timid, becomes concerned about protecting himself against the worst that can happen, and this worst is described by the lower boundary of the value graph diagram.

We have looked at the problem from the viewpoint of the player. We could similarly and equally well look at it from the viewpoint of the opponent. His picture of the game is shown in Fig. 4-4. He fears that the player will have guessed his randomized strategy $\pi(s_1) = k$, $\pi(s_2) = 1 - k$ and then have chosen the corresponding simple strategy which maximizes the value. This maximized value for different k is shown by the heavy line in Fig. 4-4. The opponent will

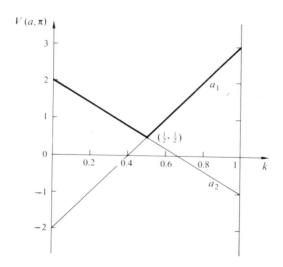

Fig. 4-4 Value graphs for a randomized strategy of the opponent and for the two simple strategies of the player. The heavy line picks out $\max\{V(a_1, \pi), V(a_2, \pi)\}$.

then choose his k to make this maximized value as small as possible. This he clearly achieves by the choice of $k = \frac{1}{2}$ when the value to the player is $\frac{1}{2}$.

It thus appears that with this air of suspicion between the contestants an equilibrium is reached, the player being content to ensure value $\frac{1}{2}$ through his randomized strategy p^*, say, with $c = \frac{3}{8}$, and his opponent content to keep the value to this level by using randomized strategy π^*, say, with $k = \frac{1}{2}$. Then

$$V(p, \pi^*) \leq V(p^*, \pi^*) \leq V(p^*, \pi) \qquad \text{for all } p \text{ and } \pi. \qquad (4\text{–}10\text{–}1)$$

Such a solution can be reached for any given matrix of utilities; the proof of this statement is beyond the scope of this book. Since the player maximizes the minimum value allowed him by the opponent, and since the opponent minimizes the maximum value securable by the player, the player's and opponent's best strategies are termed *max-min* and *min-max* strategies. The agreed value, namely $V(p^*, \pi^*)$, is the max-min (or min-max) value of the game. The max-min and min-max property can be formally expressed in terms of min and max instructions.

4–10–1 Definition *Max-min strategy.* A *max-min strategy* p^* of the player (and a corresponding min-max strategy π^* for the opponent) is defined by (4–10–1). The value to the player is then

$$V(p^*, \pi^*) = \max_p \{\min_\pi V(p, \pi)\} = \min_\pi \{\max_p V(p, \pi)\}. \qquad (4\text{–}10\text{–}2)$$

EXERCISES

1. Following the argument of this section and drawing value graphs as in Figs. 4–2 and 4–3, determine the max-min strategy of the player, the min-max strategy of the opponent, and the value of the game with the following payoff table.

	Opponent's strategy	
Player's strategy	s_1	s_2
a_1	-3	4
a_2	3	-2

2. There are two ways in which I can try to obtain an article that I want and value at 110. I may order it direct-mail at a price of 90 (post paid) and run the risk of receiving an unsatisfactory article, in which case I reckon I will lose 40 in its resale. Alternatively, I can go to the depot at a travel cost of 20 and purchase it, only if I find it satisfactory, at a price of 80. Express my problem in terms of a game and determine my max-min course of action.

3. A retailer has already decided to avail himself of a once-and-for-all offer of tourist souvenirs but is undecided about the quantity—5000, 10,000 or 20,000—that he should order. His hesitation is due to his uncertainty about whether the souvenirs will "take" or not. If they take, he estimates that his overall profits on these batches would be 2500, 7000, and 15,000, respectively; if not, then his losses would be −1000, −3000, −11,000. If he is in a pessimistic state, what must his order be?

His market research department says that the souvenir will take, and they are correct in such predictions roughly two times out of three. How will this affect the retailer's decision?

4–11 THE MAX-MIN APPROACH TO INTRODUCING A NEW PRODUCT

The max-min solution of the game of Introprod is now obvious. The heavy line of Fig. 4–2 shows the maximum value that the player can ensure for himself, and it is clear that this is minimized by the opponent's choosing π^* with k any value in the interval $\frac{1}{2} \leq k \leq 1$. The max-min value of the game is then 0. There is clearly only one strategy for the player which ensures this, and that is his strategy a_1. It really requires no subtle analysis like this to realize that if you believe that nature will do her worst, you are not prepared to introduce a new product.

There is a growing consensus that the max-min approach to problems is an altogether too pessimistic one. This is certainly borne out by the example we have just investigated. It is essentially a policy of avoiding all possible risks rather than a policy of taking a calculated risk. In the controversy that occasionally flares up between advocates of Bayesian strategies and others, there is a tendency for the two sides to argue from the extremes of their philosophies. The practicalities of life are usually somewhat different from these two extremes. Usually there is not sufficient information to pinpoint accurately the opponent's randomized strategy. In *Introducing a New Product* we may not have complete information about the variability of the product in mass production; we have not so far mass-produced it. But, equally, there is seldom no information about the randomized strategy. We may have a fairly shrewd idea at least about the range in which the proportion of defectives (the k of our model Introprod) lies. For example, if we are reasonably assured that this proportion is less than 10 percent (that is, $k < 0.1$), we would have no hesitation (see Fig. 4–2) in adopting strategy a_2, that is, introducing and selling the product without further testing of items.

Every problem must, of course, be treated on its own merits in this respect. But it is well to realize that the max-min approach is a last resort when courage fails. A more constructive approach in such circumstances is probably to investigate how the Bayesian strategy changes as different assumptions about the opponent's randomized strategy are adopted.

Computationally, too, the max-min approach is much more difficult than the case in which the player knows the opponent's randomized strategy. We have succeeded in the simple illustrative problems taken because we could obtain, with the small number of strategies available to the contestants, a graphic representation. Such a direct representation is not available to us when, as in many real problems, the number of strategies takes us into dimensions higher than three. (To appreciate the difficulties the reader may care to try to obtain the max-min solution of the game of One-two-three, which can be found from a three-dimensional representation.) Special devices, such as the conversion to an equivalent problem in linear programming, may then be necessary and the problem may then be resolved by suitably instructing an automatic computer. (For references, see Reference 20 in the list of Further Reading.)

CHAPTER 5

THE NATURE OF
STATISTICAL INFERENCE

In the game approach of Chapter 4 we met and solved our first problem in decision-making under uncertainty. What has been lacking so far has been the possibility of experimenting, of obtaining some additional information, to help the decision-making process. What we have been involved with up to now could be called the *no-data* decision-making process. We must now consider how to handle data to provide the kind of information we require for decision-making. This is the branch of our study called *statistical inference*, the subject of the present chapter.

5–1 THE CLASS OF POSSIBLE PROBABILITY MODELS

Very seldom can we specify a probability model for a basic experiment or situation, where variability is present, and say with any certainty "This is the true model, this is precisely the way nature works." We have already had instances of this in Section 2–9. There we recognized that in Problem 4 (Determine the steroid level of a baby, Section 1–5) the experiment has two possible models, one applicable when the baby is normal, the other when the baby is abnormal. For a particular baby about to be screened, we do not know which is the true model. If we did know, then we would have little further intellectual interest in it for there is nothing else to discover. We would know the state of the baby—normal or abnormal—and screening would be unnecessary. Usually we are far from being able to specify the true model, but may be in a position to say that it is one of a class of possible probability models.

Example *Trials of a new medical drug.* A new medical drug of potential value in the cure of a certain ailment is under consideration. Here the *basic experiment* is the application of the drug to a patient, and we suppose that the record set is simply $X = \{0, 1\}$, where 0 represents failure and 1 represents success. We saw in Section 2–9 that since we cannot know in advance the success rate or probability s, we must postulate a whole class of possible probability models with probability functions

$$p(0 \mid s) = 1 - s, \qquad p(1 \mid s) = s,$$

one corresponding to each s in the interval $0 \le s \le 1$, which thus constitutes the index set S.

The application of the drug to a single patient will give us little information about the unknown true index or success probability. We must determine the total number y of successes among a number n, say, of patients, and so we are led to the idea that the *informative experiment*, here a binomial counting experiment (Definition 3–6–2), may differ from the basic experiment. This informative experiment also has a whole class of probability models (Table 3–13) *indexed by the same s*. To emphasize this we would then write the probability function of Table 3–13 in the form $q(y \mid s)$ instead of $q(y)$. The purpose of such controlled trials is to narrow down the wide range of possible models, to try to obtain a clearer picture of what index s nature is using. For example, if $n = 100$ and $y = 85$, we have 85 successes out of 100 trials and this clearly tells us that some of the models (or, equivalently, indexes)—for example $s = 0.01$—can be regarded as unreasonable, whereas others—for example 0.85—are very reasonable.

Note that we have taken, and must continue to take, the necessary step of making it quite clear in our notation which model or probability function we are considering. For example, when we evaluate an expectation the result depends on which particular model is under consideration. In such circumstances we shall then write for the means and variances $\mathscr{E}(x \mid s)$, $\mathscr{E}(y \mid s)$, and $\mathscr{V}(x \mid s)$, $\mathscr{V}(y \mid s)$, to indicate that the models under consideration are those indexed by s. For instance, in our example above, we should rewrite the results of Theorem 3–9–5 as

$$\mathscr{E}(y \mid s) = ns, \qquad \mathscr{V}(y \mid s) = ns(1 - s),$$

to emphasize the dependence of the quantities on the index.

Example *Cutting edges.* It has been discovered that the apparently identical cutting edges supplied to a textile manufacturer are of two types, *soft* and *hard*. Edges can be definitely sorted into the two types only after a large number of operations. However, the pattern of necessary resharpening of eventually classified edges has suggested the probability models of Table 5–1 to describe the number x of operations between successive sharpenings for each of the two types.

TABLE 5–1

Probability models for number of operations between sharpenings

Type	x					
	1	2	3	4	5	6
s_1 (soft)	0.11	0.24	0.35	0.18	0.08	0.04
s_2 (hard)	0.02	0.09	0.22	0.33	0.22	0.12

Suppose that we are given a cutting edge of unknown type. While we know that one of the probability models applies, we do not know which particular one. If we denote the possible states of the cutting edge by

$$s_1: \quad \text{soft},$$

$$s_2: \quad \text{hard},$$

then we can conveniently index this class of (two) probability models for the basic experiment "determine the number of operations to resharpening." We can then denote the entries in the first row of Table 5–1 by $p(x \mid s_1)$ and those in the second row by $p(x \mid s_2)$. With this notation it is absolutely clear which model is being used at any particular time. Again in the computations of means and variances it is important to show which model is concerned. We have

$$\mathscr{E}(x \mid s_1) = 1 \times 0.11 + \cdots + 6 \times 0.04 = 3,$$

$$\mathscr{E}(x \mid s_2) = 1 \times 0.02 + \cdots + 6 \times 0.12 = 4,$$

$$\mathscr{V}(x \mid s_1) = (1 - 3)^2 \times 0.11 + \cdots + (6 - 3)^2 \times 0.04 = 1.54,$$

$$\mathscr{V}(x \mid s_2) = (1 - 4)^2 \times 0.02 + \cdots + (6 - 4)^2 \times 0.12 = 1.46.$$

Here also the informative experiment which we carry out to help us discover which of the models is the more reasonable may be different from the basic experiment. For example, we may record the numbers (x_1, x_2) of operations associated with two intersharpening intervals. There is then a class of probability models for this informative experiment, consisting of two product models (Definition 3–2–1), one based on the s_1 probability function of Table 5–1, the other on the s_2 probability function. This class of models is therefore indexed by the same index as the basic experiment.

These examples show that while we do not know which is the true model, we can assume that there is some true index s^*, say, which nature has chosen and which she uses. We would be extremely fortunate if we knew s^*, for then we would have a complete description of the experiment. Indeed our whole purpose in experimentation is simply to reduce our uncertainty about the true index. Can we somehow or other narrow the field of uncertainty characterized by the "size" of the set S of possible indexes? We may or we may not have some prior experience of such situations. In some circumstances we may be able to attach some weight or measure of plausibility (a concept developed in the next section) to each s; in other circumstances we may find it hard to do so. In either circumstance we shall probably, if at all possible, perform some informative experiment, which is somehow related through the indexing system to the basic experiment. Even if we are armed with measures of plausibility, we are to a considerable extent uncertain of which index s^* nature has chosen. How do we use the information from the informative experiment to reduce our uncertainty? The answer naturally depends on the underlying reasons for our wish to reduce this uncertainty. It is our purpose in this chapter to examine a number of ways to use the information to reduce this uncertainty—ways traditionally categorized as methods of statistical inference.

Since we shall be concerned mainly with the way we use the information from the informative experiment and shall not need a specific notation for the basic experiment, we shall denote the (possibly multidimensional) record set of the informative experiment by X, a typical simple record by x, and the probability function corresponding to index s by $p(x \mid s)$.

EXERCISES

1. Consider some binomial trial familiar to you (for example, recording whether the next phone call you receive will be social or business). Can you specify the probability of success precisely, or do you have to admit that there are a number of possible values for the success probability? If the latter is the case, then you have a class of possible models for the binomial trial.

2. Review Problem 4 (Section 1–5), considering the description of the experiment of examining a baby and determining its steroid level. Show that the describing class of probability models consists of just two models. Indexing these by s_1 and s_2, evaluate $\mathscr{E}(x \mid s_1)$, $\mathscr{V}(x \mid s_1)$, $\mathscr{E}(x \mid s_2)$, $\mathscr{V}(x \mid s_2)$.

3. In the example of this section on cutting edges, consider the informative experiment which records the numbers (x_1, x_2) of operations associated with two intersharpening intervals. Construct the class of probability models for this informative experiment, and from these models evaluate, using a suitable notation, the means and variances of $x_1 + x_2$. (Recall also the simple method of Theorem 3–9–4.) Evaluate also the means and variances of max (x_1, x_2).

4. Individuals may possess a character (genetically, a gene-pair) in one of three forms: dominant AA, hybrid Aa, and recessive aa. *Panmixia* is a genetic model which attempts to explain the distribution of these forms in terms of the transmission of genes (A and a)

from parents to offspring under random mating. It asserts that an offspring of a random mating takes its form according to one of the following models:

x	AA	Aa	aa
$p(x \mid s)$	s^2	$2s(1-s)$	$(1-s)^2$

where $0 \le s \le 1$.

Let $f(x)$ denote the number of A genes possessed by an offspring of type x. Show that

$$\mathscr{E}\{f(x) \mid s\} = 2s, \qquad \mathscr{V}\{f(x) \mid s\} = 2s(1-s).$$

Suppose that $g(x)$ records 1 for a dominant offspring and 0 otherwise. Evaluate $\mathscr{E}\{g(x) \mid s\}, \mathscr{V}\{g(x) \mid s\}$.

5–2 MEASURES OF PLAUSIBILITY

The index s which labels the possible models describing the basic or informative experiment may be considered a "state of nature." The fact that we do not know the true state of nature is shown in our statement that any s in S is a possible index or state of nature. The true state of nature is the unknown s^*. When we assume that nature operates at s or is in state s, we are assuming that the appropriate probability function for the informative experiment is $p(x \mid s)$. Now while we may not know, prior to performing an informative experiment, which s is the true value, we may have some previous evidence that some values of s are more plausible than others.

For example, in Problem 1 (Introducing a new product, Section 1–4), trial runs may have given us a fair idea of the relative frequencies of defective (state s_1) and effective (state s_2) items. Again in Problem 3 (Locating a machine fault, Section 1–5), the unknown states of nature are the possible locations of the fault, namely s_1, the engine, and s_2, the gearbox. Past records may show that gearbox faults are more common than engine faults. Before we are told what particular symptoms have been displayed, it is reasonable to consider the gearbox as a more likely source of fault than the engine.

One way we may use this prior information is to attempt to express varying plausibilities by specifying a measure of plausibility $\pi(s)$ to each s in S. The ratio of $\pi(s_1)$ to $\pi(s_2)$ gives the relative plausibility of s_1 to s_2. Now the extent to which $\pi(s)$ is founded in any real evidence will vary from situation to situation. In some situations we may have much information. There may be some underlying process which essentially produces s, and we may in fact have fairly reliable information about the relative frequencies of various s, which we can identify with $\pi(s)$. The examples just quoted have this feature. At the other extreme we may have very little evidence and then the $\pi(s)$ may be assigned in almost a subjective way. Many persons shudder at the thought of allowing a subjective element to creep into what they regard as an essentially objective process. There are, however, some situations in which it is impossible to exclude some subjective element. It may be that awareness of the presence of a subjective element makes the assignment of $\pi(s)$ a responsible act, whereas some other approach to the problem may conceal the subjective aspect.

If the plausibilities were firmly based on relative frequencies, then they would naturally follow the same rules as probabilities. There is some sense then in our assuming that, even when $\pi(s)$ is assigned subjectively, the plausibility function $\pi(s)$ behaves like a probability function. It is as if we believed that nature had carried out an experiment to determine her state, and that this experiment by nature has record set S and probability function $\pi(s)$. We shall, however, retain the term plausibility rather than probability to draw attention to the fact that the information on which the plausibility function is constructed may be less direct and less well founded than the information obtained from the explicitly undertaken informative experiment.

EXERCISE

A factory inspector proposes to select an item at random from a box of three items and to determine whether or not it is defective. Enumerate the appropriate class of models to describe this experiment, using the (unknown) number of defectives in the box to index the class. The inspector recently examined the entire contents of 1000 boxes and found 772, 119, 72, 37 boxes with 0, 1, 2, 3 defectives, respectively. Can you suggest a suitable plausibility function for the index set?

5–3   PLAUSIBILITIES BEFORE AND AFTER EXPERIMENTATION

Suppose that we start with a plausibility function $\pi(s)$ on S, experiment, and obtain x in the informative experiment which has class of probability functions $p(x \mid s)$ as described in Section 5–1. We have here the formal structure of a two-stage experiment (see Fig. 5–1). In Section 3–4 under the heading "An important relationship" we saw that it was possible to move to an alternative two-stage description; in this view x is recorded at the first stage with probability $p(x)$ and s at the second stage, $\pi(s \mid x)$ denoting the probability or plausibility of s, given

First-stage experiment   Second-stage experiment

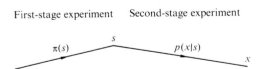

Fig. 5–1 View of the assignment of a plausibility function and the informative experiments as a two-stage experiment.

x. Here *s* and *x* play the roles of x_1 and x_2 in the setting of Section 3–4. Following the arguments of Section 3–4, we can present the construction of this alternative generation of *s* and *x* in three steps. First, we construct the "joint" probability function of *x* and *s*,

$$p(x, s) = \pi(s)p(x \mid s); \qquad (5\text{–}3\text{–}1)$$

compare (3–3–4). Second, we determine the "marginal" probability function,

$$p(x) = \sum_s p(x, s); \qquad (5\text{–}3\text{–}2)$$

compare (3–4–4). This acts as the first-stage probability function of our alternative sequential formulation. Third, we arrive at the new second-stage function by the relation

$$\pi(s \mid x) = \frac{p(x, s)}{p(x)}, \qquad (5\text{–}3\text{–}3)$$

analogous to (3–4–5). These three steps can clearly be combined into one statement:

$$\pi(s \mid x) = \frac{\pi(s)p(x \mid s)}{\sum_s \pi(s)p(x \mid s)}. \qquad (5\text{–}3\text{–}4)$$

We may interpret $\pi(s \mid x)$ as the plausibility of *s* after we have carried out the experiment and observed *x*. The effect of the experiment is to transform our plausibility assessment before experimentation, namely $\pi(s)$, into a plausibility assessment after the experiment, namely $\pi(s \mid x)$. If we are going to make decisions on the basis of the information *x*, then it is our present assessment of uncertainty through $\pi(s \mid x)$ which will be relevant to the decision and not $\pi(s)$.

The relationship (5–3–4) is generally called *Bayes's theorem* or *Bayes's formula* after its first discoverer, the Reverend Thomas Bayes (1702–61). It, or its three-step equivalent, will play a central role in the remainder of this book.

Example *Machine faults.* Consider the aspect of inference in Problem 3 (Locating a machine fault, Section 1–5). Here the basic situation is the variability of symptoms arising from the two possible fault locations. The unknown states of nature are

s_1: engine fault,
s_2: gearbox fault,

and the record set *X* of the informative experiment has three simple records,

x_1: overheating only,
x_2: irregular traction only,
x_3: overheating and irregular traction.

Table 1–3, by providing the relative frequencies of the symptom combinations for each location of fault over an extensive set of previous fault investigations, gives essentially the probability functions $p(x \mid s_1)$ and $p(x \mid s_2)$ for the two possible models. Suppose that extensive past records have also shown that the proportions of engine faults and gearbox faults are 0.6 and 0.4. Then we can use this knowledge to assign a prior plausibility function $\pi(s_1) = 0.6$, $\pi(s_2) = 0.4$. From the $\pi(s)$ and $p(x \mid s)$ functions we apply the three-step construction of the posterior plausibility functions $\pi(s \mid x)$. The first two steps are shown in Table 5–2. For example, the first entry is by (5–3–1) and Table 1–3

$$p(x_1, s_1) = \pi(s_1)p(x_1 \mid s_1) = 0.6 \times 0.1 = 0.06.$$

Then the $p(x)$ are obtained as columns sums by (5–3–2).

TABLE 5–2

Table of $p(x, s)$ and $p(x)$

	Symptom x		
Location of fault	x_1 (overheating only)	x_2 (irregular traction only)	x_4 (overheating and irregular traction)
s_1 (engine)	0.06	0.24	0.30
s_2 (gearbox)	0.20	0.12	0.08
$p(x)$	0.26	0.36	0.38

From Table 5–2 we can calculate from (5–3–5) the complete table (Table 5–3) for the three posterior plausibility functions $\pi(s \mid x_1)$, $\pi(s \mid x_2)$, $\pi(s \mid x_3)$. For example, $\pi(1 \mid x_1) = 0.06/0.26 = 0.231$. Thus the evidence that the only symptom present is overheating changes the prior plausibility ratio of 0.6 to 0.4 in

TABLE 5–3

Table of posterior plausibilities $\pi(s \mid x)$

	Symptom x		
Location of fault	x_1 (overheating only)	x_2 (irregular traction only)	x_3 (overheating and irregular traction)
s_1 (engine)	0.231	0.667	0.789
s_2 (gearbox)	0.769	0.333	0.211

favor of an engine fault to a posterior plausibility ratio of 0.769 to 0.231 in favor of a gearbox fault. Similarly for the other symptoms.

Table 5–3 completes the inference part of the problem; it summarizes our assessment of the uncertainty between engine or gearbox fault after observing the symptom. How we act on this assessment will depend on the relative costs of examining engine and gearbox. Even if the odds, given a particular symptom, point to an engine fault, it may still be more sensible to dismantle the gearbox first if this is appreciably the less costly examination. Full consideration of this point must await our fuller investigation of decision-making.

When a plausibility measure can be assigned, the whole inference story is contained in the conversion of the prior to the posterior assessment of uncertainty. Everything that the data x can supply has been extracted in this conversion. This is the essence of the Bayesian approach to inference. For those situations in which it is impossible to assign such a plausibility measure, what is the nature of the inference problem? Some kind of solution is then usually attempted by the consideration of some more special purpose to the inference than the mere extraction of all the relevant information. In later sections of this chapter we shall examine a number of those special aspects of inference.

Since $\pi(s \mid x)$ behaves in all respects like a probability function on S, we can formally obtain the mean and variance associated with this function. We can write these as $\mathscr{E}(s \mid x)$ and $\mathscr{V}(s \mid x)$ to show their association with $\pi(s \mid x)$. We shall find later that these play an important role when the index has a quantitative character (for example, probability of success, number of effective articles, number of intruder cells).

Example *Two scribes.* Extensive manuscripts of two scribes show that they differ in the relative frequencies with which they use two alternative vowel forms "e" and "œ," as shown in the following table:

	e	œ
Scribe *A*	0.3	0.7
Scribe *B*	0.5	0.5

A new manuscript fragment, known to be by one of the scribes, uses the vowel form five times, three times as "e" and twice as "œ." On previous independent evidence the odds are 7 to 3 in favor of *A*. Show that the evidence of these vowel forms is enough to turn the odds in favor of *B*.

Solution. The unknown state of nature here is which of the two scribes wrote the manuscript, so we may take $S = \{s_1, s_2\}$, where

s_1: scribe *A* wrote the manuscript,
s_2: scribe *B* wrote the manuscript.

The previous independent evidence of odds of 7 to 3 in favor of *A*, based on the extensive classified manuscripts, allows us to set

$$\pi(s_1) = 0.7, \qquad \pi(s_2) = 0.3.$$

The informative experiment is the counting of the number x of vowel forms of type "e," say, in the five (assumedly independent) uses of it in the fragment, that is, a binomial counting experiment for scribe A (index s_1) with success probability 0.3, and a binomial counting experiment for scribe B (index s_2) with success probability 0.5. Since $x = 3$, we have

$$p(x \mid s_1) = \binom{5}{3}(0.3)^3(0.7)^2 = 0.1323,$$

$$p(x \mid s_2) = \binom{5}{3}(0.5)^3(0.5)^2 = 0.3125.$$

By (5–3–1) and (5–3–2),

$$\begin{aligned}
p(x) &= \pi(s_1)p(x \mid s_1) + \pi(s_2)p(x \mid s_2) \\
&= 0.7 \times 0.1323 + 0.3 \times 0.3125 \\
&= 0.09261 + 0.09375 = 0.8636.
\end{aligned}$$

Hence, by (5–3–4),

$$\pi(s_1 \mid x) = \frac{0.09261}{0.8636}, \qquad \pi(s_2 \mid x) = \frac{0.09375}{0.8636},$$

so that the prior odds

$$\frac{\pi(s_1)}{\pi(s_2)} = \frac{7}{3}$$

in favor of A are turned, by the evidence of the vowel forms, into odds of

$$\frac{\pi(s_1 \mid x)}{\pi(s_2 \mid x)} = \frac{9261}{9375} = \frac{3087}{3125},$$

which are now in favor of B.

Note that since we are concerned here only with odds and since, from (5–3–4),

$$\frac{\pi(s_1 \mid x)}{\pi(s_2 \mid x)} = \frac{\pi(s_1)p(x \mid s_1)}{\pi(s_2)p(x \mid s_2)},$$

the step of computing $p(x)$ could have been avoided.

EXERCISES

1. For the following class of three models the prior plausibilities attaching to s_1, s_2, s_3 are 0.1, 0.4, 0.5. Find the four posterior plausibility functions associated with $x_1, \ldots, x_4$.

Index	Simple record			
	x_1	x_2	x_3	x_4
s_1	0.1	0.2	0.3	0.4
s_2	0.3	0.3	0.2	0.2
s_3	0.5	0.1	0.1	0.3

2. A plant virus can be of one of two strains A and B, and an attempt is being made to classify the strain attacking a plant from the plant symptoms displayed (leaf-yellowing only, petal-falling only, leaf-yellowing and petal-falling) instead of by costly laboratory tests. The study of a large number of plants attacked by known strains of virus suggests the following probability models for symptom variability:

Strain	Symptom		
	Leaf-yellowing only	Petal-falling only	Leaf-yellowing and petal-falling
A	0.4	0.2	0.4
B	0.6	0.2	0.2

On the assumption that strain B is twice as likely to attack a plant as strain A, evaluate the posterior plausibilities that the attacking virus is A in plants suffering from
a) leaf-yellowing only,
b) petal-falling only,
c) leaf-yellowing and petal-falling.

How are these plausibilities affected if you are told that the plants come from an area where attacks by A and B viruses are equally common?

3. A candidate in an examination is said to be of quality s if there is a probability s that he knows the answer to a multiple-choice question. If he does not know the answer he selects one of the a answers offered at random. For a candidate of quality s who has answered such a question correctly, show that the plausibility on this evidence of his having known the answer is $as/\{(a - 1)s + 1\}$. Show that this plausibility cannot be less than s. Is this intuitively reasonable?

4. A psychiatrist has been studying a test for detecting a certain kind of abnormality. He has come to the conclusion that the test has a probability 0.02 of misclassifying a

normal person as abnormal and a probability 0.01 of misclassifying an abnormal person as normal. In the population as a whole he estimates that 1 in 1000 persons has this abnormality. In a screening trial a person has been classified by the test as abnormal. What measure of plausibility should the psychiatrist assign to the conclusion that this person is genuinely abnormal?

It is pointed out to the psychiatrist that in patients referred to him the proportion of abnormals is probably as high as $\frac{1}{4}$ because of preliminary examination by the patients' doctors. For a referred patient classified by his test as abnormal, how plausible will he now regard abnormality as the true state of the patient?

What proportion of patients referred to the psychiatrist will be misclassified one way or the other?

5. During a routine three-year valuation study a car insurance company has ascertained that 1 in 40 of the cars insured by it was involved in an accident. Of its accident-involved cars the proportions that were dark, medium, and light in color tone were 0.3, 0.3, 0.4; whereas for accident-free cars these proportions were 0.2, 0.2, 0.6. You are asked by the manager to assess how the color tone of a car affects its accident proneness. What answer would you give?

6. A stamp dealer is offered a sheet of British commemoratives with the gold Queen's head missing. He is aware that it is possible to remove the gold by a chemical process which has as yet deluded detection. He has developed two independent tests to detect traces of the chemical in the stamp, but unfortunately neither of these is foolproof because one of the printing inks also contains minute quantities of the chemical. In fact, the models he constructs from his experience are as follows:

Nature of Sheet	Reaction			
	Test 1		Test 2	
	Positive	Negative	Positive	Negative
Fake	0.9	0.1	0.7	0.3
Genuine	0.2	0.8	0.4	0.6

He believes, however, that between them the tests will turn odds of 9 to 1 against the sheet's being genuine into odds in favor of its being genuine when both reactions are negative. Is he correct in this belief?

Can either test by itself achieve this turn of odds?

7. A prolific artist has bequeathed to a public art gallery a large number of rectangular abstract pictures. For all but one of these he has indicated the correct hanging orientation. The enigmatic picture has no such indication and a bitter controversy has arisen among the curators as to how it should be hung, opinion being equally divided among the four possible orientations. In an attempt to resolve the situation, the curators invite two art critics, who have never seen the pictures before, to hang, independently, the

pictures of known orientation, though they, of course, are not told the correct orientation. The following table shows the relative frequencies with which a picture hung by them had to be turned counterclockwise through 0°, 90°, 180°, 270° to reach the correct position.

	0°	90°	180°	270°
Critic *A*	0.51	0.08	0.16	0.25
Critic *B*	0.44	0.32	0.13	0.11

The sides of the enigmatic picture are numbered clockwise as 1, 2, 3, 4, and the two critics are invited to hang, again independently, this picture. Critic *A* places side 1 at the top, and critic *B* places this side at the bottom. Which orientation is most favored by all this evidence?

5–4 PLAUSIBILITY ANALYSIS OF CELL-ESTIMATION PROBLEM

We can conduct a plausibility analysis of Problem 6 (Estimating a number of cells, Section 1–7). Here there are three basic response situations corresponding to the number of intruder cells in the organism. They can be indexed by this number of intruder cells or, equivalently and more conveniently, by these three response probabilities:

$$\text{no intruder cells:} \quad s_0 = 0.3,$$
$$\text{one intruder cell:} \quad s_1 = 0.6,$$
$$\text{two intruder cells:} \quad s_2 = 0.7.$$

The informative experiment, the determination of the total number x of reactions in the three repeated tests, has a record set $X = \{0, 1, 2, 3\}$ and is a binomial counting experiment (Definition 3–6–2); and there are three possible models or probability functions corresponding to indexes s_0, s_1, s_2. We have then Table 5–4 for $p(x \mid s)$, directly computed from the binomial probability

TABLE 5-4

Table of $p(x \mid s)$

Number of intruder cells	Index	Number x of positive reactions			
		0	1	2	3
0	s_0	0.343	0.441	0.189	0.027
1	s_1	0.064	0.288	0.432	0.216
2	s_2	0.027	0.189	0.441	0.343

formula of Table 3–13. For example,

$$p(1 \mid s_0) = \binom{3}{1}(0.3)(0.7)^2 = 0.441.$$

From the extensive past records we have as prior plausibility function $\pi(s_0) = 0.2$, $\pi(s_1) = 0.5$, $\pi(s_2) = 0.3$. Table 5–5, giving $p(x, s)$, $p(x)$, and $\pi(s \mid x)$, then follows in exactly the same way as in the previous section, from Eqs. (5–3–1) through (5–3–3). Thus if we observe exactly one positive reaction ($x = 1$), we see that the relative plausibilities of the organism's having 0, 1, 2 intruder cells are now approximately 0.3, 0.5, 0.2, compared with the prior plausibilities 0.2, 0.5, 0.3.

TABLE 5–5

Table of $p(x, s)$, $p(x)$, $\pi(s \mid x)$

	Index	Number x of positive reactions			
		0	1	2	3
$p(x, s)$	s_0	0.0686	0.0882	0.0378	0.0054
	s_1	0.0320	0.1440	0.2160	0.1080
	s_2	0.0081	0.0567	0.1323	0.1029
$p(x)$		0.1087	0.2889	0.3861	0.2163
$\pi(s \mid x)$	s_0	0.6311	0.3053	0.0979	0.0250
	s_1	0.2944	0.4984	0.5594	0.4993
	s_2	0.0745	0.1963	0.3427	0.4757

EXERCISES

1. The factory inspector of Exercise 1 of Section 5–2 finds that the item he selects from the box of three items is defective. What plausibilities does he now assign to there being 0, 1, 2, 3 defectives in the box? What is the mean number of defective items in boxes in which he finds the inspected item defective?

2. Sealed batteries each contain three cells, each of which may be "live" or "dead," and experience has shown that, at the time of testing, the proportions containing 0, 1, 2, 3 live cells are 0.1, 0.2, 0.3, 0.4. Two independent tests, each producing either a positive or negative reaction, may be carried out on a battery, the probabilities of positive reactions being as follows for batteries in different states.

Number of live cells	Test 1	Test 2
0	0.3	0.1
1	0.5	0.4
2	0.7	0.6
3	0.9	0.8

A sealed battery is tested and gives a negative reaction in each test. Assign plausibilities to the possible numbers of live cells it contains.

For batteries giving negative reactions to both tests, what is the mean number of live cells per battery? What is the corresponding variance?

5-5 PLAUSIBILITY ANALYSIS OF BINOMIAL TRIALS

Suppose that an informative experiment for a basic binomial trial with success probability s records the total number x of successes in n binomial trials, and so is a binomial counting experiment (Definition 3-6-2). This situation presents us with some mathematical difficulties because the index set S does not contain a finite number of indexes but consists of the whole interval $0 \le s \le 1$. A thorough analysis would thus involve us in models associated with continuous sets, which is strictly outside the scope of this book. We hope, however, that we shall be able to demonstrate this possibility to the reader convincingly enough to enable him to accept a result which we wish to use in some of our future analyses. A prior plausibility function $\pi(s)$ assigns to each s a plausibility. Thus we can represent a plausibility function by its graph. Figure 5-2 shows three possible graphs. For example, (a) which indicates high plausibility for s in the neighborhood of $\frac{1}{2}$, might be a suitable form of prior plausibility function for the probability of obtaining a head in the toss of a coin. If we were introducing a completely new pharmaceutical product of unknown potency, we might be more inclined toward a prior of type (b), where each possible success probability is regarded as equally plausible.

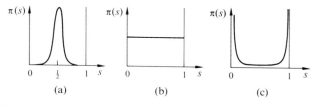

Fig. 5-2 Some prior plausibility functions for a binomial success probability.

Is there any way in which we can express in terms of a plausibility function complete prior ignorance? What do we mean by complete ignorance? Are we, in fact, ever in a state of complete ignorance? Such questions lead to knotty philosophical and semantic problems which are still far from being resolved. Answers have been given which range from the uniform plausibility function of (b) to the extreme U-shaped function of (c). The mathematical and philosophical discussion of these problems is quite beyond the scope of this book. One consolation is that if we have a large amount of information from our informative experiment—in the present case, a large number of replicates or binomial trials—then it makes little difference which of these prior plausibility functions is used. The informative experiment is then contributing so substantially to the effective analysis of the situation that the prior view is swamped by the evidence. Another way of expressing this is to say that the extent of the difference between these ignorance priors is small when measured in terms of the number of trials which would provide sufficient evidence to move from one extreme to the other. In fact, two replicates would be sufficient. Thus we see that if we have a substantial informative experiment we can afford to be a little lax about the precise nature of the prior plausibility function.

In order to apply statistical decision theory later in this book, we shall have to adopt some prior plausibility function for the success probability in binomial trials. For the sake of definiteness we shall assume the uniform version of Fig. 5–2(b). All that we shall have to know about the consequences of such an adoption is that the posterior plausibility function has mean

$$\mathscr{E}(s \mid x) = \frac{x + 1}{n + 2}, \qquad (5\text{–}5\text{–}1)$$

a result to be used in the derivation of (5–6–3). The adoption of such a prior plausibility function is by no means necessary to the arguments that follow. It is simply that we wish to use some function to illustrate the analysis.

EXERCISE

Consider some binomial situations (for example, social or business telephone call, throwing a six or otherwise with a die, next day or later delivery of a letter) and ask yourself what form the graph of your plausibility function for the "success" probability would take.

5–6 PLAUSIBLE PREDICTION

The problem of statistical inference considered thus far has been directed toward reducing uncertainty about which index is the true one by plausibility analysis. While such an activity is useful, it may not be directly relevant to certain problems where we are trying to discover from the informative experiment what will happen at future performances of experiments of a similar nature. For example, a trial run with a drug on a number of patients is not primarily aimed at placing posterior plausibilities on the possible models, but rather at giving some guide as to the future results likely to be obtained if and when the drug is administered to future patients. While plausibility analysis is no doubt useful, we can show that it may have to be developed further to give a direct assessment of the future.

Example *Choice of contracts.* We shall illustrate this aspect in relation to Problem 9 (Choosing between contracts, Section 1–9). To do this we must pose the following question: From our knowledge of the relative frequencies of the raw material categories (1 and 2) and the information from the five test components, can we define in some way the plausibility of a future component's being of poor quality or of good quality? We adopt the indexing device of Section 5–4 of using the success probability—here the probability that a component is of high quality—instead of the raw material category. Thus we have the two indexes:

$$\text{raw material category 1}: \quad s_1 = 0.5,$$

$$\text{raw material category 2}: \quad s_2 = 0.7.$$

We can readily take the first step of plausibility analysis based on the given prior plausibilities $\pi(s_1) = 0.6$, $\pi(s_2) = 0.4$, and the informative experiment. Let x be the number of components of good quality obtained in the informative experiment. Then x is the simple record of a binomial counting experiment, so the possible models for the informative experiment are given by Table 3–13 as

$$p(x \mid s_1) = \binom{5}{x}(0.5)^x(0.5)^{5-x} \quad (x = 0, \dots, 5),$$

$$p(x \mid s_2) = \binom{5}{x}(0.7)^x(0.3)^{5-x} \quad (x = 0, \dots, 5).$$

Since our observed x is 4, we have

$$p(4 \mid s_1) = 5(0.5)^5 \quad = 0.15625,$$

$$p(4 \mid s_2) = 5(0.7)^4(0.3) = 0.36015.$$

Hence, by (5–3–4),

$$\pi(s_1 \mid 4) = \frac{0.6 \times 0.15625}{0.6 \times 0.15625 + 0.4 \times 0.36015} = 0.394,$$

$$\pi(s_2 \mid 4) = \frac{0.4 \times 0.36015}{0.6 \times 0.15625 + 0.4 \times 0.36015} = 0.606.$$

We now ask: What are the plausibilities of poor quality and of good quality in a newly produced component from the batch? To answer this we imagine a future experiment with record set $Y = \{y_1, y_2\}$, y_1 and y_2 representing the outcomes "poor quality" and "good quality." Since this future experiment is a basic binomial trial, we know that the probability function is given by one of the following rows:

$$p_0(y_1 \mid s_1) = 0.5, \qquad p_0(y_2 \mid s_1) = 0.5;$$

$$p_0(y_1 \mid s_2) = 0.3, \qquad p_0(y_2 \mid s_2) = 0.7.$$

If we knew the state of the batch we would have a means of predicting quality, since this is precisely the role of the probability functions $p_0(y \mid s_1)$ and $p_0(y \mid s_2)$; if the batch is of category 1 then the probability of a component of poor quality is $p_0(y_0 \mid s_1)$. Although we do not have knowledge of the actual category, we do have our posterior plausibility assessment. We can imagine the determination of the quality of a new component as a conceptual two-stage experiment, the first-stage experiment determining the category of the batch with probability model $\pi(s \mid x)$ and the consequent second-stage experiment the quality of a component from the batch. This second-stage experiment has probability model $p_0(y \mid s_1)$ if the batch category is s_1, and $p_0(y \mid s_2)$ if the batch category is s_2. We are interested in only how x affects our prediction, not in the actual category of the raw material involved. In terms of our two-stage experiment, this means that we are interested only in what happens at the second stage. From our discussion of two-stage experiments in Section 3–3 we have here to find the marginal description of the second-stage experiment. Therefore, we can express this by the use of the notation $\pi(y_1 \mid 4)$ and $\pi(y_2 \mid 4)$ to indicate the plausibilities that the next component will be of poor quality or of good quality (given that four components of good quality have been observed in the five tested). We thus have, by the application of (3–3–6) to the present setting,

$$\pi(y_1 \mid 4) = 0.394 \times 0.5 + 0.606 \times 0.3 = 0.379, \tag{5–6–1}$$

$$\pi(y_2 \mid 4) = 0.394 \times 0.5 + 0.606 \times 0.7 = 0.621. \tag{5–6–2}$$

We shall find later that this is a very useful assessment and is absolutely necessary as a step toward the complete solution of Problem 9, Section 1–9.

Example *Binomial trials.* Another example is provided by the case of binomial trials treated in the preceding section. What is the plausibility of success at a future trial if x successes have been recorded n trials? If we use y_0 and y_1 to denote failure and success at the next trial, then we have $p(y_0 \mid s) = 1 - s$ and $p(y_1 \mid s) = s$. The use of the uniform prior plausibility function for the success probability then leads, as above and by (3–3–6), to

$$\pi(y_1 \mid x) = \sum \pi(s \mid x) p(y_1 \mid s)$$

$$= \sum_s s\pi(s \mid x)$$

$$= \mathscr{E}(s \mid x)$$

$$= \frac{x + 1}{n + 2},$$ (5–6–3)

by (5–5–1), and

$$\pi(y_0 \mid x) = 1 - \pi(y_1 \mid x) = 1 - \frac{x + 1}{n + 2}.$$ (5–6–4)

This problem of the plausibility of a future success in a binomial trial has a long history dating back to Laplace (1749–1827) who, by using the uniform prior plausibility function, reached the above conclusion. Some comments on the choice of prior plausibility functions in this connection have already been made in the preceding section. We recall our comment there that the influence of the prior plausibility function dwindles as the amount of experimentation increases. Support for this comment comes from the fact that the use of a prior plausibility function of an extreme form of Fig. 5–2(c) would have given a plausibility x/n for future success, which in most practical applications differs very little from $(x + 1)/(n + 2)$ when n is large. For example, when $n = 100$ and $x = 70$,

$$x/n = 0.700, \qquad (x + 1)/(n + 2) = 0.696.$$

EXERCISES

1. Suppose that there are two possible states of nature s_1 and s_2 with prior plausibilities 0.6 and 0.4, and that an informative experiment has possible probabilistic models:

State of nature	$p(x \mid s)$		
	x_1	x_2	x_3
s_1	0.2	0.7	0.1
s_2	0.4	0.3	0.3

The outcome of a future experiment also depends on the state of nature, and the appropriate probabilistic models are:

State of nature	$p(y \mid s)$	
	y_1	y_2
s_1	0.1	0.9
s_2	0.5	0.5

Following the argument of this section, construct the three plausible prediction functions $\pi(y \mid x_1)$, $\pi(y \mid x_2)$, $\pi(y \mid x_3)$ associated with the three possible outcomes of the informative experiment.

2. In Exercise 1 of Section 5–4 the factory inspector has already examined one item from a box of three and found it to be defective. What is the plausibility that the next item he examines is also defective?

3. For the plants of Exercise 2 of Section 5–3 it has been found that 70 percent of those attacked by virus A die compared with only 40 percent of those attacked by virus B. What is the prospect of survival for a plant suffering from yellowing leaves and falling petals?

   What proportion of plants attacked by one or other forms of the virus will survive?

4. The sun has risen every day of your life so far. On the assumption that your plausibility function at birth for the probability of a sunrise is uniform, how do you assess the chance of the sun's rising tomorrow?

5. A pharmacologist has developed a completely new drug and is so vague about its potentialities that he decides, before trials commence, to regard each possible success probability as equally plausible. In 20 applications of the drug he scores 15 successes. What is the minimum number of further trials he must conduct before he can hope to claim a plausibility of at least 0.9 for success at the next trial? Is he likely to achieve his hope in this number of trials?

6. A large batch of electrical components of a certain type has been left unlabeled, and it is difficult to determine easily whether the components are all of type A or all of type B. Twice as many type A batches as type B batches are produced and the proportion of type A components which give trouble-free operation for at least 500 hours is 0.9, whereas the corresponding proportion of type A components is 0.7. It has been reported that four components from the batch have been undergoing tests and have all survived 500 hours. What plausibility would you attach to the conclusion that the next component tested will last at least 500 hours?

5–7 DIFFICULTIES OF PLAUSIBILITY ANALYSIS

We have already encountered some of the difficulties of assigning prior plausibility functions in the preceding section, where we saw that the concept of ignorance is an elusive one. We have been particularly fortunate in the problems treated thus far (Problems 3, 6 and 9 of Chapter 1) in that extensive past records were available, and in such a form that they were directly transformable into a prior plausibility function. What if there is only scant past experience and that it is rather vague or in such a form that the prior plausibilities have to be built up indirectly? Most statisticians would agree that prior information soundly based on extensive past records is safe to use and that plausibility analysis as we have named it and described it here is a correct form of analysis. Where disagreement arises it is in these other vaguer cases. At one extreme are the subjective probabilists who would argue that it is always possible—if necessary, by an attempt to place conceptual bets on alternative states of nature—to arrive at reasonable measures of plausibility. At the other extreme are the pure frequentists who insist on a relative frequency basis for any plausibility function before they are prepared to concede its usability. The only general advice that the present writer feels he can offer the reader is a warning not to be led into the blind acceptance of the dogma or the uncritical application of the methods of any particular philosophical school; rather, he should let the particular aspects of the immediate problem lead him to whichever formulation is most appropriate.

The remainder of this chapter is devoted to a short discussion of attempts that are made to use the extreme frequentist view in situations which in traditional statistics texts are studied under the heading of statistical inference. In many ways this form of statistical analysis is an attempt to provide methods which do not require prior plausibility assessments. As we might expect, this stringent requirement will bring in its wake difficulties of another sort.

5–8 HYPOTHESIS TESTING

Study of Problem 4 (Medical screening, Section 1–5) provides a good introduction to the subject of the testing of statistical hypotheses. Faced with the result of our informative experiment, the steroid level x for the given baby, we have to draw one of two conclusions or adopt one of two possible actions,

$$a_1: \quad \text{classify the baby as normal,}$$
$$a_2: \quad \text{classify the baby as abnormal.}$$

There are here two hypotheses, "the baby is normal" and "the baby is abnormal," and these can clearly be identified with the indexes s_1 and s_2 for the two possible models for the informative experiment. Thus we can without confusion refer to the hypothesis s_1 and to the hypothesis s_2.

The two models for our informative experiment have the same record set $X = \{1, 2, \ldots, 8\}$, and the probability functions constructed from the extensive past records of Table 1–4 are given in Table 5–6. Suppose that the proportions of normal and abnormal babies in the population are not known and that information about them is so vague as to be practically useless. A plausibility analysis

TABLE 5–6

Table of $p(x \mid s)$

Category of baby	Steroid level x							
	1	2	3	4	5	6	7	8
s_1	0.05	0.35	0.45	0.10	0.04	0.01	0.00	0.00
s_2	0.00	0.00	0.01	0.07	0.24	0.47	0.15	0.06

is then not available to us. How are we to assess the proposed screening method? First note that what a screening method does is to give us an instruction of how to act for any simple record that may arise. For each x it assigns a corresponding course of action $d(x)$, say. It achieves this by a convenient partition of the complete record set X into two disjoint subsets or records R_1 and R_2 and by assigning action

$$d(x) = \begin{cases} a_1 & \text{if } x \text{ is in } R_1 = \{1, 2, 3, 4\}, \\ a_2 & \text{if } x \text{ is in } R_2 = \{5, 6, 7, 8\}. \end{cases}$$

It must be realized that in using such a procedure we are liable to make two types of errors of misclassification.

1. We may misclassify a normal baby as abnormal.
2. We may misclassify an abnormal baby as normal.

A reasonable way to assess such a procedure is to attempt to find suitable measures of our liability to commit these two types of misclassification.

   Now we misclassify a normal baby as abnormal if we are in fact dealing with a normal baby (so that the informative experiment is described by the $p(x \mid s_1)$ model) and if we observe x in R_2, so that the procedure misclassifies the baby. A suitable measure of liability is thus this misclassification probability $p(R_2 \mid s_1)$, the probability that a normal child has a steroid level of 5 or higher. Now, from (2–8–1) and Table 5–6,

$$p(R_2 \mid s_1) = p(5 \mid s_1) + \cdots + p(8 \mid s_1) = 0.04 + 0.01 + 0.00 + 0.00$$

$$= 0.05.$$

In a similar way, our liability to misclassify an abnormal baby as normal is measured by the probability that an abnormal baby will have a steroid level of 4 or lower, that is

$$p(R_1 \mid s_2) = p(1 \mid s_2) + \cdots + p(4 \mid s_2) = 0.00 + 0.00 + 0.01 + 0.07$$

$$= 0.08.$$

We can thus conclude that, in the long run, with such a procedure a proportion

0.05 of normal babies will be required to undergo the more expensive diagnostic tests, and a proportion 0.08 of abnormal babies will pass unnoticed by the screening procedure. Whether or not the screening method is useful must then be judged by whether these liabilities are tolerable on medical, social, and economic grounds, and by what alternatives are available.

An obvious question to ask here is whether the procedure can be improved. The answer is unfortunately that it cannot. We could attempt to make our liability to misclassify an abnormal baby as normal smaller by taking a lower dividing line, for example, by taking $R_1 = \{1, 2, 3\}$, $R_2 = \{4, 5, 6, 7, 8\}$. The misclassification probabilities are again easily calculated. We have

$$p(R_2 \mid s_1) = 0.15, \qquad p(R_1 \mid s_2) = 0.01,$$

so that although we have reduced the long-run proportion of misclassified abnormal babies from 0.08 to 0.01, we have increased the proportion of normal babies called back for further examination from 0.05 to 0.15. It appears that "what we lose on the swings we make up on the slides" with such statistical tests. How we choose between these two alternative procedures must depend on some consideration of the relative seriousness of the two kinds of misclassification. If some view of this can be taken, then further progress may be possible. We shall return to this point in Section 7–3.

One point of interest is that both these rules are such that they place in R_1 those steroid levels which are such that $p(x \mid s_1)/p(x \mid s_2)$ is large. The greatest support for the normal hypothesis comes from the simple record x for which the probability of observing x for a normal baby is highest relative to the probability of observing x for an abnormal baby.

In the above practical situation there were just two simple hypotheses, each associated with a single index. More complicated situations can arise in which a hypothesis—for example, "the response rate to a treatment is greater than 50 percent"—is composite and refers to more than one index, in the case cited for the set of success probability indexes satisfying $s > \frac{1}{2}$. Again there may be more than two hypotheses under review, with many more types of misclassification errors with their accompanying liabilities to be weighed against each other.

EXERCISES

1. There are only two possible models, indexed by s_1 and s_2, for a certain informative experiment:

x	0	1	2	3	4	5
$p(x \mid s_1)$	0.05	0.15	0.43	0.26	0.08	0.03
$p(x \mid s_2)$	0.26	0.11	0.06	0.09	0.15	0.33

There are two different rules for deciding which of the models is the more reasonable.

a) If $x \geq 3$, decide for s_1; otherwise decide for s_2.
b) If $x = 2$ or 3, decide for s_1; otherwise decide for s_2.

Evaluate measures of liability to commit errors with these two rules. Which do you regard as the better rule? Can you improve on this better rule?

2. A hormone deficiency is regarded as one of the main causes of a certain disease, but diagnosis by hormone level alone is uncertain because low levels do occur in healthy individuals and occasionally a sufferer from the disease appears to have an adequate level. A research worker has established that the patterns of variability follow the probability models:

State of individual	Hormone level						
	1	2	3	4	5	6	7
Healthy	0.01	0.02	0.09	0.16	0.20	0.42	0.10
Diseased	0.53	0.30	0.11	0.03	0.02	0.01	0.00

He illustrates the difficulty to his colleagues by considering a particular method of screening: If the hormone level of an individual is 3 or less, regard him as diseased; otherwise regard him as healthy. What misclassification probabilities does he use to express the uncertainty of diagnosis with this method?

A colleague points out that he could easily have reduced the proportion of sufferers regarded as healthy to 0.03 by regarding as diseased all persons with hormone level 4 or less, and as healthy all other persons. A second colleague says that he can also obtain this 0.03 with this rule: Classify a person as healthy only if his hormone level is 4. Which of these suggestions is the more sensible, and what awkward feature would you draw attention to in this more sensible suggestion?

3. An examiner has prepared a multiple-choice examination of eight unrelated questions, for each of which three suggested answers, only one of which is correct, are presented. He defines a "reasonably prepared" candidate as one who for each question has probability $\frac{2}{3}$ of answering correctly, and a "guesser" as one who chooses one of the suggested answers at random. He sets the passing mark at 7 correct answers. What is the probability that a reasonably prepared student will fail? What is the probability that a guesser will pass?

Interpret this situation in terms of testing of hypotheses, identifying appropriate measures of liability to draw wrong conclusions.

4. Two simple independent tests to separate individuals into "extroverts" and "introverts" have been proposed. In each test the individual is given a score of 1, 2, or 3, according to his response. A thorough investigation of these tests has suggested the following probability response models:

State of individual	First test			Second test		
	1	2	3	1	2	3
Extrovert	0.1	0.3	0.6	0.2	0.3	0.5
Introvert	0.4	0.3	0.3	0.7	0.2	0.1

The classification criterion chosen is total score; an individual is classified as an extrovert if his total score is under 3 and as an introvert otherwise. Provide measures of the effectiveness of this classification method.

5–9 ESTIMATION

The problem of estimation is how to convert the data x from the informative experiment into a reasonable, plausible, working value or estimate $d(x)$ of s^*, the unknown true index. We should somehow be able to harness our awareness that certain data are more likely to arise from some models, or, equivalently, indexes, than from others. For example, if 45 out of 50 items from a production line turn out to be defective, we are intuitively reluctant to suggest 0.01 as an appropriate estimate of the probability of an item's being defective, but would accept an estimate of about 0.9.

From the conceptual viewpoint, what then is this process of estimation? It involves the provision of an instruction on how to construct, for each possible simple record x, a corresponding estimate $d(x)$ for s^*. In mathematical terms, therefore, we are simply defining a function on the record set X and taking values in the index set S. We can express this by speaking of the estimator d which gives the instruction to construct the estimate $d(x)$ corresponding to x. Each such function defines a means of arriving at an estimate from any given data.

5–9–1 Definition *Estimator, estimate.* For an informative experiment with record set X and class of models with index set S, an *estimator* of the unknown true index s^* is a function on X taking values in the set S. If a performance of the experiment yields simple record x then the estimator instructs us to use $d(x)$ as our *estimate* of the unknown true index s^*.

The next very obvious question is: How should we choose d in a sensible manner? What are criteria of good estimation? One way of assessing d is to ask: What would be the consequences of repeated application of the estimator d to simple records of the replicates of the informative experiment? Just as we obtain observations from replicates of the informative experiment, so we obtain estimates in S. We would ideally like every estimate to fall on s^*, but since we do not know s^* this is an unattainable ideal. We would, however, hope that the estimates cluster around the unknown s^* in some sense. The variability in the simple record of the informative experiment is reflected in the variability in the estimate, that is, in the variability in the induced experiment which records the estimate $d(x)$ rather than the simple record x.

Example *Binomial trials.* Suppose that in our trials with a medical drug (Section 5–1) we treat 100 patients with the drug and keep simple records $x_1, \ldots, x_{100}$ in the now familiar way (0 for failure, 1 for success) for each of the patients. The simple record of our informative experiment is then $x = (x_1, \ldots, x_{100})$. We have little hesitation in suggesting as an estimate of the unknown success probability s^* the relative frequency of success in the 100 trials, namely $\frac{1}{100}(x_1 + \cdots + x_{100})$. Our model-building has been founded on the correspondence between relative frequency and probability, and in such a simple situation the equating of the two to obtain an estimate is direct and intuitive. In probing for deeper reasons for this choice, we shall consider three alternative estimators, some of them obviously ridiculous. In giving expression to this ridiculousness, we shall obtain criteria for good estimation.

Consider then the four estimators: d_1, d_2, d_3, d_4, defined as follows:

$$d_1(x) = \tfrac{1}{100}(x_1 + \cdots + x_{100}),$$

$$d_2(x) = \tfrac{1}{25}(x_1 + \cdots + x_{25}),$$

$$d_3(x) = 1 - \tfrac{1}{100}(x_1 + \cdots + x_{100}),$$

$$d_4(x) = (x_1 + \cdots + x_{50} + \tfrac{1}{2})/(x_1 + \cdots + x_{100} + 1).$$

Note that all these functions take values only in the interval $0 \leq s \leq 1$, and so are estimators in the sense of Definition 5–9–1.

Suppose then that to demonstrate the properties of these estimators in repeated applications, we simulate the 100-trial informative experiment, with s^* set equal to 0.25. (For example, the simulation of a binomial trial could be the toss of two coins, the outcome "two heads" constituting "success," with probability 0.25.) We perform altogether 40 replicates of this informative experiment (4000 trials in all) and calculate the four estimates for each informative experiment. Figure 5–3 shows the results, each square representing an estimate.

The estimator d_1, our natural choice, has succeeded in locating the target s^* and has clustered its estimates fairly closely around s^*. Estimator d_2 appears also to be aimed at the correct target s^*, but its estimates are more widely scattered about the target. This is not surprising since $d_2(x)$ is simply the relative frequency of success in the first 25 trials; it thus ignores the valuable information from the remaining 75 trials, so its straddling of the target is wider than that of d_1. Estimator d_3 assigns estimates which are 1 minus the corresponding estimate from d_1. Although its spread is thus a reflection of that of d_1, it is aiming at

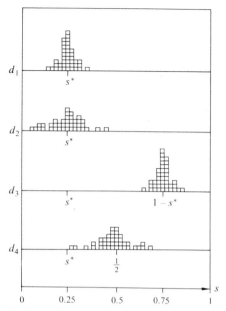

Fig. 5–3 Distribution of 40 estimates for each of the four binomial probability estimators $d_1, \ldots, d_4$.

$1 - s^*$, a completely incorrect target. The final estimator d_4 seems to aim at $s = \frac{1}{2}$, so it too is off target. That this will always be so, whatever the value of s^*, is clear from its form. Since $x_1 + \cdots + x_{50}$ is the number of successes in the first 50 trials, and since this number will tend to be half of the number of successes in all 100 trials, estimates constructed by d_4 will tend to cluster round $\frac{1}{2}$, regardless of the value of s^*. While d_4 might have proved reasonable for the particular case $s^* = \frac{1}{2}$, we want a method which chases the target whatever that target may be. Intuitively, d_1 and d_2 have such a property.

The satisfactoriness of an estimate d could thus be judged by the distribution of its estimates in S, that is, by the true probability model describing the induced experiment which records $d(x)$ rather than x. Since this true probability model is indexed by s^*, and since we do not know s^*, we are faced with the actual assessment of estimators by examination of the whole class of induced probability models. This point can be easily illustrated by an example.

Example *Estimating the number of intruder cells* (Problem 6, Section 1–7). Suppose that we wish to quote an estimate of the number of intruder cells when we have observed x reactions in the three repeated tests, and that we feel that the prior plausibility function used in Section 5–4 is unreliable. Here we take $S = \{s_0, s_1, s_2\}$ or $\{0, 1, 2\}$, the index corresponding to the number of intruder cells present; so to define an estimator, we must assign one of the indexes 0, 1, 2 to each of the possible x. For example, d_1, d_2, d_3, as specified in Table 5–7, are all possible estimators. There are only a finite number of estimators for this situation since there are just three possible indexes which can be assigned to each of four simple records, giving $3^4 = 81$ different assignments; hence 81 different estimators are possible.

TABLE 5–7

Three estimators

x	0	1	2	3
$d_1(x)$	0	0	1	2
$d_2(x)$	2	1	0	0
$d_3(x)$	0	1	2	2

We can easily apply the methods of Section 3–5 to obtain, for each index s, the corresponding induced probability function for each estimator d. The resulting nine probability functions are given in rows in Table 5–8. For example the set of x for which $d_1(x) = 0$ is $\{0, 1\}$, the associated record of Section 3–5, so the first entry in the first table is

$$p(0 \mid s_0) + p(1 \mid s_0) = 0.343 + 0.441 = 0.784,$$

from Table 5–4. Now if the true index is 0, we would like it to be as highly probable as possible that the estimate should turn out to be 0. In this respect the 0.784 of d_1 seems successful compared with the 0.216 and 0.343 of d_2 and d_3. Following this argument we see that we need as high values as possible along the main

TABLE 5–8

Induced probability functions of the three estimators

Index set	d_1 Record set			d_2 Record set			d_3 Record set		
	0	1	2	0	1	2	0	1	2
$s_0 = 0$	0.784	0.189	0.027	0.216	0.441	0.343	0.343	0.441	0.216
$s_1 = 1$	0.352	0.432	0.216	0.648	0.288	0.064	0.064	0.288	0.648
$s_2 = 2$	0.216	0.441	0.343	0.784	0.189	0.027	0.027	0.189	0.784

diagonals. In this respect thus d_1 and d_3 are more successful than d_2. But how are we to choose between d_1, which is superior in the first two entries, and d_3, which is superior in the final diagonal position? Our next step is beginning to emerge, because the difficulty seems to be that we are trying to compare entire probability functions, which is a difficult task. May there not be some simple characteristics of probability functions whose comparison would be sufficient? This question leads to the considerations of the next two sections, which give criteria for estimators.

EXERCISES

1. Place 50 beads in a bottle, 15 of one color (say red) and 35 of another (say blue). Imagine that you do not know the proportion s of red beads in the bottle. Extract 20 beads and let x_1, x_2 denote the numbers of red beads in the first and second set of 10. Consider the following estimators of s:

   a) $d_1(x_1, x_2) = \frac{1}{10}x_1$,
   b) $d_2(x_1, x_2) = x_1/(x_2 + 4)$,
   c) $d_3(x_1, x_2) = 1 - \frac{1}{10}x_1$,
   d) $d_4(x_1, x_2) = \frac{1}{20}(x_1 + x_2)$.

   Which of these estimators do you favor on intuitive grounds? Check your answer by repeating the sampling experiment a number of times displaying the distribution of estimates as in Fig. 5–3.

2. Follow the argument of this section to produce induced probability functions for the following estimators associated with the two-test experiment of Exercise 2 of Section 5–4.

x	$(+, +)$	$(+, -)$	$(-, +)$	$(-, -)$
$d_1(x)$	3	2	1	0
$d_2(x)$	0	1	2	3

   Can you draw any conclusion about the relative merits of these two estimators?

3. In a plant-raising experiment the hybrid produced by a cross-fertilization is of category 1, 2, or 3 with probabilities s^2, $1 - s$, $s(1 - s)$, where $0 \leq s \leq 1$, and the true index $s*$ is unknown. In a total of n such cross-fertilizations n_1, n_2, n_3 were of categories 1, 2, 3, where $n_1 + n_2 + n_3 = n$. Consider the relative merits of the following as estimates of $s*$:

   a) n_3/n,
   b) $1 - (n_2/n)$,
   c) $(n_2 + n_3)/n$,
   d) $(2n_2 + n_3)/(2n_1 + n_2 + 2n_3)$.

   (You can simulate such a cross-fertilization with $s* = \frac{1}{2}$ by tossing a coin twice and recording category 1 if both tosses give heads, category 2 if the first toss gives a tail, and category 3 otherwise.)

5–10 MINIMUM VARIANCE UNBIASED ESTIMATOR

In our investigation of binomial trials in the preceding section we saw that there are two essential features that an estimator should display. First, its distribution in the induced record set S should in some sense be centered on the true index s^*; in Fig. 5–3 we prefer d_1 and d_2 to d_3 and d_4. Second, subject to this centering, its distribution should be as closely clustered around s^* as possible; in Fig. 5–3 we prefer d_1 to d_2.

One way of ensuring the first requirement is to demand that the expectation of the estimator be s^*, that is

$$\mathscr{E}\{d(x) \mid s^*\} = s^*.$$

The notation here must show the dependence of the expectation on the model assumed to be operating. Since we do not know s^*, the only way to ensure that such a condition holds is to demand it for all indexes.

5–10–1 Definition *Unbiased estimator.* An estimator d is *unbiased* (and estimates provided by it are also termed unbiased) if

$$\mathscr{E}\{d(x) \mid s\} = s \qquad \text{for every } s \text{ in } S. \tag{5–10–1}$$

If d is unbiased, then (5–10–1) is satisfied. Thus the long-run average of estimates provided by an unbiased estimator from replicates of the informative experiment is s^*. We are here harnessing nature to our aid by a kind of feedback system. Regardless of what s^* nature chooses, she will produce an x which reflects her choice and the subsequent use of an unbiased estimate $d(x)$ is aimed back on the target s^*.

While the property of unbiasedness ensures that estimates cluster around s^*, we want further to make the clustering around s^* as close as possible, to use d_1 rather than d_2 (Fig. 5–3). We can do this by choosing some suitable measure of variability about s^* in the induced model and selecting from all the possible unbiased estimators one which makes this measure of dispersion or spread a minimum, again for all s in S since we do not know s^*. One of the most convenient measures of spread is the variance $\mathscr{V}\{d(x) \mid s\}$; recall Section 3–8 and note again the dependence on s in the notation. We have thus arrived at a reasonable set of criteria for a good estimator and we give these in the following definition.

5–10–2 Definition *Minimum variance unbiased estimator.* A *minimum variance unbiased estimator* satisfies these two conditions:

1. $\mathscr{E}\{d(x) \mid s\} = s$ for every s in S; that is, d is unbiased.
2. $\mathscr{V}\{d(x) \mid s\} \leq \mathscr{V}\{d_1(x) \mid s\}$ for every unbiased estimator d_1; that is, d has minimum variance among all unbiased estimators.

We have answered the questions posed at the end·of Section 5–9 by adopting the mean and variance as measures of the location and spread of the induced distribution and using them as summarizing characteristics. It requires some degree of mathematical sophistication to establish that an estimator has the minimum variance unbiased property, and such tools are of no relevance to our purpose here. We can, however, illustrate the concepts by reference to simple examples.

Illustrative Example Suppose that the informative experiment has class of probability functions

x	0	1	2	3
$p(x \mid s)$	s^2	$s(1 - s)$	$s(1 - s)$	$(1 - s)^2$

with index set S the interval $0 \le s \le 1$. Consider the estimator defined by

x	0	1	2	3
$d(x)$	a_0	a_1	a_2	a_3

Then

$$\mathscr{E}\{d(x) \mid s\} = a_0 s^2 + a_1 s(1 - s) + a_2 s(1 - s) + a_3(1 - s)^2$$
$$= a_3 + (a_1 + a_2 - 2a_3)s + (a_0 - a_1 - a_2 + a_3)s^2.$$

For unbiasedness of d we therefore require, by Definition 5–10–1, that

$$a_3 + (a_1 + a_2 - 2a_3)s + (a_0 - a_1 - a_2 + a_3)s^2 = s$$

for every s in the interval $0 \le s \le 1$. This will be so if and only if the coefficients of s^0 (the constant term), s and s^2 on both sides of this equality are equal. Thus the condition for unbiasedness becomes

$$a_3 = 0, \qquad a_1 + a_2 - 2a_3 = 1, \qquad a_0 - a_1 - a_2 + a_3 = 0,$$

or, equivalently,

$$a_3 = 0, \qquad a_2 = 1 - a_1, \qquad a_0 = 1.$$

Hence we see that there is a whole class of unbiased estimators, one for each value that a_1 can take. We can write

x	0	1	2	3	
$d(x)$	1	a	$1 - a$	0	$(0 \le a \le 1)$

as a typical unbiased estimator. Let us now calculate the variance of d and then find the value of a that minimizes the variance. Since $d(x)$ has, by unbiasedness, mean s, we have

$$\mathscr{V}\{d(x) \mid s\} = (1 - s)^2 \times s^2 + (a - s)^2 \times s(1 - s) + (1 - a - s)^2 \times s(1 - s)$$
$$+ (0 - s)^2 \times (1 - s)^2$$
$$= s(1 - s)\{s(1 - s) + (a - s)^2 + (1 - a - s)^2 + s(1 - s)\}$$
$$= s(1 - s)\{2a^2 - 2a + 1\}.$$

The expression in braces can be written as

$$2(a - \tfrac{1}{2})^2 + \tfrac{1}{2},$$

a form which shows that this variance is smallest when $a = \tfrac{1}{2}$, whatever the value of s. Thus we have found a unique minimum variance unbiased estimator

x	0	1	2	3
$d(x)$	1	$\tfrac{1}{2}$	$\tfrac{1}{2}$	0

with minimum variance

$$\tfrac{1}{2}s(1 - s).$$

Example *Binomial trials* (Section 5–9). For the estimator d_1 we have

$$\mathscr{E}\{d_1(x) \mid s\} = \tfrac{1}{100}\mathscr{E}(x_1 + \cdots + x_{100} \mid s) \qquad \text{by Theorem 3–9–1,}$$
$$= s \qquad \text{by Theorem 3–9–5,}$$

so d_1 is unbiased. Also

$$\mathscr{V}\{d_1(x) \mid s\} = (\tfrac{1}{100})^2\mathscr{V}(x_1 + \cdots + x_{100} \mid s) \qquad \text{by Theorem 3–9–2,}$$
$$= \frac{s(1 - s)}{100} \qquad \text{by Theorem 3–9–5.}$$

By a similar argument d_2 is also unbiased, but has larger variance

$$\mathscr{V}\{d_2(x) \mid s\} = \frac{s(1 - s)}{25}.$$

Since $d_3(x) = 1 - d_1(x)$ we have, by Theorem 3–9–1,

$$\mathscr{E}\{d_3(x) \mid s\} = 1 - s,$$

so d_3 can be discarded as biased. We have already discarded d_4 on intuitive grounds; we could show mathematically that it too is biased.

All that we have established here is that d_1 is the only contender among d_1, d_2, d_3, d_4 for the title of minimum variance unbiased estimator. We cannot say whether or not we have exhausted the class of unbiased estimators. This is the underlying difficulty of the problem. How can we find the whole class of unbiased estimators in this case? Such an undertaking would take us beyond the scope of this book, and we shall merely record the fact that d_1 is indeed the unique minimum variance unbiased estimator.

Example *Estimating the number of intruder cells* (Section 5–9). Consider here the estimator defined by

x	0	1	2	3
$d(x)$	a_0	a_1	a_2	a_3

where the a_i are all members of the set $S = \{0, 1, 2\}$. The requirements of unbiasedness are

$$\mathscr{E}\{d(x) \,|\, s_0\} = 0, \qquad \mathscr{E}\{d(x) \,|\, s_1\} = 1, \qquad \mathscr{E}\{d(x) \,|\, s_2\} = 2,$$

or

$$0.343a_0 + 0.441a_1 + 0.189a_2 + 0.027a_3 = 0,$$
$$0.064a_0 + 0.288a_1 + 0.432a_2 + 0.216a_3 = 1,$$
$$0.027a_0 + 0.189a_1 + 0.441a_2 + 0.343a_3 = 2.$$

It is obvious that these cannot be satisfied, for the first relationship would demand that $a_0 = a_1 = a_2 = a_3 = 0$, and then the second and third relationships are not satisfied. Thus we have a situation in which an unbiased estimator does not exist, far less a minimum variance unbiased estimator.

The nonexistence of a minimum variance unbiased estimator does not mean that the situation is hopeless, for we must realize that there is a certain arbitrariness in the choice of the expectation or mean as the centering measure and also of the variance as the measure of dispersion. For example, what would we choose if we discovered an estimator which, although slightly biased, had a variance of much smaller magnitude than the minimum variance unbiased estimator? We raise such questions to leave the reader in a fairly critical mind about the merits and demerits of minimum variance unbiasedness. When a minimum variance unbiased estimator exists, it is usually a not unreasonable tool; when it does not exist, all may not yet be lost.

We point out here that there is a common practice to quote with an estimate as obtained above, a measure of its accuracy implied by $\mathscr{V}\{d(x) \,|\, s^*\}$. Since s^* is not known, it is usual to replace s^* by its estimate $d(x)$ in the expression for this variance, and then to quote the square root of the resulting quantity under the name *estimated standard error* of the estimate.

EXERCISES

1. Find the class of unbiased estimators of θ for the informative experiment with class of models

x	0	1	2	3
$p(x \mid s)$	s^2	$\frac{1}{2}s(1-s)$	$\frac{3}{2}s(1-s)$	$(1-s)^2$

where $0 \le s \le 1$, and hence find a minimum variance unbiased estimator of s^*, the unknown true index. What is the minimum variance of this estimator?

2. Show that, for the informative experiment with class of probability models

x	0	1	2
$p(x \mid s)$	s^2	$s(1-s)$	$1-s$

where $0 \le s \le 1$, there is a unique unbiased estimator of s^*, the unknown true index, and hence a minimum variance unbiased estimator. What is the minimum variance?

3. Show that, for the informative experiment with class of probability models

x	0	1	2
$p(x \mid s)$	$\frac{2}{3}s$	$\frac{1}{3}(1-s)$	$\frac{1}{3}(2-s)$

where $0 \le s \le 1$, no unbiased estimator of s^*, the unknown true index, exists.

4. In $n_1 + n_2$ binomial trials x_1 and x_2 are the total numbers of successes in the first n_1 and in the last n_2 trials, respectively. Show that the estimators d_1 and d_2 defined by

$$d_1(x_1, x_2) = \frac{1}{2}\left(\frac{x_1}{n_1} + \frac{x_2}{n_2}\right),$$

$$d_2(x_1, x_2) = \frac{x_1 + x_2}{n_1 + n_2}$$

are both unbiased. Which of the two estimators do you prefer? As an application, consider the following problem.

A clinician has recorded the responses of 50 patients to a new drug in two separate columns, 30 in the first and 20 in the second. Of the 30, 21 responded, but of the 20, only 10 responded. Estimate the response probability, and provide an estimated standard error of your estimate.

5–11 MAXIMUM LIKELIHOOD ESTIMATES

One awkwardness about minimum variance unbiased estimators is that their definition provides no construction by which to produce them. Another method of estimation is based on the following argument. Suppose that only two indexes s_1 and s_2 are possible and that x has been observed. Then $p(x \mid s_1)$

and $p(x \mid s_2)$ are the probabilities of observing x on the two possible models. Now if $p(x \mid s_1) > p(x \mid s_2)$ we may argue that since x is more probable on model s_1 than on model s_2 and since we have actually observed x, it is reasonable to assume that s_1 is more plausible than s_2. For example, suppose that we do not know which of two coins—a specially biased one s_1 with probability $\frac{3}{4}$ of falling heads, or an ordinary mint one s_2 with probability $\frac{1}{2}$ of falling heads—is about to be tossed. We regard 20 heads in 20 tosses of the coin as strong evidence that the biased coin has been tossed because the probability of 20 heads in 20 tosses of the biased coin is $p(20 \mid s_1) = 0.003171$ which, while not large absolutely, is huge relative to the corresponding probability $p(20 \mid s_2) = 0.000001$ for the mint coin. If there were a third coin s_3 with probability $\frac{1}{4}$ of falling heads, then we would regard "6 heads in 20 throws" as supporting s_3 more strongly than s_1 or s_2. Again, on inspection of

$$p(6 \mid s_1) = 0.00003, \qquad p(6 \mid s_2) = 0.03696, \qquad p(6 \mid s_3) = 0.16861,$$

we see that $p(6 \mid s_3)$ is "large" compared with the other two values.

These arguments suggest that in the general case after we have observed x we may regard the relative magnitudes of $p(x \mid s)$ as measures of support for the various s as the value of the true unknown index s^*. It is thus not unnatural to choose as our estimate of s^* that s which maximizes $p(x \mid s)$. For different x this will give different estimates $d(x)$. The function so generated is an estimator.

5–11–1 Definition *Maximum likelihood estimator.* For given x, let $d(x)$ be a value of s which maximizes $p(x \mid s)$ over S. Then the estimator so defined is called a *maximum likelihood estimator* of the unknown true index s^*.

Such estimators can be shown to possess many desirable properties and are especially useful when the informative experiment is large (for example, consists of a fair number of replicates), since they then tend to concentrate their distribution around s^* in a minimum variance unbiased sense. This comment about their large-experiment behavior does not, of course, rule out the possibility that they are also reliable for some small experiments. We shall not go more deeply into this aspect but content ourselves with brief comments on the three examples of Section 5–10.

Illustrative Example

$p(0 \mid s) = s^2$, and this is a maximum for $s = 1$,
$p(1 \mid s) = s(1 - s) = \frac{1}{4} - (s - \frac{1}{2})^2$, and this is a maximum for $s = \frac{1}{2}$,
$p(2 \mid s)$ is similarly a maximum for $s = \frac{1}{2}$,
$p(3 \mid s) = (1 - s)^2$, and this is a maximum for $s = 0$.

Hence, by Definition 5–11–1, we obtain as maximum likelihood estimator the estimator defined by

x	0	1	2	3
$d(x)$	1	$\frac{1}{2}$	$\frac{1}{2}$	0

so the maximum likelihood estimator turns out to be the same as the minimum variance unbiased estimator found in Section 5–10.

Example *Binomial trials.* It can be shown that

$$p(x \mid s) = s^{x_1 + \cdots + x_{100}}(1 - s)^{100 - (x_1 + \cdots + x_{100})}$$

is maximized when $s = \frac{1}{100}(x_1 + \cdots + x_{100})$, so the maximum likelihood estimator coincides with d_1. In this example too the maximum likelihood and minimum variance unbiased estimators are identical.

Example *Estimating the number of intruder cells.* To obtain the maximum likelihood estimator d here we must, by Definition 5–11–1, choose for each simple record x the index s for which $p(x \mid s)$ of Table 5–4 is maximum, that is, the largest entry in the column headed x. For example, 0.441 is the largest entry in the column headed $x = 2$, and since this entry corresponds to 2 intruder cells, we must set $d(x) = 2$. We arrive at the maximum likelihood estimator:

x	0	1	2	3
$d(x)$	0	0	2	2

We already know from the argument of Section 5–10 that no unbiased estimator exists, so this maximum likelihood estimator cannot possess the minimum variance unbiased property.

We shall reexamine the problem of estimation from the viewpoint of statistical decision theory in Section 7–3.

EXERCISE

Find the maximum likelihood estimators associated with the informative experiments of Exercises 2 and 3 of Section 5–9, and 1 through 3 of Section 5–10.

CHAPTER 6

THE STRUCTURE OF
STATISTICAL DECISION THEORY

Now that we are able to use the language of probability to quantify uncertainty, have learned how to analyze competitive situations through the theory of games, and have found a means of extracting information from data through the principles of statistical inference, we are poised for our attack on the wider problem of decision-making under uncertainty. We shall lead up to the general form of the problem by consideration of an example which is already familiar.

6–1 THE BASIC INGREDIENTS

Let us examine in detail the decision-making aspect of Problem 3 (Locating a machine fault, Section 1–5). A straightforward investigation of this problem will reveal certain basic ingredients common to all problems of decision-making under uncertainty.

The Feature of Uncertainty Suppose that we are a manager charged with the task of devising an efficient procedure or set of rules by which our mechanics will locate faults. The root cause of our difficulty is that we do not know at the time of making a decision where the fault lies in the particular machine under scrutiny. There is an unknown true state of nature, which is one of two possibilities:

s_1: the fault is in the engine,
s_2: the fault is in the gearbox.

Together s_1 and s_2 constitute a set $S = \{s_1, s_2\}$ of unknown states of nature. We have already noted this feature in Chapter 5.

The Information Available Although we do not know where the fault is, we do have available information about the symptom displayed when the machine broke down. There are three such possible symptom combinations or symptoms:

$$x_1: \quad \text{overheating only,}$$
$$x_2: \quad \text{irregular traction only,}$$
$$x_3: \quad \text{overheating and irregular traction.}$$

We can regard the observing and recording of the symptom as an informative experiment with record set $X = \{x_1, x_2, x_3\}$.

Relation of Information to Uncertainty From our previous studies we realize that there is a structure associated with the two sets S and X. The rows of Table 1–3 give the long-run relative frequencies of the symptoms for the two types of fault, and are thus simply the two possible probability models for the informative experiment corresponding to the two possible states of nature. Thus the elements of S act as indexes for the class of probability models for the informative experiment. We may denote the probability functions associated with those two models by $p(x \mid s_1)$ and $p(x \mid s_2)$, so the table of Problem 3 may be expressed in the following terms (Table 6–1).

TABLE 6–1

Probability functions $p(x \mid s)$ for the informative experiment

Location of fault	Symptom x		
	x_1 (overheating only)	x_2 (irregular traction only)	x_3 (overheating and irregular traction)
s_1 (engine)	0.1	0.4	0.5
s_2 (gearbox)	0.5	0.3	0.2

We must use the information obtained (here our knowledge of the actual symptom x displayed) to remove some of our uncertainty about the unknown state of nature and so to help us determine our course of action.

The Possible Courses of Action Let us suppose that we have a flow of machines arriving for repair, each accompanied by the information of the particular symptom displayed at breakdown. For any particular machine there are just two possible actions open to us:

a_1: examine the engine first; if it is not faulty proceed to examine the gearbox;

a_2: examine the gearbox first; if it is not faulty proceed to examine the engine.

We shall denote by $A = \{a_1, a_2\}$ the set of possible actions.

The Gains and Losses Involved From the information about the expenses of examining and repairing the engine and the gearbox and the profit from repairs we may build up a table of rewards associated with the various eventualities; reread Problem 3. The cost of locating the fault in the machine will depend on

1. the actual location of the fault, that is, on the true state of nature;
2. the action taken.

For example, if the fault is in the engine and we take action a_1, then we shall examine the engine only, and so the cost of discovering and repairing the fault is simply 1. For the repair of the fault we charge 4, and so our net gain or utility is $4 - 1 = 3$. If, however, the fault is in the engine and we take action a_2, we shall examine the gearbox at expense 2, find that the fault is not there, and so have subsequently to examine and then repair the engine at additional expense 1, thus incurring altogether a cost of $2 + 1 = 3$ in discovering the fault and overall utility $4 - 3 = 1$. We can thus fill up a table of gains, Table 6–2, showing a utility $U(a, s)$ associated with each combination of action and state of nature.

TABLE 6–2

Utilities $U(a, s)$

Action	Location of fault	
	s_1 (engine)	s_2 (gearbox)
a_1 (examine engine first)	3	1
a_2 (examine gearbox first)	1	2

Decision Procedures The next step is to consider how we can relate the information available to the action taken. In order not to have our mechanics referring decisions to us for every machine, we must specify a clear procedure associating with each possible symptom a definite action to be taken. One such procedure would be the following. If symptom x_1 is displayed, take action a_2; if x_2, take action a_2; if x_3, a_1. Such a decision procedure or decision function can be regarded as the assignment, for each symptom x, of a unique action, say $d(x)$. Since there are here two possible actions, either of which may be adopted for any of the three symptoms, we see that there are in fact eight (2^3) possible decision procedures. These can be labeled $d_1, \ldots, d_8$, and arranged as in Table 6–3. It is convenient to have a symbol to denote the class of decision procedures. We shall write $D = \{d_1, \ldots, d_8\}$.

TABLE 6–3

Possible decision procedures

Symptom	Decision procedure							
	d_1	d_2	d_3	d_4	d_5	d_6	d_7	d_8
x_1 (overheating only)	a_1	a_1	a_1	a_1	a_2	a_2	a_2	a_2
x_2 (irregular traction only)	a_1	a_1	a_2	a_2	a_1	a_1	a_2	a_2
x_3 (overheating and irregular traction)	a_1	a_2	a_1	a_2	a_1	a_2	a_1	a_2

Thus if we adopt decision procedure d_7 we shall examine the gearbox first if there is only overheating or if there is only irregular traction, and we shall examine the engine first if there is both overheating and irregular traction.

EXERCISES

1. A decision problem has been formally expressed in terms of $S = \{s_1, s_2, s_3\}$, $X = \{x_1, x_2\}$, $A = \{a_1, a_2, a_3\}$, with class of probability models and utility function

$p(x \mid s)$	x_1	x_2
s_1	0.2	0.8
s_2	0.4	0.6
s_3	0.7	0.3

$U(a, s)$	s_1	s_2	s_3
a_1	1	3	5
a_2	4	2	2
a_3	2	6	1

Enumerate all the possible decision procedures. (This exercise will be developed in later sections.)

The following exercises will be developed further in subsequent sections. For the moment, identify for each

a) the sets S, X and A,

b) the informative experiment and its class of models $p(x \mid s)$,

c) the utility function,

and tabulate

d) the class of possible decision procedures.

2. A factory process simultaneously uses wool supplied by two spinning machines A and B to produce knitted garments. A check on the correct operation of the machine is supplied by the quality of the finished garments; the nature of any symptom displayed gives some indication of whether the fault lies in machine A or B. Extensive past records of faulty operation have shown the following proportions of machine-symptom combinations for each machine individually.

Location of fault	Symptom		
	Knots only	Holes only	Knots and holes
Machine A	0.3	0.3	0.4
Machine B	0.2	0.5	0.3

The costs of dismantling (and where necessary repairing) are 3 for machine A and 5 for machine B, and the gain from completing a repair is 10. As company statistician you are asked to provide a set of working rules for determining the best order of dismantling the machines corresponding to each of the possible symptoms.

3. An agricultural research station report runs as follows. "The yield from the new variety depends crucially on soil condition which can be one of three types. The soil test necessary to determine the condition is unfortunately not foolproof, experience having established the following probabilities of correct and wrong categorizations for the three soil types.

Soil type	Probability of classification as type		
	1	2	3
1	0.7	0.2	0.1
2	0.1	0.8	0.1
3	0.1	0.3	0.6

Yield is estimated at 11, 12, 13 per acre for soil types 1, 2, 3. For soil types 1 and 2 it is possible to apply a soil conditioner at a cost of 0.5 per acre and the effect is to change the soil type to 2 and 3, respectively. Application to type 3 soil does not alter the soil condition, and two applications of the conditioner are no more effective than one."

A farmer has already decided to have the soil test carried out and then to consider his best course of action. The cost, including cultivation cost, of the new variety is 4 per acre, and he has also the option of growing a completely different crop at a profit of 7.8 per acre regardless of soil condition. What advice would you give him?

4. An insurance company offers short-term "unit" policies at an ordinary premium of 50, but may demand a special premium of 70 if it considers this necessary. In addition to paying claimants, at 1000 per unit policy, the company returns 30 of any special premium paid by a nonclaimant.

An actuary has classified the past policies into claimants and nonclaimants and has observed the variability in points scored on a system devised for assessing answers to proposal form questions. He arrives at the following probabilistic pattern.

Class of policy	Score					
	0	1	2	3	4	5
Claimant	0.05	0.15	0.24	0.36	0.13	0.07
Nonclaimant	0.24	0.15	0.09	0.11	0.17	0.24

How should he relate score to premium?

5. In the interval since I wrote Exercises 2 of Section 4–2 and 2 of Section 5–2, my dentist and some colleagues have conducted a large-scale controlled clinical trial. A scoring system they have devised to take account of the many historical factors has been applied to the trial patients, each of whom had one root infection. Among patients whose root infections proved amenable to treatment the proportions having scores 1, 2, 3, 4 were 0.6, 0.2, 0.1, 0.1; among patients eventually requiring extractions these proportions were 0.2, 0.3, 0.3, 0.2. With my present root infection I have scored 2. What is my best course of action?

6–2 THE ASSESSMENT OF PROCEDURES

How are we to choose from among the eight possible procedures of Table 6–3? We must clearly assess the effectiveness of any chosen procedure by the utilities arising from successive applications of the procedure. For this we can calculate the long-run average utility of locating and repairing the two kinds of faults. We illustrate the calculations for procedure d_7. Consider machines which are in state s_1 and so have an engine fault. In the long run a proportion 0.1 of these machines displays symptom x_1, in which case action a_2 is taken and a utility 1 obtained; similarly, a proportion 0.4 of these machines displays symptom x_2, leading to action a_2 and utility 1; finally, a proportion 0.5 shows symptom x_3, and we then take action a_1 with utility 3. Thus for machines in state s_1 the long-run average utility of locating and repairing the fault is

$$W(d_7, s_1) = 1 \times 0.1 + 1 \times 0.4 + 3 \times 0.5 = 2.0.$$

Note that we use a notation $W(d, s)$, which shows the dependence of the long-run average on the procedure operated and on the state of nature. By similar reasoning we can calculate the long-run average utility $W(d_7, s_2)$ of using d_7 to locate and repair faults in machines with gearbox trouble:

$$W(d_7, s_2) = 2 \times 0.5 + 2 \times 0.3 + 1 \times 0.2 = 1.8.$$

Thus, for this procedure, we have in those two long-run averages, 2.0 and 1.8, measures of the effectiveness of locating engine faults and gearbox faults. Such long-run averages can be calculated for each of the other seven procedures; Table 6–4 displays the results.

TABLE 6–4

Long-run average utilities $W(d, s)$

Location of fault	Decision procedure							
	d_1	d_2	d_3	d_4	d_5	d_6	d_7	d_8
s_1 (engine)	3.0	2.0	2.2	1.2	2.8	1.8	2.0	1.0
s_2 (gearbox)	1.0	1.2	1.3	1.5	1.5	1.7	1.8	2.0

Note that we can provide a formula for $W(d, s)$. For example,

$$\begin{aligned} W(d_7, s_1) &= U(a_2, s_1)p(x_1 \mid s_1) + U(a_2, s_1)p(x_2 \mid s_1) + U(a_1, s_1)p(x_3 \mid s_1) \\ &= U\{d_7(x_1), s_1\}p(x_1 \mid s_1) + U\{d_7(x_2), s_1\}p(x_2 \mid s_1) \\ &\quad + U\{d_7(x_3), s_1\}p(x_3 \mid s_1) \\ &= \sum_x U\{d_7(x), s_1\}p(x \mid s_1). \end{aligned}$$

It is also convenient to have a terminology for $W(d, s)$: we present this in a definition.

6–2–1 Definition *Worth of a procedure.* The *worth* of using a procedure d when the state of nature is s is

$$W(d, s) = \sum_x U\{d(x), s\}p(x \mid s).$$

EXERCISES

1. Evaluate $W(d, s_1)$, $W(d, s_2)$, $W(d, s_3)$ for each of the possible decision procedures of Exercise 1 of Section 6–1.

2. Review Exercises 2 through 5 of Section 6–1, calculating the worth for each procedure and each state of nature.

3. Carry the analysis of the following problem to the stage of the calculation of worths.

   The performance of a water diviner has been scrutinized and the following conclusions have been drawn. Where there is a good subterranean supply of water there is a probability 0.7 that he will divine water; where the supply is moderate this probability is 0.5; where there is no water this probability is 0.3. The financing of a properly constructed well is assumed to cost the equivalent of 40 each year and the output would give a return of 240 a year from a good supply, 90 a year from a moderate supply. An alternative hole-in-the-ground method costing the equivalent of 15 each year brings 85 a year from a good supply, 65 a year from a moderate supply. What advice would you give to someone who had contracted to use this diviner?

6–3 ADMISSIBLE AND INADMISSIBLE PROCEDURES

Inspection of the worths in Table 6–4 shows that we can immediately dismiss as unsound some of these eight procedures. For example, procedure d_2 has worths 2.0 and 1.2 which are both smaller than the corresponding worths 2.8 and 1.5 of procedure d_5. It would therefore clearly pay us to adopt procedure d_5 rather than procedure d_2. Similarly, we can dismiss procedures d_3 and d_4; also d_6 is clearly inferior to procedure d_7. We shall use the term *inadmissible* to describe a procedure d which is such that, for some other procedure d',

$$W(d, s_1) \leq W(d', s_1), \qquad W(d, s_2) \leq W(d', s_2),$$

with strict inequality for at least one of s_1 and s_2. Thus d_2, d_3, d_4, d_6 are inadmissible, d_5 or d_7 acting as the superior opponent d' in the above inequalities. The formal definition takes the form:

6–3–1 Definition *Admissible and inadmissible procedures.* A decision procedure d is *inadmissible* if there is another decision procedure d' such that

$$W(d, s) \leq W(d', s) \qquad \text{for } \textit{every } s \text{ in } S,$$

with strict inequality for *some s* in *S*. A procedure which cannot be so dismissed as inadmissible is naturally called *admissible*.

Removal of inadmissible procedures leaves us with the reduced set of admissible procedures displayed for convenience in Table 6–5.

It is inherent in the definition of the term admissible that the comparison of any two admissible procedures (for example, d_1 and d_5) shows that while one

TABLE 6–5

Admissible procedures and their worths

Decision procedure	Symptom			Location of fault	
	x_1	x_2	x_3	s_1	s_2
d_1	a_1	a_1	a_1	3.0	1.0
d_5	a_2	a_1	a_1	2.8	1.5
d_7	a_2	a_2	a_1	2.0	1.8
d_8	a_2	a_2	a_2	1.0	2.0

(say d_1) has greater worth in dealing with engine faults, the other (procedure d_5) has greater worth in locating gearbox faults. There is unfortunately no procedure which stands out as best in locating both kinds of faults.

A Uniformly Best Procedure Had the utility structure been as given by Table 6–6, then the worths of the various procedures when confronted with engine

TABLE 6–6

$U(a, s)$ **for a different utility structure**

Action	Location of fault	
	s_1	s_2
a_1	3	1
a_2	1	1

faults and when confronted with gearbox faults would have been easily calculated as in Table 6–7.

TABLE 6–7

$W(d, s)$ **for the different utility structure**

Location of fault	Decision procedure							
	d_1	d_2	d_3	d_4	d_5	d_6	d_7	d_8
s_1	3.0	2.0	2.2	1.2	2.8	1.8	2.0	1.0
s_2	1.0	1.0	1.0	1.0	1.0	1.0	1.0	1.0

Procedure d_1, which examines the engine first regardless of the symptom, emerges as the only admissible procedure. This is clearly an overall best procedure and is called a *uniformly best procedure*. This is a rather obvious result since the utilities involved in a_1 compared with those involved in a_2 for this utility structure are higher for engine faults and as good for gearbox faults. Again, if the descriptions of the informative experiment had been different, as in Table 6–8, then the presence of the symptom x_1 would imply that the fault

TABLE 6–8

$p(x \mid s)$ for a different informative experiment

Location of fault	Symptom		
	x_1	x_2	x_3
s_1	0	0.5	0.5
s_2	1	0	0

is in the gearbox and the presence of symptom x_2 or x_3 that the fault is in the engine. It is then clear that, with any reasonable utility structure, procedure d_5 will be uniformly best. This is demonstrated with the original utility structure by the worths displayed in Table 6–9.

TABLE 6–9

$W(d, s)$ for the different informative experiment

Location of fault	Decision procedure							
	d_1	d_2	d_3	d_4	d_5	d_6	d_7	d_8
s_1	3	2	2	1	3	2	2	1
s_2	1	1	1	1	2	2	2	2

We emphasize that in very few real situations will such a clear-cut uniformly best procedure emerge. The removal of inadmissible procedures will usually leave an appreciable number of admissible procedures. The question that we must now pose is: What procedure do we adopt if no uniformly best procedure emerges? What do we, as manager, decide in our problem of locating a fault?

One line of argument, which is defensible but carries little consolation for the practical man, is that we have done all that we can do by the elimination of inadmissible procedures. So long as we employ one of the four admissible procedures we are acting in a rational way.

Any advance on this position must involve either

1. the introduction of some criterion or principle of choice additional to that of the comparison of the worths, or
2. the introduction of additional information.

In the remainder of this section we discuss very briefly under 1 two principles that are sometimes advocated. We shall consider alternative 2 in some detail in later sections of this chapter.

The Principle of Invariance   The principle of invariance is sometimes useful as a means of legitimately excluding some admissible procedures in the hope that there will emerge only one admissible invariant procedure. The principle of exclusion used is based on some inherent invariance property of the structure of the decision problem under consideration. For example, if the purpose of the experiment is to estimate the mean lifetime of a component, we should want our procedure to be such that we obtain the same result whether we measure the lifetimes of the tested components in seconds, minutes, or hours. A great number of possible procedures of estimation would not have this invariant property and could be summarily dismissed. It may then turn out to be the case that only one admissible procedure has this property; this procedure would then be *uniformly best invariant*. This is a problem which is of importance mainly in situations in which measurements are being made on a continuous scale, so we cannot provide a useful illustration within the context of finite models. In particular, it is of no relevance to our immediate decision problem.

The Max-Min Principle   Another line of approach is to adopt the very pessimistic philosophy that things will go against us; recall Sections 4–10 and 4–11. We then look at each of the four admissible procedures and say: If we use procedure d_1, the worst that can happen is that in the future all machines will have gearbox faults and we shall obtain average utility or worth 1;...; if we use procedure d_8, then the worst that can happen is that in the future all machines will have engine faults, and the worth to us will be 1. This leads us to Table 6–10, which shows the minimum worths associated with each admissible procedure. We would then argue as follows. To prepare against the worst, we must choose a procedure for which this worst possible worth is largest. We will therefore adopt procedure d_7, and so maximize the minimum procedural worth. Although the max-min procedure we have arrived at in this case is a reasonable one, this is by no means always the case. We have already seen in Section 4–11 that the

TABLE 6–10

Table of minimum worths

Decision procedure	d_1	d_5	d_7	d_8
Minimum worth	1.0	1.5	1.8	1.0

max-min principle can lead to an absurdly pessimistic view of a problem. It is often unrealistic to hedge one's bets against the very worst that can happen.

In the above argument we have confined our attention to the simple strategies or decision procedures of the decision-maker. It is, however, possible to introduce, as in the study of games, the concept of randomized decision procedures, whereby the simple decision procedure adopted at an application is preselected by a prior ancillary experiment, for example, d_1, d_5, d_7, d_8 might be chosen with probabilities p_1, p_5, p_7, p_8. It can be shown that such a complication strengthens the decision-maker's hand by thwarting nature's supposed ability to detect his strategy and allowing him to increase his expected utility per application. In the present context this increase is from 1.80 to 1.83, and can be achieved by the randomized procedure which operates d_7 or d_8 with probabilities $\frac{1}{6}$ and $\frac{5}{6}$. Since we shall not seriously apply the max-min principle to any of the problems of Chapter 1 we shall not enter into the details of this extension; but see the comment in Section 6–10.

EXERCISES

1. Classify each of the possible decision procedures of Exercise 1 of Section 6–1 as admissible or inadmissible, and tabulate the reduced set of admissible procedures and their worths. From this table select a max-min simple action.

   Show that if $U(a_1, s_1)$ and $U(a_1, s_2)$ had been 4 and 6 instead of 1 and 3, then a uniformly best procedure would have been available, and identify it.

2. For each of Exercises 2 through 5 of Section 6–1 and 3 of Section 6–2 draw up a table of the reduced set of admissible procedures and their worths.

   Consider some of the procedures you have declared inadmissible and ask yourself whether their dismissal could have been foreseen on intuitive grounds.

3. Carry the following problem to the stage of tabulating the reduced set of admissible procedures and their worths.

   The return per batch of manufacturered items depends on the grade—high or low—of the load of a raw material input, being 10 and 7 for high- and low-grade loads, respectively. The grade of the raw material can be ascertained easily only by the quality of finished product, but preliminary, though by no means foolproof, tests are always carried out on each load. The following probability models can be assumed to describe the variability in overall test scores:

Grade	Score			
	1	2	3	4
High	0.1	0.2	0.3	0.4
Low	0.3	0.3	0.3	0.1

Two buying contracts are offered for each load of raw material:

a) a flat rate of 5 for each load regardless of quality,

b) a deferred rate of 6 per high-grade load and 3 per low-grade load, payable immediately after batch processing.

How may the test score be used in helping to decide which contract to choose?

4. An industrial process operates at a low or high level depending on a variety of undeterminable circumstances. If a decision is made early enough, it is possible to convert a naturally low-level run into a high-level run by an adjustment costing 2. The adjustment does not affect a run which is naturally at the high level. To help reach a decision, the manufacturer can determine the grade of an early test specimen and can construct models to describe the variability in grade. If the process is operating at the low level the probabilities are 0.1, 0.3, 0.6 that the specimen will be of grade A, B, C; a process operating at the high level yields these grades with probabilities 0.2, 0.3, 0.5. The returns from low- and high-level runs are 7 and 11, respectively. No information is yet available about what proportions of future runs left unadjusted would operate at the low level.

Provide as full an analysis of the situation as you can on the basis of the information provided.

6–4 THE STRUCTURE OF THE DECISION PROBLEM

It is worth while to pause in our pursuit of procedures to form a picture of the structure of the decision problem as we have defined it so far. We recognize that mathematically speaking it is the story of three interrelated sets, the index set S of possible states of nature, the record set X of the informative experiment, and the set A of actions open to us; see Fig. 6–1.

1. The sets S and X are interrelated in the description of the informative experiment. Corresponding to each index s in S there is a probability model in the form of a probability function $p(x \mid s)$ on X. As in previous chapters, we have, in fact, a class of probability functions and this structure is the content of Table 6–1.

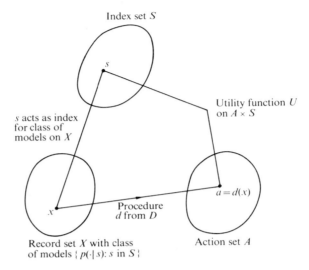

Fig. 6–1 Schematic representation of the structure of the problem of decision-making under uncertainty.

2. The sets A and S are related through the utility structure. Indeed mathematically speaking Table 6–2 is nothing more than the specification of a function U on the product set $A \times S$, since it defines for each pair (a, s), consisting of an action a and a state of nature s, a utility $U(a, s)$.

3. Is there any structure associated with the sets X and A? The answer to this question is to be found in the concept of a decision procedure. Mathematically speaking a procedure is simply a function d on X taking values in A. Given a simple record x of the informative experiment the function d directs us to take action $d(x)$; it transforms observation into action. There may be many decision procedures, so we have to consider the whole class D of possible decision procedures.

The elements in a confrontation of a decision procedure with a real situation can be imagined as emerging in sequence; see Fig. 6–2. We are presented with a machine in a specific state s (not disclosed to us); we observe the symptom x (disclosed by the informative experiment whose probabilistic structure depends on s); this information x through the decision procedure d (selected from the class D) leads us to take action $d(x)$. Then comes the reckoning and we find that we gain $U\{d(x), s\}$.

The principle on which the choice of decision procedure is being based is essentially that of maximizing our long-run average utility or worth.

Decision-Making against the Background of Repeated Decision-Making Suppose that we are going to apply a decision procedure d repeatedly on a number of

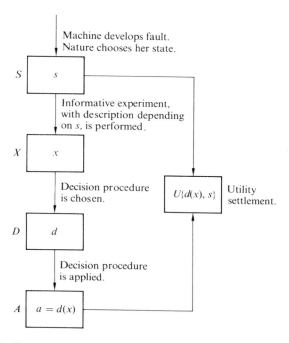

Fig. 6–2 Sequence of steps in the application of a decision procedure.

occasions in which nature always chooses the same s from S. We would then have a sequence of outcomes $x_1, \ldots, x_n$ from the n occasions on which the informative experiment was performed and the corresponding actions would be $d(x_1), \ldots, d(x_n)$. If utilities are additive over repetitions of the decision-making situation, the total utility gained in the use of the decision procedure d is

$$U\{d(x_1), s\} + \cdots + U\{d(x_n), s\}$$

and the average utility per operation of the procedure is

$$\frac{1}{n}[U\{d(x_1), s\} + \cdots + U\{d(x_n), s\}].$$

If in reality this average (or even the concept of this average) is a reasonable assessment, this draws our attention to its counterpart in the model, the expectation of $U\{d(x), s\}$ with respect to the model which actually operates, namely that corresponding to s. Thus the assessment of decision procedure d is made on the expected utility or worth

$$W(d, s) = \sum_x U\{d(x), s\} p(x \mid s).$$

Since this depends on the procedure d and on s (we have averaged or "expected" over x), we may write it in the form $W(d, s)$, as in Definition 6–2–1.

Uniformly Best Procedure If, therefore, we are faced with such a repetitive decision-making process, it would seem not unreasonable to try to choose a procedure d^* in such a way that $W(d^*, s)$ is as large as possible. The difficulty about this is that we do not know what the true state of nature is. We might then try to ensure that d^* does in fact have the desired property by requiring that

$$W(d^*, s) \geq W(d, s) \qquad \text{for every } s \text{ in } S \text{ and every } d \text{ in } D,$$

and so in particular for the true state of nature s^*. Such a d^* is called a uniformly best (best for all possible s) decision procedure. As we have seen, it is an unfortunate fact of life that such a d^* rarely exists. This is so because essentially a very great deal is being demanded of d^*.

Admissible Procedures If for each procedure we were to plot $W(d, s)$ against s, the worth graphs that emerged might be as in Fig. 6–3, where we suppose that there are just four possible procedures $d_1, \ldots, d_4$. A procedure d is defined as inadmissible if there is some better procedure d' in the sense that

$$W(d, s) \leq W(d', s) \qquad \text{for every } s \text{ in } S,$$

and there is some s' for which strict inequality holds, namely

$$W(d, s') < W(d', s').$$

Thus in Fig. 6–3, $d = d_3$ is inadmissible since $d' = d_2$ and s' satisfy the conditions of the definition. An inadmissible procedure has a worth graph which never

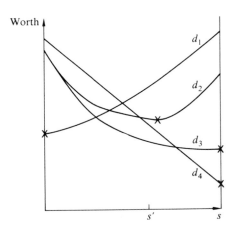

Fig. 6–3 Worth graphs of four typical procedure $d_1, \ldots, d_4$ for convenience with a continuous index set.

rises above the graph of some other procedure and is somewhere below this graph.

Formally an admissible procedure d, being not inadmissible, is such that, for any other d', either

$$W(d, s) = W(d', s) \qquad \text{for every } s \text{ in } S$$

or there is some s' such that

$$W(d, s') > W(d', s').$$

Expressing this in terms of the graphic picture we see that when we compare the worth graph of an admissible procedure with that of any other procedure either the graphs coincide or the graph of d has points above the other graph.

Max-Min Procedure We can set out formally the definition of a max-min procedure, d^* say, by using max and min instructions; compare Section 4–10. It will have the property

$$\min_S W(d^*, s) = \max_D \min_S W(d, s);$$

that is, it is a procedure which maximizes the minimum (over s) worth. In Fig. 6–3 the $\times$ depicts $\min_S W(d, s)$ for each d; it is merely the lowest point of the graph. We then select as d^* a procedure whose $\times$ is highest. In Fig. 6–3 d_2 is clearly the max-min procedure.

EXERCISE

Review each of the exercises given so far in this chapter, noting carefully the common structure of the problems as set out in Fig. 6–1.

6–5 THE INTRODUCTION OF ADDITIONAL INFORMATION

The reader is probably growing impatient at the absence of any consideration of additional information that may be available. We have already seen in Chapter 5 that the records which allowed us to derive models for the informative experiment of recording symptoms may have been built up from the experience of machines arriving at the machine repair shop. If this is so then they must contain information about the relative frequency of engine and gearbox faults. Cannot we use this kind of additional information? The answer is that we *can* use it, and this is the purpose of the present section.

Let us suppose that from a long run of previous records we have observed a certain proportion, say 0.6, of engine faults. We may then feel it reasonable to assume in our subsequent arguments that, prior to any information we have about the symptom of the particular machine at present under consideration, there is a probability, or better a plausibility, 0.6 (the observed relative frequency) that the machine has an engine fault and a plausibility $0.4 = 1 - 0.6$ that the machine has a gearbox fault.

We can now consider the long-run average utility obtainable from diagnosing and repairing the faults in the whole stream of machines, in contrast to our previous need to consider separately the stream of engine-faulty machines and the stream of gearbox-faulty machines. In fact the long-run average utility of a given procedure per machine repair, regardless of the type of fault, is the weighted average of the two worths of locating the two particular types of machine faults. For procedure d_7, for example, we have for this long-run average over all machines:

$$B(d_7, \pi) = 2.0 \times 0.6 + 1.8 \times 0.4 = 1.92.$$

Note again that we show in the notation the dependence of this long-run average on the procedure under consideration and the prior plausibility function assumed. We call $B(d, \pi)$ the *Bayesian worth of the procedure d relative to the prior plausibility function* π. We can similarly evaluate the Bayesian worths for the other admissible procedures. These are given in the first row of Table 6–11. We would then select as our best procedure one which gives the

TABLE 6–11

Bayesian worths $B(d, \pi)$

Prior plausibility		Decision procedures			
$\pi(s_1)$	$\pi(s_2)$	d_1	d_5	d_7	d_8
0.6	0.4	2.20	2.28	1.92	1.40
0.2	0.8	1.40	1.76	1.84	1.80

maximum Bayesian worth, in this situation d_5 with maximum Bayesian worth 2.28. This best procedure we call the *Bayesian procedure relative to* π. Note that if the prior plausibility function were different—for example, with plausibility 0.2 for engine faults—then we would have a different set of Bayesian worths (see the second row of the table) and a different Bayesian procedure d_7.

We are here supposing the existence of a prior plausibility function π defined on S, as we did in Section 5–3. Formal definitions of the main concepts of this section can then be easily provided.

6–5–1 Definition *Bayesian worth.* The *Bayesian worth* of a decision procedure d relative to a prior plausibility function π on S is

$$B(d, \pi) = \sum_s W(d, s)\pi(s),$$

where the worths $W(d, s)$ are computed as in Definition 6–2–1.

The Bayesian worth represents the long-run average utility per decision from the use of procedure d in the face of a stream of decision problems in which nature chooses her state s with probability $\pi(s)$.

Bayesian Procedure Relative to π If a decision-maker has prior plausibility function π on S, then his best decision procedure d^*, the *Bayesian decision procedure relative to* π, is simply the procedure which maximizes the Bayesian worth; in terms of the max instruction, choose d^* such that

$$B(d^*, \pi) = \max_D B(d, \pi).$$

EXERCISES

1. a) From your previous work on Exercise 1 of Section 6–1 compute the Bayesian worth of each admissible procedure relative to the prior plausibility function π defined by

$$\pi(s_1) = 0.3, \qquad \pi(s_2) = 0.5, \qquad \pi(s_3) = 0.2,$$

and hence select the Bayesian procedure relative to π.
   b) Illustrate the dependence of a best procedure on the prior plausibility function by showing that the Bayesian procedure relative to

$$\pi(s_1) = 0.2, \qquad \pi(s_2) = 0.5, \qquad \pi(s_3) = 0.3$$

is different from that found in (a).

2. For the process of Exercise 2 of Section 6–1 it is known that the frequencies of machine A and machine B faults are in the ratio 3 : 7. Provide the best set of working rules asked for in that exercise.

   Would your answer be affected if the gain from completing a repair were 12 instead of 10?

   What is the average dismantling-repair cost per repair with your set of rules?

3. For the geographical area in which the farm of Exercise 3 of Section 6–1 is situated the report suggests that the likely proportions of farming land of soil types 1, 2, 3 are 0.4, 0.5, 0.1. Complete your analysis of the farmer's problem on the basis of this additional information. What should the farmer do with a field classified as of soil type 1 by the test?

4. Only 4 percent of past unit policies were found to be claimants by the actuary of Exercise 4 of Section 6–1. Show how he may complete his score-premium relationship on the basis of this knowledge.

   How will his analysis be affected if he anticipates that in the future the proportion of claimants will rise to 5 percent?

5. Amalgamate the information of Exercises 2 of Sections 4–2, 2 of Section 4–5, and 5 of Section 6–1 to resolve my dental dilemma, on the assumption that I assign equal prior plausibilities to necessary extraction and amenability to root treatment for my particular tooth.

6. The contractor of Exercise 3 of Section 6–2 reckons that of the sites he considers only a proportion 0.05 have a good water supply but a proportion 0.25 have a moderate water supply. Complete your analysis of the situation for him.

7. Complete Exercise 3 of Section 6–3 on the assumption that low-grade loads are three times as frequent as high-grade loads.

8. At a certain road junction truck drivers must choose between crossing a river by bridge or by ferry. Conditions on the two approach roads are very variable, and in an attempt to provide some guidance to its drivers a trading company tries to formulate a simple model which will exploit the dependence of the time taken to reach the junction from the depot on the prevailing conditions on the two approach roads ahead. Conditions on each of these roads are classified as light or heavy, and from observations the following probability models are constructed for the distribution of times to the junction.

Condition on approach road to:		Time taken to junction		
Bridge	Ferry	Under 2 hours	2–3 hours	Over 3 hours
Light	Light	0.65	0.25	0.10
Light	Heavy	0.37	0.37	0.26
Heavy	Light	0.43	0.23	0.34
Heavy	Heavy	0.20	0.40	0.40

The plausibilities associated with each of the four combinations of road conditions are assumed, for future operations, to be 0.2, 0.3, 0.3, 0.2 for (light, light), (light, heavy), (heavy, light), (heavy, heavy).

The profit for each journey is 18 by bridge and 20 by ferry under light conditions, but these are decreased by 2 and 6, respectively, under heavy conditions.

What rules should be suggested to the truck drivers on the basis of this translation of the problem?

6–6 SOME COMMENTS ON MATHEMATICS AND PHILOSOPHY

At first sight it appears that the investigation of $W(d, s)$ in an attempt to find a uniformly best or max-min procedure and the maximization of $B(d, \pi)$ are mathematically about equally difficult. The investigation of $W(d, s)$ involves the selection of a procedure or function d from a whole set D of possible functions. There is little doubt that this may prove an extremely difficult task. First we have to enumerate in some convenient way all the possible procedures, and in many real problems this may turn out to be a very large set. Then we have to evaluate $W(d, s)$ for every d and every s, or, equivalently, draw the worth graphs to dismiss inadmissible procedures and to try to identify a uniformly best (if it exists) or a max-min procedure. The mathematical difficulties are apparently overwhelming and it is little wonder that, despite the excitement in the statistical world created by Wald's theory, which centers on $W(d, s)$, no great practical tool has emerged from this theory. Its main importance is that it gave the first clear formulation of the nature of the statistical decision problem. It gave statisticians a deeper insight into their subject. (See also Section 7–1.)

In searching for a d^* which maximizes $B(d, \pi)$ we are apparently again investigating a set of functions. But there is one vital difference. The problems involving $W(d, s)$ are awkward simply because we do not know s and are trying to make allowances for this. In constructing $B(d, \pi)$ we have averaged over s, and $B(d, \pi)$, as our notation implies, does not depend on s. We shall see that this allows us to obtain d^* by actual *construction* rather than by a search or equivalent technique applied to the whole set D of decision procedures.

The investigation of $W(d, s)$ is often referred to as the *frequentist* or *classical approach*, since it does not use the plausibility function. It recognizes only probability statements which are capable of a relative frequency interpretation. As our terminology has already suggested, the use of $B(d, \pi)$ is commonly referred to as the *Bayesian approach*, after Bayes who first discussed plausibility functions. In recent years statisticians have tended to divide themselves into roughly defined factions—Bayesians and frequentists. The argument tends to be a general philosophical one, the contestants trying to establish and defend some general theory which will cover all practical problems. The author's own view is that such an undertaking has no great merit. Problems that arise are so varied and so subtle in their differences that to be tied to some general philosophy seems positively unscientific. There will be occasions when the investigation of $B(d, \pi)$ is perfectly legitimate, as for example in our problem of locating faults. There will be other times when the specification of a plausibility function is an extremely hazardous activity. The Bayesian and frequentist should be prepared to learn from each other's analyses. For example, the frequentist may gain considerable insight into his problem by investigating the Bayesian approach with a number of different plausibility functions. A frequentist uniformly best procedure, when it exists, may be used by the Bayesian since it can easily be shown to be the Bayesian procedure relative to every π.

6–7 THE CONSTRUCTION OF A BAYESIAN PROCEDURE

As conducted in the preceding section, the search for a Bayesian procedure by the evaluation of $B(d, \pi)$ for every procedure d can be almost impossibly long. There is thus some point in rethinking the steps by which we arrive at $B(d, \pi)$ to see whether some simpler search process is available. As an incentive to the careful study of this section we can promise as compensation a dramatic simplification in the process of determining a sensible course of action.

Let us consider in more detail the computation of $B(d, \pi)$. The following array (Table 6–12) consists of six terms, each term corresponding to a particular symptom or simple record x and a particular state of nature s. By Definition 6–2–1 the row sums are simply $W(d, s_1)\pi(s_1)$ and $W(d, s_2)\pi(s_2)$, and the sum of these row sums is $B(d, \pi)$. Hence the sum of all six terms in the array is $B(d, \pi)$. Let us now compute this sum by first calculating the column sums. To do this we can replace each $p(x \mid s)\pi(s)$ by $p(x)\pi(s \mid x)$ in each of these terms; this simply involves the application of Bayesian inference as described in Section 5–3, since we are converting by (5–3–4) the prior plausibility function into the posterior plausibility function. Knowing that this embodies the whole of statistical inference, we have a right to hope that something interesting will emerge. To simplify the notation we introduce an alternative computation.

6–7–1 Definition *Value of an action.* The *value* of action a for a given simple record x is

$$V(a, x) = \sum_{s} U(a, s)\pi(s \mid x)$$

relative to a prior plausibility function π. (Note that the expression depends on π but that we have not shown this in the notation for the sake of brevity.)

We then see that the column sums can be expressed as in Table 6–12. If we now take $d(x_1)$ as that action which gives the largest value $V(a, x_1)$, $d(x_2)$ as that action which gives the largest value $V(a, x_2)$, and so on, we shall clearly obtain the largest sum of column sums possible. In this construction we are thus arriving at the Bayesian procedure d^* relative to π. This is an extremely easy operation mathematically. Indeed we see that there is no need to construct the whole procedure if we are not going to apply it repeatedly. It is sufficient to construct only the $V(a, x)$ for the observed x, and then choose the action which gives the largest value.

Bayesian Action Relative to π To obtain the Bayesian action relative to π and based on information or simple record x we construct $V(a, x)$ for every action a in A, and choose an action a^* which gives the largest *value*. In terms of the max instruction,

$$V(a^*, x) = \max_A V(a, x).$$

Corresponding to each x, such a construction gives a Bayesian *action*; this correspondence defines a Bayesian *procedure* relative to π.

Example *Machine faults.* We can demonstrate the construction of a Bayesian action by this method. Consider the first prior plausibility function with

TABLE 6–12

Two ways of computing Bayesian worth

Location of fault	Symptom			Row sums
	x_1 (overheating only)	x_2 (irregular traction only)	x_3 (overheating and irregular traction)	
s_1 (engine)	$U\{d(x_1), s_1\}p(x_1 \mid s_1)\pi(s_1)$	$U\{d(x_2), s_1\}p(x_2 \mid s_1)\pi(s_1)$	$U\{d(x_3), s_1\}p(x_3 \mid s_1)\pi(s_1)$	$W(d, s_1)\pi(s_1)$
s_2 (gearbox)	$U\{d(x_1), s_2\}p(x_1 \mid s_2)\pi(s_2)$	$U\{d(x_2), s_2\}p(x_2 \mid s_2)\pi(s_2)$	$U\{d(x_3), s_2\}p(x_3 \mid s_2)\pi(s_2)$	$W(d, s_2)\pi(s_2)$
Column sums	$V\{d(x_1), x_1\}p(x_1)$	$V\{d(x_2), x_2\}p(x_2)$	$V\{d(x_3), x_3\}p(x_3)$	$B(d, \pi)$

TABLE 6–13

Table of $\pi(s \mid x)$

	Symptom x		
Location of fault	x_1 (overheating only)	x_2 (irregular traction only)	x_3 (overheating and irregular traction)
s_1 (engine)	0.231	0.667	0.789
s_2 (gearbox)	0.769	0.333	0.211

$\pi(s_1) = 0.6$, $\pi(s_2) = 0.4$. In Table 5–3 we constructed the posterior plausibility functions corresponding to the different possible symptoms, and we reproduce the table here for ease of reference (Table 6–13).

Consider the construction of $d^*(x_1)$. We calculate

$$V(a_1, x_1) = U(a_1, s_1)\pi(s_1 \mid x_1) + U(a_1, s_2)\pi(s_2 \mid x_1)$$

$$= 3 \times 0.231 + 1 \times 0.769$$

$$= 1.462;$$

$$V(a_2, x_1) = U(a_2, s_1)\pi(s_1 \mid x_1) + U(a_2, s_2)\pi(s_2 \mid x_1)$$

$$= 1 \times 0.231 + 2 \times 0.769$$

$$= 1.769.$$

Hence if we observe x_1 (overheating only), we shall take action a_2 (inspect the gearbox first), so that $d^*(x_1) = a_2$, with value 1.769. Similar calculations give

$$V(a_1, x_2) = 2.333, \qquad V(a_2, x_2) = 1.333,$$

$$V(a_1, x_3) = 2.578, \qquad V(a_2, x_3) = 1.211,$$

so that

$$d^*(x_2) = a_1 \qquad \text{with value 2.333,}$$

$$d^*(x_3) = a_1 \qquad \text{with value 2.578.}$$

Thus we have readily constructed the Bayesian procedure relative to $\pi(s_1) = 0.6$, $\pi(s_2) = 0.4$, and have found it to be d_5, as before. The reader may care to verify by similar computation that d_7 is the Bayesian procedure relative to $\pi(s_1) = 0.2$, $\pi(s_2) = 0.8$.

By our previous method in Section 6–5 we had to enumerate eight procedures, compute 16 worths and, from these, eight Bayesian worths to find a Bayesian procedure. Even in this simple example the present method involves only the calculation of nine *values*. For more complex problems this constructive method gives an even more dramatic simplification; see Exercise 1 of this section.

The analysis of Table 6–12 has shown that there are two ways of calculating the Bayesian worth; as a sum of the row sums or as a sum of the column sums. The former, which uses the worths $W(d, s)$ and forms a weighted average with weights $\pi(s)$, has already been applied in the analysis of the preceding section, where we saw that the Bayesian worth of procedure d_5 relative to $\pi(s_1) = 0.6$, $\pi(s_2) = 0.4$ is 2.28. The other method uses the values and forms a weighted average, the weights being the $p(x)$ which were calculated in Table 5–2—as a step towards the construction of $\pi(s \mid x)$. Thus for the Bayesian procedure d_5 relative to $\pi(s_1) = 0.6$, $\pi(s_2) = 0.4$ we have the Bayesian worth

$V(a_2, x_1)p(x_1) + V(a_1, x_2)p(x_2) + V(a_1, x_3)p(x_3)$

$$= 1.769 \times 0.26 + 2.333 \times 0.36 + 2.578 \times 0.38$$

$$= 2.28,$$

as before.

We set out the equivalence of the two methods of computing the Bayesian worth as a theorem.

6–7–1 Theorem *Bayesian worth.* The following forms for computing the Bayesian worth $B(d, \pi)$ are equivalent:

$$B(d, \pi) = \sum_s W(d, s)\pi(s)$$

$$= \sum_x V(a, x)p(x),$$

where $W(d, s)$ and $V(a, x)$ are given by Definitions 6–2–1 and 6–7–1, and

$$p(x) = \sum_s p(x \mid s)\pi(s).$$

EXERCISES

1. The following tables completely define a statistical decision problem.

	$\pi(s)$	$p(x\mid s)$				$U(a, s)$		
		x_1	x_2	x_3	x_4		s_1	s_2
s_1	0.3	0.1	0.2	0.3	0.4	a_1	8	5
s_2	0.7	0.2	0.5	0.2	0.1	a_2	14	−3
						a_3	−2	7

Construct the posterior plausibility functions $\pi(s \mid x)$ and hence $V(a_1, x)$, $V(a_2, x)$, $V(a_3, x)$ for each x. Hence construct the Bayesian decision procedure relative to the given prior plausibility function, and evaluate its Bayesian worth.

Compare the ease of this construction with the alternative of enumerating all the 81 possible decision procedures, calculating the 162 worths, eliminating the inadmissible procedures, and then evaluating for each procedure in the reduced set its Bayesian worth, eventually selecting as best procedure that with maximum Bayesian worth.

2. For Exercise 1 of Section 6–5 construct directly as in this section the Bayesian procedure relative to the prior plausibility function $\pi(s_1) = 0.3$, $\pi(s_3) = 0.5$, $\pi(s_2) = 0.2$. Verify that this coincides with the answer you obtained in that exercise. Which method do you prefer?

    For this Bayesian procedure fill in the entries of Table 6–12, verifying that the column and row sums are related to the values and worths in the form suggested, and that the sum of the column sums and the sum of the row sums both give the same Bayesian worth as calculated in Exercise 1 of Section 6–5.

3. Reconsider all the decision problems already posed in exercises in this chapter and convince yourself of the effectiveness of the direct constructive method of this section compared with the method of enumeration of procedures previously employed.

4. The problem of locating faults causing transient errors of computations in its desk calculators is causing concern in the maintenance department of a computer firm. It may reasonably be assumed that the fault in any machine requiring repair lies in one and only one of three possible parts—the store, the operating system, the input-output mechanism—and that the frequencies with which these parts are the sources of fault are in the ratios $1 : 1 : 3$. So far no foolproof diagnostic test has been devised; the best available shows the following probabilistic pattern for known locations of fault.

Location of fault	Probability that test result is	
	Positive	Negative
Store	0.8	0.2
Operating system	0.5	0.5
Input-output mechanism	0.3	0.7

It has been decided to carry out four such tests independently and on the evidence provided to select one location which is then replaced at a cost of 10, whatever the location. If this turns out to be the wrong location then the eventual additional cost of making good the wrong diagnosis is 30.

The firm intends to charge a standard sum for each repair, and to make an average profit of 10 per repair. What repair policy should be adopted and what standard sum per repair should be charged?

5. Consideration is being given to the use of a next-day's weather forecaster as an aid to the night-before setting of the level of heating in a large factory in a location of very variable temperature. Five broad categories of daily weather conditions—cold, cool, moderate, warm, hot—are defined and assessed to occur with probabilities 0.2, 0.2, 0.4, 0.1, 0.1. A study of the reliability of the weather forecaster for each of these conditions suggests the following probability pattern.

Actual condition of next day's weather	Probability that forecaster says next day will be				
	Cold	Cool	Moderate	Warm	Hot
Cold	0.5	0.3	0.1	0.1	0.0
Cool	0.2	0.4	0.3	0.1	0.0
Moderate	0.1	0.2	0.4	0.2	0.1
Warm	0.1	0.1	0.2	0.5	0.1
Hot	0.0	0.1	0.2	0.3	0.4

Provided that the heating level is suited to the weather conditions, a day's production brings a profit of 100. An overheated factory, however, involves an unnecessary loss of fuel amounting to 5 for each category by which the heating level is overestimated. An underheated factory inevitably leads to a loss of production amounting to 8 for each category by which heating level is underestimated.

What is the best heating policy based on such forecasts?

What advantage is there in the use of this best policy over that which assumes that conditions are always moderate?

6–8 STATISTICAL DECISION-MAKING AS A GAME

Given a prior plausibility function π and given the outcome x of the informative experiment, we can immediately, as we have seen, derive the posterior plausibility function $\pi(s \mid x)$. We can view this posterior plausibility function as

TABLE 6–14

Decision problem as a game

Player's simple strategy	Opponent's randomized strategy	
	$\pi(s_1 \mid x)$	$\pi(s_2 \mid x)$
	s_1	s_2
a_1	$U(a_1, s_1)$	$U(a_1, s_2)$
a_2	$U(a_2, s_1)$	$U(a_2, s_2)$

our assessment just prior to action of the way that nature has chosen s. We are thus engaged as the player in a game with nature, whom we assume to be operating a randomized strategy $\pi(s \mid x)$, in the role of the opponent. The payoff is a utility to us of $U(a, s)$ if we take action a against a choice of s by nature. We can display this in a game table (Table 6–14) as in Chapter 4. For example, suppose that we have observed symptom x_1. Then our previous calculations (Table 5–3) show that we are faced with the game in Table 6–15. The decision-maker's optimum strategy is a_2, as before.

TABLE 6–15

"Locating a machine fault" as a game

Player's simple strategy	Opponent's randomized strategy	
	0.231	0.769
	s_1	s_2
a_1	3	1
a_2	1	2

What is essentially happening here is that we are separating the statistical decision problem into two natural and well-defined components. The first, statistical inference, involves the conversion of $\pi(s)$ into $\pi(s \mid x)$. Having removed the element of statistical inference, we are then left with a game, the player or decision-maker having a set A of possible strategies or actions, the opponent having a set S of possible strategies, and with payoff or utility structure $U(a, s)$. The opponent plays a randomized strategy $\pi(s \mid x)$ which is known to the player.

EXERCISE

Separate the statistical decision problems of Exercises 1 and 5 of Section 6–7 into their components of statistical inference and game theory. By solving these games with randomized strategy of the opponent known to the player, confirm your previous analysis of the problems.

6–9 THE RATIONAL MAN CONCEPT

Our analysis of the decision problem has been reached by consideration of a long run of repeated decision-making situations of the same kind. We have seen that when a prior plausibility function can be assigned, the way to reach an action is to maximize the value or the expected utility, expectation being taken with respect to the posterior plausibility function. A further assumption that was relevant to this long-run view of the problem was that utilities for successive confrontations were added together to get the overall assessment. We may ask whether this kind of analysis is relevant to the problem of making a single or once-for-all decision. Some comfort is to be found in the so-called rational man theory evolved by von Neumann and Savage. If one postulates a rational decision-maker, and states very reasonable assumptions about how he would act in certain circumstances (for example, if in given circumstances he prefers a_1 to a_2 and also a_2 to a_3, then he prefers a_1 to a_3), then it can be established that in reaching decisions he behaves as if he had a utility function and a plausibility function and reaches an action in precisely the way we have described. This is not to say that it is impossible to be a rational decision-maker without specifying these entities, but it does support the view that this method of decision-making is a very reasonable one.

6–10 GRAPHIC INVESTIGATION

A graphic investigation of the class of all Bayesian procedures throws considerable light on the interrelations of the various approaches. Let us consider procedure d_5 of Table 6–4, and suppose that we have found that $\pi(s_1 \mid x) = k$, so that $\pi(s_2 \mid x) = 1 - k$. We can then compute the corresponding Bayesian worth for procedure d_5. We obtain

$$\begin{aligned}
B(d_5, \pi) &= kW(d_5, s_1) + (1 - k)W(d_5, s_2) \\
&= 2.8k + 1.5(1 - k) \\
&= 1.5 + 1.3k.
\end{aligned}$$

If we plot $B(d_5, \pi)$ against k we obtain a straight line and we can clearly do the same for each of the procedures. Figure 6–4 shows the picture for the four admissible procedures d_1, d_5, d_7, d_8. From this picture we can pick out the Bayesian procedure for any given posterior plausibility. To do this we merely compute $\pi(s_1 \mid x)$ and then from the graphs pick out that procedure whose graph at $k = \pi(s_1 \mid x)$ is highest above the k-axis. We can mark out the Bayesian procedure corresponding to each k. This gives the heavy upper boundary line in Fig. 6–4. We can thus divide the interval $0 \le k \le 1$ to show subintervals for which the different admissible procedures are Bayesian procedures.

Note that the max-min randomized procedure mentioned in Section 6–3 corresponds to the lowest point of the upper boundary, that is, to the point where the d_7 and d_8 graphs intersect. We see that this corresponds to the Bayesian worth 1.83 and to the least favorable proportion $k = \frac{1}{6}$ of faulty engines that can face us.

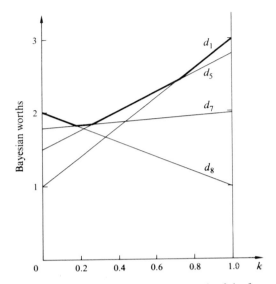

Fig. 6-4 Bayesian worth plotted against k for each of the four admissible procedures d_1, d_5, d_7, d_8.

EXERCISES

1. For the decision problem defined by

	$p(x \mid s)$			$U(a, s)$	
	x_1	x_2		s_1	s_2
s_1	0.3	0.7	a_1	2	6
s_2	0.6	0.4	a_2	5	4

show that only one of the four possible decision procedures is inadmissible. How is such inadmissibility recognized in the graphic analysis of this section?

From a graphic analysis show that for any $k = \pi(s_1) < \frac{8}{29}$ it is best to take action a_1 regardless of the outcome of the informative experiment. What information does the graph provide about how to act if $k \geq \frac{8}{29}$?

2. In Exercises 2 of Section 6–1 and 2 of Section 6–5 the incidence of machine A faults was assumed to be the proportion 0.3. Instead of making this assumption, carry out the graphic form of analysis discussed in this section, dividing the range of possible incidence into intervals for which a particular decision procedure is best. Confirm that the constructed interval containing 0.3 has as associated decision procedure the one selected by you as best in Exercise 2 of Section 6–5.

6–11 DESIGN OR CHOICE OF EXPERIMENT

We now extend Problem 3 (Locating a machine fault, Section 1–5) by supposing that we need not reach our decision only on the information about the symptom presented. We can now, if we wish, perform one, but only one, of two diagnostic tests (for example, we can check the oil supply system or check the ignition system). The result of each test may be positive, denoted by y_1, or negative, denoted by y_2. We assume that for a given location of fault the symptom presented and the result of a test are independent, and that the probabilistic descriptions of these tests are shown in Table 6–16. The assumption of independence

TABLE 6–16

Probability models for the two diagnostic tests

	Test 1 $p_1(y \mid s)$		Test 2 $p_2(y \mid s)$	
Location of fault	y_1 (positive)	y_2 (negative)	y_1 (positive)	y_2 (negative)
s_1 (engine)	0.7	0.3	0.9	0.1
s_2 (gearbox)	0.2	0.8	0.1	0.9

has been taken for convenience; it is not an essential part of the analysis, and could be easily dropped provided that we had sufficient information to construct the table of $p(x, y \mid s)$ (Table 6–17). Finally, we suppose that the cost of operating test 1 is 0.10 and of operating test 2 is 0.12. It is clear that test 2 is better in the sense that it discriminates better between the two faults, but it achieves this at a higher cost. The question we have to answer is whether this greater cost is more than compensated for by the better discrimination. Moreover, we have to convince ourselves that the cost of testing will provide a sufficient improvement in the procedure for locating the fault to make it more appealing than our already derived procedure based on knowledge of the symptom alone.

The complication here is thus that we have a choice of three possible experiments,

$$e_0: \quad \text{no further test,}$$
$$e_1: \quad \text{apply test 1,}$$
$$e_2: \quad \text{apply test 2,}$$

and the consequential complication that the utility function depends now also on the experiment chosen. This, however, involves us in little additional complication. All we have to do is to discover, for each of the three possible experiments, the Bayesian procedure relative to the prior plausibility function $\pi(s_1) = 0.6$, $\pi(s_2) = 0.4$, and from the subsequently computed Bayesian worths to choose that experiment with largest Bayesian worth. This we now proceed to do.

For e_0 we have already found that the Bayesian procedure relative to $\pi(s_1) = 0.6$, $\pi(s_2) = 0.4$ is d_5 with Bayesian worth 2.28. If we perform e_1, then we shall have available not only the symptom x but also the test result y, so we have the enlarged informative experiment which records (x, y). We first require the class of probability functions which describe this experiment. Since the test result and symptom displayed are assumed independent, the appropriate model is the product one of Definition 3–2–1 with $p(x, y \mid s) = p(x \mid s)p_1(y \mid s)$ displayed in Table 6–17.

TABLE 6–17

Table of $p(x, y \mid s)$ for diagnostic test 1

Location of fault	Simple records					
	(x_1, y_1)	(x_1, y_2)	(x_2, y_1)	(x_2, y_2)	(x_3, y_1)	(x_3, y_2)
s_1	0.07	0.03	0.28	0.12	0.35	0.15
s_2	0.10	0.40	0.06	0.24	0.04	0.16

From this table we obtain, as in Section 5–3, the joint probability function

$$p(x, y, s) = \pi(s)p(x, y \mid s),$$

then the marginal probability function for (x, y) by

$$p(x, y) = \sum_s p(x, y, s),$$

TABLE 6–18

Table of $p(x, y, s)$ and $p(x, y)$

	(x_1, y_1)	(x_1, y_2)	(x_2, y_1)	(x_2, y_2)	(x_3, y_1)	(x_3, y_2)
s_1	0.042	0.018	0.168	0.072	0.210	0.090
s_2	0.040	0.160	0.024	0.096	0.016	0.064
$p(x, y)$	0.082	0.178	0.192	0.168	0.226	0.154

TABLE 6–19

Table of $\pi(s \mid x, y)$

	(x_1, y_1)	(x_1, y_2)	(x_2, y_1)	(x_2, y_2)	(x_3, y_1)	(x_3, y_2)
s_1	0.512	0.101	0.875	0.429	0.929	0.584
s_2	0.488	0.899	0.125	0.571	0.071	0.416

and finally the posterior plausibility function $\pi(s \mid x, y)$ by

$$\pi(s \mid x, y) = p(x, y, s)/(p(x, y)).$$

These steps are presented in Tables 6–18 and 6–19. The utility function is the same as the previous one except that every entry in the table has to have deducted from it the cost 0.10 of test 1. Instead of altering this utility table we can produce the same effect by using the unadjusted utility table and then deducting from the unadjusted $B(d, \pi)$ a final 0.10.

This enables us, as in the previous analysis, to compute $V(a, x, y)$, the value of action a when the information is (x, y). For example,

$$V(a_1, x_1, y_1) = \sum_s U(a_1, s)\pi(s \mid x_1, y_1)$$

$$= 3 \times 0.512 + 1 \times 0.488$$

$$= 2.024.$$

From these we can, by the constructive method, obtain the Bayesian procedure for experiment e_1. The complete table of values of $V(a, x, y)$ is shown in Table 6–20.

The maximum unadjusted Bayesian risk is

$$W(d^*, \pi) = 2.024 \times 0.082 + 1.899 \times 0.178 + \cdots + 2.168 \times 0.154 = 2.324.$$

TABLE 6–20

Table of values $V(a, x, y)$ associated with diagnostic test 1

	(x_1, y_1)	(x_1, y_2)	(x_2, y_1)	(x_2, y_2)	(x_3, y_1)	(x_3, y_2)
a_1	2.024	1.202	2.750	1.858	2.858	2.168
a_2	1.488	1.899	1.125	1.571	1.071	1.416
Bayesian procedure d^*	a_1	a_2	a_1	a_1	a_1	a_1

Adjusted to take account of the cost 0.10 of testing, this becomes 2.224. Since this is smaller than 2.28, the Bayesian worth corresponding to no test, we see immediately that test 1 is not advisable.

A similar technique may be followed for test 2; Table 6–21 gives the essential computations.

TABLE 6–21

Construction of Bayesian procedure associated with diagnostic test 2

		(x_1, y_1)	(x_1, y_2)	(x_2, y_1)	(x_2, y_2)	(x_3, y_1)	(x_3, y_2)
$p(x, y \mid s)$	s_1	0.09	0.01	0.36	0.04	0.45	0.05
	s_2	0.05	0.45	0.03	0.27	0.02	0.18
$p(x, y, s)$	s_1	0.054	0.006	0.216	0.024	0.270	0.030
	s_2	0.020	0.180	0.012	0.108	0.008	0.072
$p(x, y)$		0.074	0.186	0.228	0.132	0.278	0.102
$\pi(s \mid x, y)$	s_1	0.730	0.032	0.947	0.182	0.971	0.294
	s_2	0.270	0.968	0.053	0.818	0.029	0.706
$V(a, x, y)$	a_1	2.460	1.064	2.894	1.364	2.942	1.588
	a_2	1.270	1.968	1.053	1.818	1.029	1.706
Bayesian procedure		a_1	a_2	a_1	a_2	a_1	a_2

The maximum unadjusted Bayesian worth is therefore

$$2.460 \times 0.074 + 1.968 \times 0.186 + \cdots + 1.706 \times 0.102 = 2.440,$$

so the maximum Bayesian worth, adjusted for cost 0.12 of testing, is 2.32. Since this is greater than 2.28, we conclude that, of the three experiments e_0, e_1, e_2, we should choose e_2. Thus we recommend that test 2 be carried out and that the information available from this be used together with the symptom presented in the operation of the procedure of Table 6–22. It may be noted that, since a_1 is the action always associated with the observation of y_1 and a_2 with y_2, diagnostic test 2 is really turning out to be so good that it completely dwarfs the importance of the information in the symptom presented. Note that this is not true of diagnostic test 1; at its most effective it uses the information from both the symptom observation and the diagnostic test.

TABLE 6–22

The Bayesian procedure

Simple record	(x_1, y_1)	(x_1, y_2)	(x_2, y_1)	(x_2, y_2)	(x_3, y_1)	(x_3, y_2)
Bayesian action	a_1	a_2	a_1	a_2	a_1	a_2

To sum up, what we should do is to disregard completely the information offered (presumably by the customer) about the symptom at breakdown and to carry out diagnostic test 2. If the result of this test is positive, we examine the engine first; if negative, the gearbox first. The long-run average profit per repair is then 2.32, which is 0.096 per repair better than we could obtain with diagnostic test 1, and 0.04 per repair more than we would obtain if we did not use any diagnostic test.

EXERCISES

1. For a decision problem with

$$S = \{s_1, s_2, s_3\}, \qquad A = \{a_1, a_2\},$$
$$\pi(s_1) = 0.2, \qquad \pi(s_2) = 0.3, \qquad \pi(s_3) = 0.5,$$

and

$U(a, s)$			
	s_1	s_2	s_3
a_1	1	3	5
a_2	2	4	2

two informative experiments e_1 and e_2 are available, each with record set $X = \{x_1, x_2\}$ and with the following classes of models

	x_1	x_2		x_1	x_2
s_1	0.3	0.7	s_1	0.7	0.3
s_2	0.5	0.5	s_2	0.2	0.8
s_3	0.8	0.2	s_3	0.9	0.1

The costs of experiments e_1 and e_2 are 1 and 2, respectively.

It is worth while to incur the cost of experimentation and, if so, which is the better experiment to use? What is the best decision procedure associated with your choice?

2. In Exercise 2 of Section 6–1 and its continuation in Exercise 2 of Section 6–5 a diagnostic test, yielding a positive or negative result independently of the displayed symptom and at an additional cost of 0.4, is available for the location of the fault. The probabilistic response pattern of this test is as follows:

Location of fault	Probability that result is	
	Positive	Negative
Machine A	0.6	0.4
Machine B	0.2	0.8

Is it worth while to make use of this test? Express in quantitative terms the advantage or disadvantage in adopting it.

3. If the payment for the services of the water diviner of Exercises 3 of Section 6–2 and 6 of Section 6–5 is the equivalent of 4 per year, is it worth while engaging his services?

4. In the problem of determining the best contract policy in Exercises 3 of Section 6–3 and 7 of Section 6–5 the cost of the preliminary test was ignored. Clearly, if the test is very expensive it will not be worth while applying it. Can you determine the break-even cost k, in the sense that a test with cost higher than k is not worth while, whereas a test with cost lower than k is worth while?

5. In certain cases of acute pain commonly referred to the hospital there is particular difficulty in diagnosing whether the cause of pain is of a temporary physical nature or whether an organ is diseased. As some guide to the two possible courses of action—medication or surgery—two tests have been developed. The first, a simple blood test, gives a positive or negative reaction; the second, a consistency test, has three categories of response: hard, normal, soft. Case histories of diagnosed patients suggest that the tests are essentially independent and that, of referred patients with diseased organs, a proportion 0.9 reacts positively to the blood test, and proportions 0.2, 0.3, 0.5 yield hard, normal, and soft responses to the consistency test; for referred patients without diseased organs the respective proportions are 0.2 and 0.6, 0.2, 0.2. Of referred patients a proportion 0.3 has diseased organs.

Although there has naturally been much heated argument about the quantitative assessments of the consequences of right and wrong decisions, it has been agreed, if only to gain some insight into the relative merits of the two tests, to postulate the following utilities, measured in "utiles":

operating on a diseased organism: 20,
operating on a healthy organism: −20,
medication for a diseased organism: −20,
medication for a healthy organism: 10.

In the time available before a decision has to be taken only one test is possible. Show that if it is possible to assign costs c_1 and c_2 (measured in utiles) to the blood and consistency tests, then the blood test is the better if and only if $c_1 - c_2 < 4.8$.

6. Two art "experts" *A* and *B* have undergone tests of their reliability in which each has separately pronounced judgment—genuine or counterfeit—on a large number of art objects of known origin. From these it appears that *A* has probability 0.8 of detecting a counterfeit and probability 0.7 of recognizing a genuine object; *B* has higher probability 0.9 of detecting a counterfeit but unfortunately has probability 0.4 of denouncing as counterfeit a genuine object.

I have been offered an objet d'art at what seems to me a bargain price of 100. If it is genuine, I reckon that I can immediately resell it for 300. I believe that there is an even chance that it is genuine but am prepared, if it is to my advantage, to call on the services of either *A* or *B* before deciding whether to buy or not. Their charges are 30 and 40, respectively, per assessment.

What should I do and what can I best expect to gain?

6–12 UTILITY DEPENDENT ON THE OUTCOME OF THE INFORMATIVE EXPERIMENT

Let us now examine Problem 5 (Choice of a batch-sentencing rule, Section 1–6). We again emphasize that the batch size in practice will usually be much larger than 3, and that our limitation to such a small size is simply for the purpose of easy illustrative computation. The principles applying to larger batches are exactly as presented here.

There are three possible states of nature or batch composition indexes, say s_0, s_1, s_2, s_3, the subscript indicating the number of effective items in the batch. Let us suppose that the informative experiment consists of selecting two of the items at random and submitting both to a test which tells us whether an item is effective or defective. The information from this informative testing experiment is thus represented by x_0, x_1, x_2, the subscript here indicating the number of effective items in the sample. We can immediately write down the class of possible probability models (Table 6–23). For example, the fact that $p(x_1 \mid s_2) = \frac{2}{3}$ arises from the consideration that the probability of drawing at random one

TABLE 6–23

Class of probability models for sampling experiment

Batch composition index (number of effective items)	Number of effective items in sample		
	$x_0 = 0$	$x_1 = 1$	$x_2 = 2$
$s_0 = 0$	1	0	0
$s_1 = 1$	$\frac{1}{3}$	$\frac{2}{3}$	0
$s_2 = 2$	0	$\frac{2}{3}$	$\frac{1}{3}$
$s_3 = 3$	0	0	1

effective and one defective from a batch consisting of 2 effectives and 1 defective is $\frac{2}{3}$.

We have now defined the first two sets, namely S and X, of our three sets. The reader will soon convince himself that the following four actions exhaust the reasonable possibilities, and $A = \{a_0, a_1, a_2, a_3\}$ is the third set required:

a_0 :   scrap the batch regardless of the result of the test;

a_1 :   scrap all the tested items, whether or not they are defective, but place the untested item on the market;

a_2 :   scrap any tested items which turn out to be defective, but place all others including the untested one on the market;

a_3 :   place the whole batch on the market, irrespective of the result of the test.

The utility function here is more general than that previously considered since it depends not only on the unknown state of nature and on the action taken but also on the particular outcome which led us to that action. Thus the utility function is in fact a function of three elements, the action a, the state of nature s, and the experimental outcome x. Consider then $U(a_2, s_1, x_1)$. Here the batch consists of one effective and two defectives and in our sample experiment we have one effective and one defective. Since the action is to scrap the tested defective (with reward -1) and to sell the remaining two articles (thus receiving 1 for the tested debilitated item and 2 for the untested and, as it happens, defective item, resulting in a claim for replacement of the untested defective item and so the further negative reward -5), the overall utility associated with (a_2, s_1, x_1) is

$$-1 + 1 + 2 - 5 = -3.$$

The dependence of this utility on x_1 arises from the fact that the number of items scrapped depends crucially on the number of defective items observed and this information is contained in x_1. In a similar way we can construct the utility corresponding to any combination of a, s, x. Since we are going to investigate the decision problem from a Bayesian point of view and hence from a knowledge of the x actually recorded, it is convenient to tabulate the utilities associated with x_0, x_1, and x_2 separately; see Table 6–24. Note that all these utilities have been calculated on the assumption that the cost of testing is nil. There is no loss of generality here by this omission, since a cost of testing would reduce each entry by the same amount. If, as in the next section, we wish to compare experiments, that is, ask what is the optimum number of items to test, we can easily adjust the Bayesian worths as we did in our examination of which was the better diagnostic test in locating a machine fault. Note also that we do not need to quote $U(a, s, x)$ for all (a, s, x) combinations, since some combinations of (s, x), for example (s_1, x_2), are impossible.

TABLE 6–24

Table of utilities $U(a, s, x)$

Action	Simple record, state of nature					
	x_0		x_1		x_2	
	s_0	s_1	s_1	s_2	s_2	s_3
a_0	-3	-3	-3	-3	-3	-3
a_1	-5	0	-5	0	-5	0
a_2	-5	0	-3	2	-1	4
a_3	-9	-6	-6	-1	-1	4

We can immediately dismiss a_3 from consideration since its utilities are dominated by those of a_2. Action a_1, which is equally nonsensical under real conditions, could be similarly dismissed, but we retain it to show its automatic rejection in the subsequent analysis. We suppose that past records have given us the proportions of the different batch compositions. These proportions give us the prior plausibility function of Table 6–25.

TABLE 6–25

Prior plausibility function

Batch composition	s_0	s_1	s_2	s_3
$\pi(s)$	0.10	0.15	0.45	0.30

The construction of $\pi(s \mid x)$ then follows in Table 6–26 in the now familiar way.

To select a Bayesian procedure, all we must now do is, for the given observed x, to construct the value

$$V(a, x) = \sum_s U(a, s, x)\pi(s \mid x)$$

for each of the remaining actions a_0, a_1, a_2, and choose that one which gives the greatest value. We have, for example,

$$V(a_2, x_1) = -3 \times \tfrac{1}{4} + 2 \times \tfrac{3}{4} = \tfrac{3}{4}.$$

The complete table can then be computed in a similar way and the resulting Bayesian procedure d^* relative to π easily constructed (see Table 6–27).

TABLE 6–26

Construction of posterior plausibility functions

		x_0	x_1	x_2
	s_0	0.10	0	0
$p(x, s)$	s_1	0.05	0.10	0
	s_2	0	0.30	0.15
	s_3	0	0	0.30
$p(x)$		0.15	0.40	0.45
	s_0	$\frac{2}{3}$	0	0
$\pi(s \mid x)$	s_1	$\frac{1}{3}$	$\frac{1}{4}$	0
	s_2	0	$\frac{3}{4}$	$\frac{1}{3}$
	s_3	0	0	$\frac{2}{3}$

TABLE 6–27

Table of $V(a, x)$ and Bayesian procedure

Action	x_0	x_1	x_2
a_0	-3	-3	-3
a_1	$-\frac{10}{3}$	$-\frac{5}{4}$	$-\frac{5}{3}$
a_2	$-\frac{10}{3}$	$\frac{3}{4}$	$\frac{7}{3}$
Bayesian procedure d^*	a_0	a_2	a_2

The maximum Bayesian worth (unadjusted for cost of testing) is by Theorem 6–7–1:

$$B(d^*, \pi) = -3 \times 0.15 + \tfrac{3}{4} \times 0.40 + \tfrac{7}{3} \times 0.45 = 0.90.$$

EXERCISES

1. A decision problem with utilities dependent on the outcome of the informative experiment is defined by the following tables:

	$\pi(s)$	$p(x \mid s)$	
		x_1	x_2
s_1	0.8	0.3	0.7
s_2	0.2	0.6	0.4

U(a, s, x)				
	x_1		x_2	
	s_1	s_2	s_1	s_2
a_1	6	−8	−2	15
a_2	−1	5	1	−5

Derive the best decision procedure and determine the maximum Bayesian worth.

2. Items are produced in batches of three at a cost of 4 per item, and records show that the frequencies with which batches contain 0, 1, 2, 3 effective items are in the ratios 1 : 3 : 3 : 5. To help in determining the quality of the batch, one item is selected at random and submitted to a nondebilitating test which reveals whether or not it is effective. If the tested item is effective, then the three items of the batch may be sold as a lot at 16 per item. If the tested item is defective, then the other two items may be sold as a lot, again at 16 per item. The customer, wishing to ensure that any lot (whether of two or three items) sold to him contains at least two effective items, negotiates a penalty from the manufacturer of 96 for any lot failing to reach this standard. The manufacturer may, however, sell any tested defective items or untested items as seconds to another customer at 6 per item without penalty.

Show that the manufacturer's best policy is to sell a lot to his first customer if and only if the tested item proves effective, and otherwise to dispose of the batch as seconds. If he follows this policy, what is the average profit per batch if the cost of the test is ignored?

3. In a batch-refining process the grade—A or B—of the input material is not easily determined, but experience suggests that there is a probability 0.6 that it is of grade A. The process can be carried out in two stages, the quality attained after the first stage acting as an indicator of whether or not it is worth while to proceed with the second stage. Detailed investigation with input of determined grade A has shown that the first stage reaches qualities 1, 2, 3, 4 with probabilities 0.3, 0.4, 0.2, 0.1, whereas with grade B the corresponding probabilities are 0.5, 0.3, 0.2, 0. The second stage will certainly take grade A input to quality 4, but will take grade B only to quality 3. The return from the sale of batches of qualities 3 and 4 are 3 and 4, respectively, and the cost of the second stage is 0.5.

At the end of the first stage a batch has reached quality 3. Is it worth while to complete the second stage?

What is the minimum change in this cost which would make you alter your choice?

4. A simplified version of a marketing research problem runs as follows. Past products from the development department have been classified as "successful" or "unsuccessful," 25 percent having proved successful. For each product a preliminary marketing trial had been run in which 200 units were offered for sale. The variability in trial sales for each type of product was then assessed in terms of the probabilities of selling 50, 100,

150, 200 units, these being 0.1, 0.2, 0.3, 0.4 for eventually successful and 0.3, 0.4, 0.2, 0.1 for eventually unsuccessful products. (We assume that the sales are multiples of 50 simply to make the necessary calculations easier.) The eventual total sales of successful products turned out to be eight times the preliminary sales, whereas the total sales of unsuccessful products was just double the preliminary sales.

Such a preliminary trial has been conducted for a new product and 150 units sold. Future products can be produced only in batches of 200 and the profit per sold item is 1; the loss from an unsold item -2. How many more batches should be produced?

6–13 GENERAL UTILITY STRUCTURE DEPENDENT ON ACTION, STATE OF NATURE, OUTCOME OBSERVED, AND EXPERIMENT UNDERTAKEN

It is now easy to present an example of a statistical decision problem whose utility structure involves all the cases so far considered; for the example of the last section is clearly not completely analyzed until we have answered this question: Are we correct in examining two items? Because of the cost and the debilitating effect of testing, may it not be better to test just one item, or even none at all? On the other hand, the replacement cost of a defective item is so great that perhaps it will pay us to ascertain the precise composition of the batch before we take action; that is, perhaps we should test all three items. How do these conflicting tendencies balance out in our best interest? Thus we have once more the problem of selecting the best experiment from the following four available experiments:

$$e_0: \quad \text{examine no items,}$$
$$e_1: \quad \text{examine 1 item,}$$
$$e_2: \quad \text{examine 2 items,}$$
$$e_3: \quad \text{examine 3 items.}$$

We must again adopt the practice of determining, for each experiment separately, the maximum Bayesian worth, now of course suitably adjusted to take account of the cost of testing. We carried out a typical analysis, for e_2,

TABLE 6–28

Table of $U(a, s)$

Action	State of nature			
	s_0	s_1	s_2	s_3
a_0	-3	-3	-3	-3
a_3	-9	-4	1	6

in the preceding section and found the maximum unadjusted Bayesian worth to be 0.90. The maximum adjusted Bayesian worth is then equal to $0.90 - 0.12 = 0.78$, since the cost of testing is 2×0.06.

In Tables 6–28 through 6–33 we summarize the relevant computations for the other three experiments. Unadjusted utilities are first used and then finally adjusted.

Experiment e_0. Actions a_0 and a_3 are the only possible ones (see Table 6–28). There is no record x to be considered. The values of the actions are then easily computed by the formula

$$V(a) = \sum_s U(a, s)\pi(s)$$

to be

$$V(a_0) = -3, \qquad V(a_3) = \tfrac{3}{4},$$

so the Bayesian action is a_3 with maximum unadjusted Bayesian worth 0.75 and, of course, maximum adjusted Bayesian worth 0.75, since there is no cost of testing.

Experiment e_1. Possible outcomes are x_0 and x_1 (Tables 6–29 and 6–30).

TABLE 6–29

Construction of posterior plausibility functions for experiment e_1

		x_0	x_1
$p(x \mid s)$	s_0	1	0
	s_1	$\frac{2}{3}$	$\frac{1}{3}$
	s_2	$\frac{1}{3}$	$\frac{2}{3}$
	s_3	0	1
$p(x, s)$	s_0	0.10	0
	s_1	0.10	0.05
	s_2	0.15	0.30
	s_3	0	0.30
$p(x)$		0.35	0.65
$\pi(s \mid x)$	s_0	$\frac{2}{7}$	0
	s_1	$\frac{2}{7}$	$\frac{1}{13}$
	s_2	$\frac{3}{7}$	$\frac{6}{13}$
	s_3	0	$\frac{6}{13}$

TABLE 6–30

Table of utilities $U(a, s, x)$ for experiment e_1

Action	Simple record, state of nature					
	x_0			x_1		
	s_0	s_1	s_2	s_1	s_2	s_3
a_0	-3	-3	-3	-3	-3	-3
a_1	-7	-2	3	-7	-2	3
a_2	-7	-2	3	-5	0	5
a_3	-10	-5	0	-5	0	5

Action a_3 is dominated by a_2 (Table 6–31).

TABLE 6–31

Table of $V(a, x)$ and Bayesian procedure for experiment e_1

Action	x_0	x_1
a_0	-3	-3
a_1	$-\frac{9}{7}$	$-\frac{1}{13}$
a_2	$-\frac{9}{7}$	$\frac{25}{13}$
Bayesian procedure d^*	a_1 or a_2	a_2

Maximum unadjusted Bayesian risk $= -\frac{9}{7} \times 0.35 + \frac{25}{13} \times 0.65 = 0.80$,

maximum adjusted Bayesian risk $= 0.80 - 0.06 = 0.74$.

Experiment e_3. Possible outcomes are x_0, x_1, x_2, x_3 (Tables 6–32 and 6–33).

The actions a_0, a_1, a_3 are dominated by a_2 and hence the optimum action whatever the outcome is a_2.

Maximum unadjusted Bayesian worth

$$= -3 \times 0.10 - 1 \times 0.15 + 1 \times 0.45 + 3 \times 0.30$$

$$= 0.90,$$

TABLE 6–32

Construction of posterior plausibility functions for experiment e_3

		x_0	x_1	x_2	x_3
$p(x \mid s)$	s_0	1	0	0	0
	s_1	0	1	0	0
	s_2	0	0	1	0
	s_3	0	0	0	1
$p(x, s)$	s_0	0.10	0	0	0
	s_1	0	0.15	0	0
	s_2	0	0	0.45	0
	s_3	0	0	0	0.30
$p(x)$		0.10	0.15	0.45	0.30
$\pi(s \mid x)$	s_0	1	0	0	0
	s_1	0	1	0	0
	s_2	0	0	1	0
	s_3	0	0	0	1

TABLE 6–33

Table of utilities $U(a, s, x)$ for experiment e_3

Action	Simple record, state of nature			
	(x_0, s_0)	(x_1, s_1)	(x_2, s_2)	(x_3, s_3)
a_0 or a_1	-3	-3	-3	-3
a_2	-3	-1	1	3
a_3	-12	-7	-2	3

maximum adjusted Bayesian worth

$$= 0.90 - 3 \times 0.06 = 0.72.$$

Collecting the maximum adjusted Bayesian worths into Table 6–34 for easy comparison we see clearly that the best experiment to perform is e_2, the examination of two items, and then the best procedure to adopt is that found in the preceding section. We can then hope to gain a return on average of 0.78 per batch.

TABLE 6–34

Bayesian worths for the four possible experiments

	e_0	e_1	e_2	e_3
Maximum unadjusted Bayesian worth	0.75	0.80	0.90	0.90
Maximum adjusted Bayesian worth	0.75	0.74	0.78	0.72

EXERCISES

1. An alternative informative experiment for the decision problem of Exercise 1 of Section 6–12 is available with class of models

$p(y \mid s)$

	y_1	y_2
s_1	0.5	0.5
s_2	0.9	0.1

and utility structure

$U(a, s, y)$

	y_1		y_2	
	s_1	s_2	s_1	s_2
a_1	1	1	0	20
a_2	3	-2	2	-25

   The first experiment costs 0.3 to perform, and this alternative costs 0.8. Which is the better experiment to use, and what is the best decision procedure?

2. Suppose that the cost of carrying out the test in Exercise 2 of Section 6–12 is 1 per item. Show that it is still better to carry out the test than to make decisions without it.

   Would there be any advantage in testing two items before reaching a decision?

3. In Exercise 3 of Section 6–12 the cost of stopping to record the quality attained at the end of the first stage is k. An alternative procedure allows a different, cheaper first stage at cost l, and gives attained qualities 1, 2, 3, 4 with probabilities 0.4, 0.3, 0.2, 0.1 for grade A input, with probabilities 0.5, 0.3, 0.1, 0.1 for grade B input. The mechanism of the second stage remains the same.

   Under what conditions on k and l is this alternative better than the original procedure?

CHAPTER 7

APPLICATIONS AND EXTENSIONS OF STATISTICAL DECISION THEORY

In this chapter we shall complete our analysis of all the outstanding challenging problems of Chapter 1. To achieve this we must introduce three new concepts. The first, which is of considerable practical value, fortunately does not lead to any complication of the analysis. It is designed to take care of situations in which the utility of an action is most directly assessable in terms not of the existing state of nature but rather of the results that are likely to arise in future experiments. We must prognosticate on the consequences of our action in order to assess its utility, so we shall call this type of statistical decision theory *prognosis analysis*. The second innovation is that we shall allow the possibility of hesitating after an experiment has been performed and of choosing between taking action now and calling for more information from further experimentation. We thus obtain a picture of a sequence of experiments after any one of which we must decide whether or not to continue. If we decide to stop, then we must choose whatever action is most appropriate on the information collected. We are thus involved in *sequential decision-making*. There is considerable added difficulty in this complication, but we shall see that the introduction of a simple principle, which is little more than an expression of the correct way of viewing the problem, ensures a successful analysis. Finally we allow greater freedom in the sequential aspect of the problem in that we may have more control over the situation than the mere choice of continuing or stopping. In these *control problems*, if we choose to continue we may select which of a number of possible experiments we wish to perform at the next stage.

Before we undertake these extensions we shall briefly review the position reached, showing the structure of decision-making in terms of decision trees, and shall also indicate the relation of statistical decision theory to the hypothesis-testing and estimation aspects of statistical inference.

7–1 DECISION TREES

We can imagine the decision problem as arising in a series of steps arranged as branches of a tree diagram, and the solution of the problem is seen to involve a journey from the tips of the branches back to the trunk of the tree. It will be seen that the Bayesian and frequentist approaches are associated with different trees. We shall discuss these forms of analysis in sequence. After a general discussion of each form we shall illustrate the associated tree analysis by the following simple example.

Example *The angler's dilemma. Preliminary analysis.* As an angler I am interested in catching a certain type of predatory seafish (mackerel). I can either use artificial bait or spend a period attempting to catch natural bait in the form of the prey (herring) of the predator. From past experience I have recognized that conditions can be classified as *plentiful* or *scarce* so far as the predator is concerned. When the predator is plentiful there is usually prey around and I estimate the probability of obtaining natural bait at 0.7; when the predator is scarce there are fewer prey and the probability of obtaining natural bait is then 0.4. At this point of the season the odds are 3 to 2 in favor of the predator's being plentiful rather than scarce.

At this stage of the presentation of the problem we recognize two possible states of nature:

$$s_1: \quad \text{predator scarce,}$$
$$s_2: \quad \text{predator plentiful.}$$

There are two "experiments" available to us:

$$e_1: \quad \text{do not fish for prey,}$$
$$e_2: \quad \text{fish for prey.}$$

The record set for experiment e_2 consists of two simple records:

$$x_1: \quad \text{no prey caught,}$$
$$x_2: \quad \text{some prey caught.}$$

"Experiment" e_1, since it is strictly never performed, has no authentic record set, but for the sake of symmetry of argument, we can give this nonexperiment a unique dummy simple record x_0. Since

$$x_0: \quad \text{dummy simple record}$$

always occurs if we choose experiment e_1, we have introduced a harmless convention.

We have now reached a position in which we can formulate the class of probability models and also complete the plausibility analysis in readiness for the various forms of decision analysis. For e_2 these are displayed in Tables 7–1 and 7–2. For experiment e_1 the posterior and prior plausibility functions are, of course, identical:

$$\pi(s \mid x_0) = \pi(s).$$

TABLE 7–1

Class of probability functions $p(x \mid s)$ for e_2

State of nature	$\pi(s)$	$p(x \mid s)$	
		x_1 (no prey caught)	x_2 (some prey caught)
s_1: predator scarce	0.4	0.6	0.4
s_2: predator plentiful	0.6	0.3	0.7

TABLE 7–2

Posterior plausibility analysis for e_2

		x_1	x_2
$p(x, s)$	s_1	0.24	0.16
	s_2	0.18	0.42
$\eta(x)$		0.42	0.58
$p(s \mid x)$	s_1	$\frac{4}{7}$	$\frac{8}{29}$
	s_2	$\frac{3}{7}$	$\frac{21}{29}$

After I have chosen one of those experiments and performed it, I must choose between two courses of action open to me:

a_1: give up the idea of fishing and go for a round of golf,
a_2: fish for predator with natural bait if available, otherwise with artificial bait.

I will not bore the reader with the introspective process by which I constructed my utility function, but will merely present the determined utilities in a convenient form later in Fig. 7–2. These utilities have taken account of the cost of artificial bait, the loss of time through fishing for prey, my greater expectation of catching a predator when the predator is plentiful and also when I can use natural bait rather than artificial bait, the satisfaction of catching a predator when they are scarce, the relative attractions of fishing and golf, and so on.

Bayesian Analysis Imagine the following sequence:

  i) We choose an informative experiment e from a set E of possible experiments.
 ii) Nature presents us with a record x chosen by probability function $p(x)$.
iii) We choose a course of action a from a set A of possible actions.
 iv) Nature declares her true state s, selected by way of the probability function $\pi(s \mid x)$.

At the end of these four steps we receive a reward or utility based possibly on all four of e, x, a, and s.

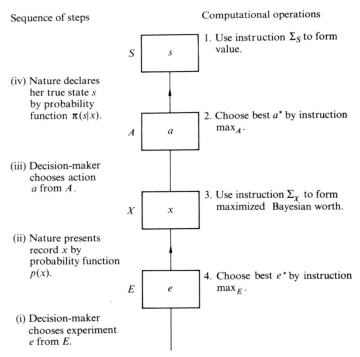

Fig. 7–1 The sequence of steps and the computational operations in the Bayesian approach to decision-making under uncertainty.

Figure 7–1 gives a picture of one possible branch of this process. The way in which an informative experiment is chosen and a course of action is arrived at can be described in terms of operations at each of these steps, the analysis taking place at four operations starting from the top and working back along the branches to the base. Two of the four steps involve a choice by the decision-maker (steps (i) and (iii)); the remaining two involve the introduction of chance or uncertainty by nature. The decision problem can therefore be described succinctly as the problem of how we exercise choice against chance. There are two basic instructions (in terms of the mathematical instructions Σ and max) which the decision-maker must use at the four operations.

a) At any stage of the analysis where the decision-maker sees chance operating, all he can do is to compute the appropriate expectation of the quantity of interest. This involves him in the use of the instructions Σ_S and Σ_X at operations 1 and 3.

b) When faced by a choice between alternatives leading to different effects, he must choose that alternative which produces the maximum effect. This is the position at operations 2 and 4 where the instructions $\max_A$ and $\max_E$ are the appropriate ones.

Operation 1. Form the expected utility with respect to $\pi(s \mid x)$. This process produces the value and uses the instruction Σ_S.

Operation 2. Choose an action which gives the largest value. This involves the instruction $\max_A$ (values) and provides the maximized value.

Operation 3. Form the expectation of the maximized value, expectation being with respect to $p(x)$. This produces the maximized Bayesian worth and uses the instruction Σ_X.

Operation 4. Choose an experiment for which the maximum Bayesian worth is largest. This requires the instruction $\max_E$.

The result of operation 4 tells us which experiment we should undertake, and operation 2 tells us what action we should take when faced with data x.

Bayesian Analysis of the Angler's Dilemma Figure 7–2 presents the complete decision tree for the Bayesian analysis of my angling problem. As already mentioned, the utilities have been directly inserted at the tips of the highest branches. For example,

$$U(e_2, x_1, a_2, s_2) = 32;$$

if I decide to fish for bait, obtain none, but decide to fish (with artificial bait) and the predator is plentiful, my utility is 32 whoopees of enjoyment. Again

$$U(e_1, x_0, a_1, s_1) = U(e_1, x_0, a_1, s_2) = 35;$$

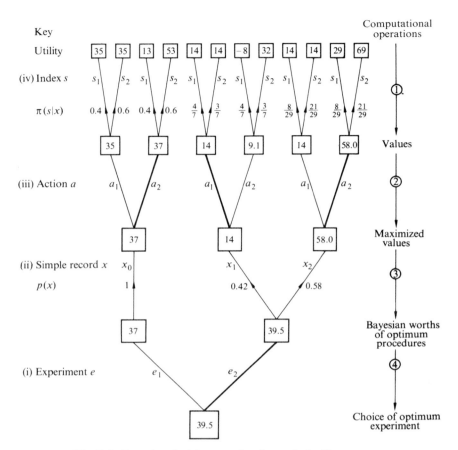

Fig. 7–2 Bayesian decision tree for the angler's dilemma.

if I decide not to fish for bait and in fact have a game of golf instead of fishing (and thereby remain blissfully ignorant of fishing conditions), I enjoy 35 whoopees. And so on.

Two comments, corresponding to (a) and (b) in the general discussion, should suffice to explain the complete construction and interpretation of Fig. 7–2.

a) Where arrows are shown (at computational operations 1 and 3) along branches leading from a node, uncertainty is present and the numbers attaching to the arrows are assessments of uncertainty in terms of probabilities or plausibilities. The evaluation of the entry at such a node requires only the multiplication of the entries at the extremities of these arrowed branches by the corresponding numbers attached to the arrows, and the summation of these products.

For example, the entry 9.1 is the value of action a_2 following the observation of x_1 in experiment e_2, and arises from

$$-8 \times \tfrac{4}{7} + 32 \times \tfrac{3}{7} = 9.1.$$

Similarly, the 39.5 at the node at the end of the e_2-branch is the Bayesian worth of the optimum decision procedure based on experiment e_2, and is found to be

$$14 \times 0.42 + 58.0 \times 0.58 = 39.5.$$

b) Where no arrows are shown (at computational operations 2 and 4) along branches leading from a node, a max instruction has to be carried out. For example, at operation 2 we have to choose the greater of 14 and 58, and the greater value 58 is carried down to the lower node. The Bayesian action a_2 at this point is then conveniently indicated by a thickening of the branch labeled a_2.

These features (a) and (b) are common to each of the trees, but in the max-min tree a min instruction replaces one of the max instructions here.

What I must do to attain the greatest enjoyment from my dilemma is then clear from the tree. The thick branch leading to e_2 indicates that I should fish for prey. If I then catch no prey (branch x_1), the thick branch leading to a_1 indicates that I should go off and golf; if I catch prey (branch x_2), the thick branch leading to a_2 indicates that I should now use this natural bait and fish for the predator. The expected number of whoopees from such a choice of experiment and decision procedure is 39.5 whoopees, compared with the 37 whoopees I could expect from the alternative choice of e_1 with its immediate fishing for the predator with artificial bait.

Frequentist Analysis We give first the frequentist sequence of steps leading to the calculation of the Bayesian worth through the introduction of the prior plausibility function, and then see how the concepts of uniformly best and max-min may be presented. The frequentist approach also depends on four steps though in a different order from the Bayesian approach and with the introduction at step (iii) of a decision procedure, whereas the Bayesian interpretation introduced an action at step (iii). Now that the reader has seen the Bayesian tree analysis the steps shown in Fig. 7–3, as well as the sequence of four operations, should be self-explanatory. If a complete prior plausibility function is available, there is no doubt that the Bayesian form of tree is easier to operate, for the simple reason that it can be used to construct bit by bit a best decision procedure through individual choice of best actions, whereas the frequentist tree requires consideration of the whole set of decision procedures. The mathematical difference here can be described for the mathematical reader as the distinction between a problem of differential calculus and one of the calculus of variations.

Sequence of steps   Computational operations

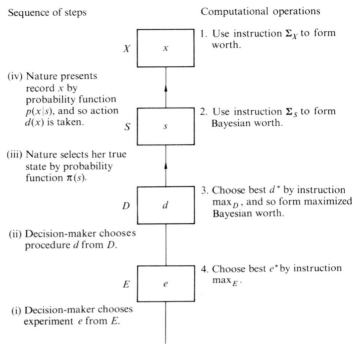

1. Use instruction Σ_X to form worth.

(iv) Nature presents record x by probability function $p(x|s)$, and so action $d(x)$ is taken.

2. Use instruction Σ_S to form Bayesian worth.

(iii) Nature selects her true state by probability function $\pi(s)$.

3. Choose best d^* by instruction $\max_D$, and so form maximized Bayesian worth.

(ii) Decision-maker chooses procedure d from D.

4. Choose best e^* by instruction $\max_E$.

(i) Decision-maker chooses experiment e from E.

Fig. 7–3 The sequence of steps and the computational operations in the frequentist approach to decision-making under uncertainty.

Frequentist Analysis of the Angler's Dilemma We must first enumerate the possible decision procedures. To retain a symmetric development we can, for e_1, introduce formal procedures d^1 and d^2 (the superscript is a labeling, not a squaring, device), which direct us to actions a_1 and a_2, respectively. These, together with the obvious four procedures for experiment e_2, are shown in Table 7–3.

Points (a) and (b) of the Bayesian analysis again apply to Fig. 7–4, and the reader should easily follow the computation of the entries, moving from the tips of the branches back towards the ground, and also the thickening of branches. The interpretation of the completed tree is also straightforward. The thick branch leading to e_2 again indicates that I should fish for prey. The secondary thick branch leading to decision procedure d_2 then instructs me, by Table 7–3, to play golf if I fail to catch prey and to fish for predator with natural bait if I catch some prey. This agrees with the previous Bayesian analysis.

Note that the rows of worths allows us for each experiment to identify the admissible procedures (here d^1, d^2, d_2, d_4) and the inadmissible procedures

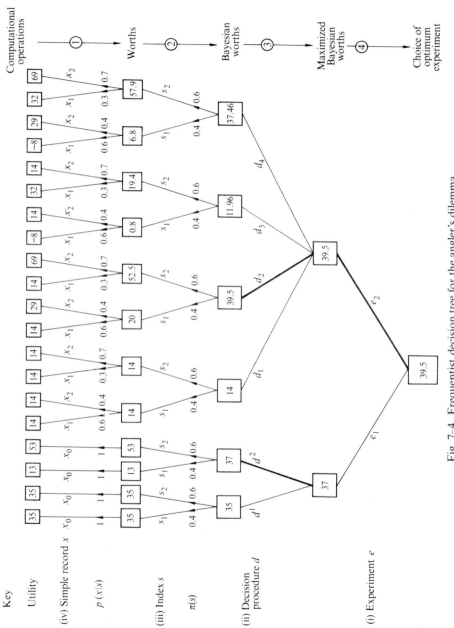

Fig. 7-4 Frequentist decision tree for the angler's dilemma.

TABLE 7-3

Possible decision procedures for the angler's dilemma

For experiment e_1			For experiment e_2				
Simple record	Decision procedure		Simple record	Decision procedure			
	d^1	d^2		d_1	d_2	d_3	d_4
x_0 (dummy)	a_1	a_2	x_1 (no prey caught)	a_1	a_1	a_2	a_2
			x_2 (some prey caught)	a_1	a_2	a_1	a_2

(here d_1, d_3) in the manner discussed in Section 6–3. Note also that the greater computational difficulty of the frequentist approach manifests itself in the greater number of branches in Fig. 7–4 compared with Fig. 7–2.

Uniformly Best and Max-Min Analysis The modifications to Figs. 7–1 and 7–3 which are necessary to produce a uniformly best solution (if such exists) and a max-min solution are shown in Figs. 7–5 and 7–6. Note that the max-min

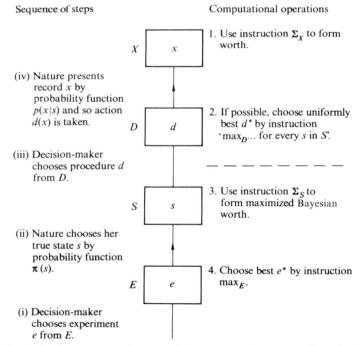

Fig. 7–5 The sequence of steps and the computational operations for the determination of a uniformly best procedure where this exists.

approach operates one expectation instruction before operating a double min and max operation, and that the uniformly best approach does not come back as far as nature's selection of her state before choosing a best decision procedure.

We have already seen in the frequentist analysis that a uniformly best procedure cannot exist for the angler's dilemma, since neither experiment has a unique admissible strategy associated with it. We shall therefore move on to the max-min analysis of this example.

Max-Min Analysis of the Angler's Dilemma The decision tree for the max-min analysis of my angling problem is shown in Fig. 7–7. In my now pessimistic mood I imagine the worst conditions possible at computational operation 2, and therefore consider the minimum worth at this stage. Note that because a min operation is used here no arrows appear along the branches leading to s_1 and s_2. Note also that where two worths are equal, either or both branches can be thickened to indicate the minimum. Once completed, the decision tree is easily interpreted. The thickened branch leading to e_1 tells me that I should not fish for bait, and the subsequent thickened branch leading to d^1 says that I should go and play golf. In short, as a pessimistic angler I am happier playing golf.

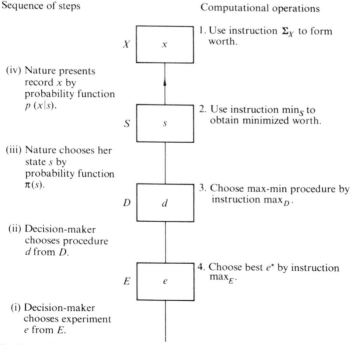

Fig. 7–6 The sequence of steps and the computational operations in the max-min approach to decision-making under uncertainty.

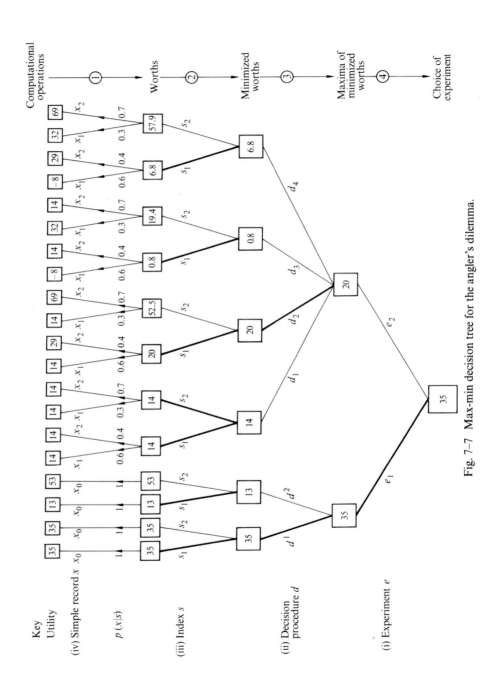

Fig. 7-7   Max-min decision tree for the angler's dilemma.

A General Point on Choice of Experiment   One general point remains to be made. Many frequentists would argue that the introduction of a prior plausibility function is legitimate at the design stage of an investigation, that is, at the time of the choice of the informative experiment; but that in the analysis of the informative experiment the prior plausibility function should be ignored to ensure an "objective" analysis—for example, through the medium of frequentist testing or estimation. While this is no doubt effective in practice and is tenable on pragmatic grounds, a number of logical objections could be leveled against it. For instance, if a prior plausibility function can be specified for one part of the decision problem, why does it not apply equally well in the other?

EXERCISES

1. My angling friend assesses his utilities at the tips of the branches of the decision tree of Fig. 7–2, from left to right, as

$$33, 33, 20, 46, 15, 15, -5, 35, 15, 15, 29, 58.$$

   Following the argument of this section, complete the counterparts of Figs. 7–2, 7–4, and 7–7, and advise my angling friend on what he should do.

2. Reconsider some of the previous exercises in Chapter 6 and construct for them decision trees as in Figs. 7–2, 7–4, and 7–7. Verify that the tree analysis conforms with your previous conclusions.

7–2 LOSS STRUCTURES

In all our applications so far, both in game theory and in statistical decision theory, we have expressed the final settlement after strategy or action a has been adopted to meet a state of nature s as a utility $U(a, s)$, the gain to the player or decision-maker. While it is clear that there is no loss of generality in this specification, since an overall loss can be expressed as a negative utility, it is convenient in some practical situations to work directly in terms of the loss $L(a, s)$ to the player or decision-maker. The considerations of preceding chapters then go through in a most obvious way, each concept such as utility U, value V, worth W, Bayesian worth B having its counterpart, say *loss L, misfortune M, risk N, Bayesian risk C*. Figure 7–8 reminds the reader of the interconnections between these concepts, each arrow indicating a summation or expectation instruction with respect to the attached probability function. In the definitions of such concepts as admissibility, inequality signs reverse their directions and max and min instructions give way to min and max instructions.

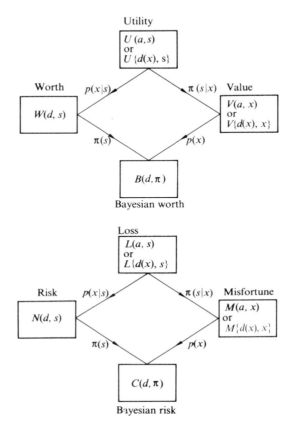

Fig. 7–8 The interrelations of utility, value, worth and Bayesian worth, and of loss, misfortune, risk and Bayesian risk.

7–3 RELATION OF DECISION THEORY TO STATISTICAL INFERENCE

We have already said that the whole of statistical inference is contained in the transformation of a prior plausibility function $\pi(s)$, through the record x of an informative experiment, into the corresponding posterior plausibility function $\pi(s \mid x)$. Thus one answer to the question "What is the relation of statistical inference to decision theory?" is that given in Chapter 6, where we saw that statistical inference, together with the theory of games, form the two components of statistical decision theory. What we propose to investigate in this section is simply how decision theory is related to those frequentist aspects of statistical activity—the hypothesis testing and estimation of Sections 5–8 through 5–11.

Hypothesis Testing   The special feature of hypothesis testing from the viewpoint of statistical decision theory is that the action set consists of an action for each hypothesis. Let us for simplicity confine our attention to Problem 4 (Medical screening, Section 1–5), where the two hypotheses are simple; review the concepts and notation of Section 5–8. We might attempt to construct a loss function along the following lines. If we make a correct classification, we are involved in no loss, so $L(a_1, s_1) = L(a_2, s_2) = 0$. If we misclassify a normal baby as abnormal, then we subject it unnecessarily to the further expensive test. If this test costs l, then $L(a_2, s_1) = l$. If we misclassify an abnormal baby as normal, there may be harm caused by the delay in diagnosis and additional costs of cure may be incurred by the need to treat a more advanced stage of the abnormality. It may be very difficult to place a numerical value on the loss due to these consequences, but let us suppose that we can set $L(a_1, s_2) = k$. Table 7–4 gives the complete loss structure.

TABLE 7-4

Loss function $L(a, s)$ for problem of medical screening

Action	State of nature	
	s_1 (normal)	s_2 (abnormal)
a_1 (conclude baby is normal)	0	k
a_2 (conclude baby is abnormal)	l	0

The risks are then easily computed as

$$N(d, s_1) = lp(R_2 \mid s_1), \qquad N(d, s_2) = kp(R_1 \mid s_2),$$

which are simply scaled measures of the liabilities of the two kinds of misclassification error discussed in Section 5–8. We have already seen there the impossibility of choosing R_1 and R_2 to minimize these two risks simultaneously, so no uniformly best test procedure exists. There are a number of procedures which are admissible.

It is interesting in this case to ask what sort of procedure would emerge from a Bayesian analysis. Suppose that we have evaluated the posterior plausibility function $\pi(s \mid x)$. Then

$$M(a_1, x) = k\pi(s_2 \mid x), \qquad M(a_2, x) = l\pi(s_1 \mid x).$$

It follows that x will lead to action a_1 if and only if

$$k\pi(s_2 \mid x) < l\pi(s_1 \mid x)$$

or, by (5–3–4),

$$\frac{p(x \mid s_1)}{p(x \mid s_2)} > \frac{k\pi(s_2)}{l\pi(s_1)}.$$

This result supports what we hinted at as a successful means of test construction in Section 5–8; that those x which have highest claim for entry into the set R_1 are precisely those for which the ratio $p(x \mid s_1)/p(x \mid s_2)$ is highest. Thus the Bayesian approach gives some support to the frequentist approach in that a frequentist "most powerful" test does just this kind of thing.

Estimation   The characteristic of an estimation problem is that the action set A is simply a copy of the index set S. An estimate a of unknown index s should ideally always be s, and the lack of success in the use of a as an estimate of s clearly increases, though in perhaps some complicated way, the farther a is from s. It is thus popular to consider estimation as a statistical decision problem with a loss $L(a, s)$ proportional to some measure of the distance from the estimate a to the index s.

The most popular measure is the squared distance or *quadratic loss function*

$$L(a, s) = (a - s)^2.$$

The reason for this preference is largely the mathematical tractability of this function. With a quadratic loss function we can, in fact, obtain very simply a general result. Suppose that the posterior plausibility function $\pi(s \mid x)$ has been evaluated. Then we wish to choose that estimate a which minimizes

$$M(a, x) = \sum_s (a - s)^2 \pi(s \mid x).$$

Now, by Theorem 3–9–3, this misfortune can be expressed in the form

$$M(a, x) = \mathscr{V}(s \mid x) + \{\mathscr{E}(s \mid x) - a\}^2,$$

its minimum value for variation in a being achieved when the expression in braces is smallest, that is, when it is zero. Hence the Bayesian estimator is given by

$$d^*(x) = \mathscr{E}(s \mid x),$$

the mean of the posterior plausibility function.

This, of course, is a Bayesian form of analysis. It produces an estimator which minimizes the expectation (relative to the posterior plausibility function) of the squared distance from the true value. It is interesting to ask whether the frequentist concept of minimum variance unbiased estimator fulfils the corresponding requirement of frequentist decision theory. For this the minimum variance unbiased estimator would have to minimize the risk $N(d, s)$ for every s.

We can write, by Theorem 3-9-3,

$$N(d, s) = \mathscr{V}\{d(x) \mid s\} + [\mathscr{E}\{d(x) \mid s\} - s]^2,$$

but such a resolution does not separate out the effect of changes in the decision procedure d as the Bayesian resolution did for the action a. The minimization of $N(d, s)$ may not in fact be achieved by consideration of only unbiased estimators (making $[\ldots]^2 = 0$) and the subsequent choice of unbiased estimator with minimum first term. In other words, a minimum variance unbiased estimator d^* does not necessarily give a uniformly best estimation decision procedure associated with a quadratic loss function. To see this we can refer to the illustrative example in Section 5–10. There

$$N(d^*, s) = \tfrac{1}{2}s(1 - s).$$

Consider, for example, the estimator

x	0	1	2	3
$d(x)$	1	0	0	0

This is, of course, biased but it demonstrates that d^* is not uniformly best in the above sense, since

$$N(d, s) = (1 - s)^2 s^2 + (0 - s)^2 (1 - s)^2$$
$$= 2s^2 (1 - s)^2$$

and

$$N(d, s) < N(d^*, s) \qquad \text{for } s \neq \tfrac{1}{2}.$$

7-4 UTILITY FUNCTION INVOLVING A PREDICTION ASSESSMENT: PROGNOSIS ANALYSIS

It is sometimes necessary to look more directly to the future to assess the merits and demerits of a particular course of action. Simple examples of this arise in contract and tariff selection, where the advantages and disadvantages of a particular choice have to be measured against the future level of production, the future quality of the goods, or the future consumption of electricity. The problems that we have already examined have allowed us to make a direct evaluation of an action in terms of the plausibilities $\pi(s \mid x)$ at the time of taking the action.

The reader will recall that we examined the predictive aspect of Problem 9 (Choosing between contracts, Section 1–9) in Section 5–6. In this problem we see that the return from a component depends on its quality and on which of three contracts is chosen. Here the set A of possible actions consists of $a_1, a_2, a_3,$

the subscripts indicating the contract chosen by the action. In Section 5–6 we imagined a future experiment with simple records y_1 and y_2 corresponding to poor- and good-quality components. We saw that we could obtain by prediction analysis the plausibility of y for given x, namely $\pi(y \mid x)$. Since the return from a component depends on only its quality and the action of choosing a contract, we can clearly regard y, the quality of a future component, as the only unknown "state of nature." The effect of the unknown "category" has been taken account of in the prediction analysis. With this interpretation we are back to a straightforward decision problem of the simple type described in Chapter 5, with the following (y takes the place of s):

$$\text{states of nature:} \quad \{y_1, y_2\},$$
$$\text{set of possible actions:} \quad \{a_1, a_2, a_3\},$$
$$\text{posterior plausibility function:} \quad \pi(y_1 \mid 4), \pi(y_2 \mid 4) \text{ as defined in Section 5-6.}$$

The 4 refers to the information that four out of five test components proved to be of good quality. The utility structure is shown in Table 7–5. For example,

TABLE 7–5

Table of $U(a, y)$

Action	Quality of future component	
	y_1	y_2
a_1	1.6	1.6
a_2	1.0	2.0
a_3	1.4	1.8

$U(a_3, y_1) = 1.4$, because if we select contract 3 and a unit of poor quality arises, we are paid 1.4. Note that we are basing our assessment on the return per future component. The corresponding value is then easily computed for each of the three actions. For example,

$$V(a_3, 4) = U(a_3, y_1)\pi(y_1 \mid 4) + U(a_3, y_2)\pi(y_2 \mid 4)$$
$$= 1.4 \times 0.379 + 1.8 \times 0.621$$
$$= 1.648,$$

from Table 7–5 and (5–6–1), (5–6–2). Table 7–6 shows the complete set of values. From this we see that contract 3 is our best choice; with it we can hope for a return of 1.648 per component.

TABLE 7-6

Values of the three contracts

Action	a_1	a_2	a_3
$V(a, 4)$	1.600	1.621	1.648

We call the above form of analysis *prognosis analysis*.

There is an alternative, and equivalent, way in which we could analyze this problem. We could argue that for a batch of category s_1 there will result a long-run proportion 0.5 of poor-quality components and a long-run proportion 0.5 of good-quality components. Hence, for example with contract 3, we will receive on the average an amount

$$U'(a_3, s_1) = 1.4 \times 0.5 + 1.8 \times 0.5 = 1.60$$

per component from a batch of category s_1. Similarly, from a batch of category s_2 our long-run average return per component will be

$$U'(a_3, s_2) = 1.4 \times 0.3 + 1.8 \times 0.7 = 1.68.$$

We can construct such long-run averages for the other two contracts. As our notation implies, we can clearly regard this U' as an induced utility function to be confronted with the posterior plausibility function $\pi(s \mid 4)$. We can thus look on the problem as one of straightforward type with utility structure and posterior plausibility function as specified in Table 7-7.

TABLE 7-7

Utilities $U(a, s)$ and posterior plausibility function $\pi(s \mid 4)$

	Action	Batch category	
		s_1	s_2
$U(a, s)$	a_1	1.60	1.60
	a_2	1.50	1.70
	a_3	1.60	1.68
$\pi(s \mid 4)$		0.394	0.606

The values associated with the different contracts are then easily computed. For example,

$$V(a_3, 4) = U'(a_3, s_1)\pi(s_1 \mid 4) + U'(a_3, s_2)\pi(s_2 \mid 4)$$

$$= 1.60 \times 0.394 + 1.68 \times 0.606$$

$$= 1.648,$$

as before. The reader should confirm for himself that the other two values are the same as before.

The reason for the equivalence of the two forms of analysis is easily found. The value $V(a, x)$ is in each case the sum of the quantities in the rectangular array of Table 7–8. The row and column sums show that the first analysis is accomplished by an initial summation over columns, and then a summation of

TABLE 7–8

Equivalence of the two forms of analysis

Raw material category	Index	Quality of future component		Row sums
		y_1	y_2	
1	s_1	$U(a, y_1)\pi(y_1 \mid s_1)\pi(s_1 \mid x)$	$U(a, y_2)\pi(y_2 \mid s_1)\pi(s_1 \mid x)$	$U'(a, s_1)\pi(s_1 \mid x)$
2	s_2	$U(a, y_1)\pi(y_1 \mid s_2)\pi(s_2 \mid x)$	$U(a, y_2)\pi(y_2 \mid s_2)\pi(s_2 \mid x)$	$U'(a, s_2)\pi(s_2 \mid x)$
Column sums		$U(a, y_1)\pi(y_1 \mid x)$	$U(a, y_2)\pi(y_2 \mid x)$	

these column sums, whereas the second form of analysis is achieved by first a summation over the entries in each row and then the accumulation of these row sums. This "array" approach is effectively regarding the unknown state of nature as a composite one (s, y) with unknown category and unknown future quality. The special feature that we have exploited then arises from the fact that the utility depends on only the aspect y of the unknown state of nature.

EXERCISES

1. Give the formal argument of prognosis analysis as discussed in this section for the decision problem defined by the following tables.

State of nature	Prior plausibilities	Informative experiment		Future experiment	
	$\pi(s)$	$p(x \mid s)$		$p(y \mid s)$	
		x_1	x_2	y_1	y_2
s_1	0.7	0.6	0.4	0.1	0.9
s_2	0.3	0.2	0.8	0.5	0.5

$U(a, y)$	y_1	y_2
a_1	5	-1
a_2	-2	1

Derive the best decision procedure. What is the expected utility per decision for this procedure?

Confirm your answers by carrying out the alternative form of analysis given in the second part of this section.

2. At a new oil refinery tankers will discharge crude oil directly into the system so that it will not be possible to determine the grade (A, B or C) of any particular delivery. Similar past deliveries to an old refinery were of known grades, the proportions of grade A, B and C deliveries being 0.1, 0.6, 0.3. An output of refined oil from a delivery can be of quality 1 or quality 2; the pattern of variability in quality is such that from grade A, B, C deliveries the probabilities of an output of quality 1 are, respectively, 0.9, 0.5, 0.3.

At an intermediate stage of the refining process an index of impurity may be determined without cost. The following tables show the probabilistic way in which this index depends on the grade of crude oil input.

Grade of crude oil	Probability that index of impurity is				
	1	2	3	4	5
A	0.3	0.3	0.2	0.1	0.1
B	0.1	0.2	0.4	0.2	0.1
C	0.3	0.3	0.2	0.1	0.1

The problem facing the management is how to label the outputs. Correctly labeled outputs of qualities 1 and 2 each give profits of 10 and 9, respectively. An output of quality 1 labeled as quality 2 involves the obvious loss of profit; an output of quality

2 labeled as quality 1 brings a complaint from the customer and entails a recompense of 3. How may the impurity index be used most effectively for the labeling of the output? What can the management expect to make on an output with the best labeling policy? What proportion of all outputs will be labeled incorrectly?

3. It was assumed in the previous exercise that there is no cost in determining the index of impurity. Unfortunately, it has turned out that each determination costs 0.06. Is it still worth while to use it?

4. In a small Scottish town the "ice-cream man" has found that the demand for his home-made ice cream depends on the weather, which unfortunately is very variable. He has classified summer days as moderate and warm, and warm and moderate days are about equally frequent. Study of his records suggests that the demands for 1, 2, 3, 4 "freezers-ful" occur with probabilities 0.4, 0.3, 0.2, 0.1 on moderate days and with probabilities 0.1, 0.3, 0.4, 0.2 on warm days.

The ice cream for a particular day has to be made on the previous evening and the only guides to the next day's weather are independent local and national forecasts. The following table shows the reliabilities of these two forecasts for each of the two types of weather.

Next day's weather	Probability that forecast is correct	
	Local forecast	National forecast
Moderate	0.8	0.7
Warm	0.7	0.6

For any freezerful sold the ice-cream man makes a profit of 2, but any unsold freezerful goes "off" before the following day and involves a loss of 1. Are these weather forecasts of any use to him in his planning?

7–5 APPLICATION TO THE NEGOTIATION OF A WAGE STRUCTURE

Problem 10 (Negotiating a wage structure, Section 1–9) is again essentially a problem which involves a prediction assessment, for the wage contract chosen will eventually be tested against the actual production obtained. That wage rate will be best which gives the best average return per day. The simplest form of analysis is to denote by (y, z) the output for a day, where y denotes the total number of units produced and z denotes the assessed quality of the day's output. We can then regard this (y, z) for a typical future day as the unknown state for that day, so (y, z) can be any one of the six possible states

$$(1, 1), (2, 1), (2, 2), (3, 1), (3, 2), (3.3)$$

constituting the set of possible states of nature.

TABLE 7–9

Prior plausibility function

State	(1, 1)	(2, 1)	(2, 2)	(3, 1)	(3, 2)	(3, 3)
$\pi(y, z)$	0.04	0.18	0.31	0.21	0.16	0.10

We can now regard the records of production as providing a prior plausibility function associated with those states, so setting observed relative frequencies equal to plausibilities, we have Table 7–9. If we do this then we have no informative experiment, so the problem is a "no-data" decision problem in the sense of Chapter 4. The utility structure is easily constructed. The action set A consists of three actions a_1, a_2, a_3, corresponding to the three wage structures. Then

$$U(a_1, y, z) = 4,$$
$$U(a_2, y, z) = 1.6y,$$
$$U(a_3, y, z) = y + z,$$

and, displaying these in detail, we have Table 7–10 for the complete utility structure.

TABLE 7–10

Table of $U(a, y, z)$

Action	State of nature					
	(1, 1)	(2, 1)	(2, 2)	(3, 1)	(3, 2)	(3, 3)
a_1	4	4	4	4	4	4
a_2	1.6	3.2	3.2	4.8	4.8	4.8
a_3	2	3	4	4	5	6

What remains to be done is simply the computation of the value of each of the possible actions. Thus, for a_3, we have

$$V(a_3) = \sum_{y,z} U(a_3, y, z)\pi(y, z)$$

$$= 2 \times 0.04 + 3 \times 0.18 + \cdots + 6 \times 0.10$$

$$= 4.10.$$

TABLE 7–11

Values of the three wage structures

Action	a_1	a_2	a_3
$V(a)$	4.000	3.888	4.100

The completed set of values is presented in Table 7–11. From this we see that the best wage rate is rate 3, with an expected daily wage of 4.1. This assessment is of course on the assumption that the pattern of production will be similar to that in the past. It may be that the added incentive in wage rate 3 to the increased production of good-quality components will in fact change the pattern of production in favor of higher-quality products and so further increase the average daily wage.

An alternative and more sophisticated, though not necessarily better, approach to this problem is to assume that there is some class of possible models, indexed by t, say, which describes the variability in (y, z), the daily output. If we had some prior plausibility function for t, then we could regard the past records as an informative experiment and so move to a posterior plausibility function for (y, z). This would then replace the prior plausibility function for (y, z) of the naive approach above. It is likely that any reasonable assumption about the prior plausibility function for t will lead to something very similar to the prior plausibility function for (y, z) which we have adopted in our naive approach. Support is given to this view by our discovery through prediction analysis in Section 5–6 that the posterior plausibility for a future success, based on some form of "ignorance" prior plausibility function and the information of x successes in n trials, lies between x/n and $(x + 1)/(n + 2)$. Thus in prognosis analysis of binomial trials there is little difference between the use of an ignorance prior plausibility function with subsequent posterior analysis based on a fair amount of information and the use of the observed relative frequencies in the informative experiment as the prior plausibilities in a no-data decision theory approach. This result can in fact be shown to carry over to the "multinomial" situation of the present example.

EXERCISES

1. The daily numbers of pieces of equipment produced by a small factory over a period of 200 days are as follows:

Number of pieces produced	0	1	2	3	4	5	6
Number of days	12	20	36	56	44	24	8

The owner of a truck, which can carry two pieces at once, is offered the following alternative contracts under which he will each day convey all the factory's output:

a) a daily payment of 5.1,
b) a payment of 3 per load or, where unavoidable, per half-load,
c) a payment of 1.7 per piece.

Which contract should he accept?

2. Reels of artificial fiber produced by operations of an extrusion process are of variable durability index and tensile strength index. From 500 such operations the reels have been sorted into durability–strength categories and the following numbers counted:

Durability index	Tensile strength index		
	1	2	3
1	80	165	55
2	70	85	45

A customer offers to purchase all future reels produced under one of four contracts.

a) For a reel of durability index x and tensile strength index y the payment is $2x + 3y$.
b) For reels of durability index 1 and 2 the payments are 7.8 and 9.7 per reel, respectively, regardless of tensile strength.
c) For reels of tensile strength index 1, 2, and 3 the payments are 5.6, 9.0, 11.8 per reel, respectively, regardless of durability.
d) A flat rate of 8.6 per reel is paid.

Which contract is most advantageous to (i) the producer, (ii) the consumer?

3. As an incentive to waiters in a popular quick-service restaurant to increase turnover at lunchtime, the management offers its waiters a lunchtime rate of 2 per complete sitting of a waiter's 16 places, plus a bonus of 2 per complete sitting after the fifth. The waiters say that they would prefer to continue with their lunchtime wage of 11, irrespective of the number of sittings. An arbiter is called in and he suggests that a flat rate of 2.25 per complete sitting would be more advantageous to the waiters and also would provide an incentive to increase turnover. Before putting forward his recommendation, the arbiter had observed 20 waiters over 25 lunchtimes and recorded that out of these 500 waiter–lunchtime combinations the numbers of occasions on which there were 3, 4, 5, 6, 7 complete sittings were 45, 90, 215, 105, 45.

Should the waiters accept the arbiter's recommendations?

7-6 APPLICATION TO THE REPLACEMENT PROBLEM

Problem 2 (Replacing capital equipment, Section 1–4) can again be treated either in a naive or a more sophisticated way. We deal here with the naive form of analysis. Put in the framework of decision theory, we have an action set A

consisting of only two elements:

a_0:   continue with the present equipment,
a_1:   scrap the old equipment and hire the new equipment.

We suppose that the relevant unknown state of nature is the quality that we shall obtain at a typical future application of the manufacturing process. This future experiment has a record set of three symbols y_1, y_2, y_3, corresponding to the three qualities with prices 1, 2, 3. The utility structure can then be easily expressed as a function $U(a, y)$ of the action a and the unknown future record y; see Table 7–12.

TABLE 7–12

Table of $U(a, y)$

Action	Future quality		
	y_1	y_2	y_3
a_0	$1 - k$	$2 - k$	$3 - k$
a_1	$1 - h$	$2 - h$	$3 - h$

The interesting new feature in this example is that our plausibility function, being different for the two kinds of equipment, is therefore dependent on the action taken. We shall express this dependence in our notation. The prior plausibility function $\pi(y \mid a_0)$ for quality from present equipment, found by equating plausibilities to observed relative frequencies or proportions, is the first row of Table 7–13. The prior plausibility function $\pi(y \mid a_1)$ for quality with hired equipment is given in the bottom row of the table.

TABLE 7–13

Prior plausibility functions $\pi(y \mid a)$ for two possible actions

Action	y_1	y_2	y_3
a_0 (continue with present equipment)	0.10	0.60	0.30
a_1 (hire new equipment)	0.08	0.42	0.50

The value for a_0 may then be computed:

$$V(a_0) = \sum_Y U(a_0, y)\pi(y \mid a_0)$$

$$= (1 - k) \times 0.10 + (2 - k) \times 0.60 + (3 - k) \times 0.30$$

$$= 2.20 - k.$$

Similarly, the value for a_1 is $2.42 - h$, and we conclude that we should adopt the new hire arrangement if and only if the rental per operation is less than $k + 0.22$.

EXERCISES

1. A consumers' guidance bureau has been investigating for its subscribers the relative merits of first- and second-class mail services within a region. Of 1000 "packets" posted under each class the record of deliveries was as follows

Class of mail	Number of letters arriving				
	(1) Next morning	(2) Next afternoon	(3) Second morning	(4) Second afternoon	Total
First	451	369	140	40	1000
Second	301	299	287	113	1000

A packet costs 50 by first-class mail and 40 by second-class mail. Subscribers have been asked to express in monetary terms their degrees of satisfaction with the various delivery times, and the picture formed from these for the "average subscriber" is 100, 80, 60, 40 for deliveries (1), (2), (3), (4).

On the combined criterion of cost and satisfaction, which of the two services do you recommend as a best buy to the average subscriber?

2. The bureau of the previous exercise has also been investigating the variability in the number of days taken to repair a television set by three service firms. Each firm's performance with 100 sets is recorded below.

Service firm number	Number of days taken to complete repair						Total number of sets
	1	2	3	4	5	Over 5	
1	43	21	15	10	7	4	100
2	28	45	20	6	1	0	100
3	57	20	9	2	3	9	100

Subscribers are again asked to express their degrees of annoyance at undue delay in monetary terms, and the "average subscriber" evolving from this information experiences 0, 10, 20, 30, 40, 60 of annoyance corresponding to 1, 2, 3, 4, 5, over 5 days of repair time. The standard charges for repair are 10, 13, 12 for firms number 1, 2, 3.

Taking account of cost and annoyance, which of the three firms do you recommend to the average subscriber?

7–7 APPLICATIONS TO THE CHOICE OF TREATMENT

The Introduction of a Treatment Problem 7 of Section 1–7 asks whether a new treatment should or should not be introduced. Here the unknown state of nature can be regarded as the unknown probability of success, say s, from an application of the treatment to a future individual. The basic experiment has therefore the probability model (Table 7–14) of a binomial trial. The informative

TABLE 7–14

Probability model for application of treatment

Future result	y_0 (failure)	y_1 (success)
$p(y \mid s)$	$1 - s$	s

experiment is then a binomial counting experiment recording the total number x of successes in n replicates of this basic experiment (Definition 3–6–2).

There are two actions which we may take:

a_0:   reject the treatment,

a_1:   adopt the treatment.

The assessment of the action adopted can be made directly in terms of its behavior at a future experiment, with the utilities of Table 7–15. We use the

TABLE 7–15

Table of $U(a, y)$

Action	Future result	
	y_0	y_1
a_0 (reject)	0	0
a_1 (adopt)	$-k$	$l - k$

plausible prediction function (5–6–3), (5–6–4),

$$\pi(y_0 \mid x) = 1 - \frac{x+1}{n+2}, \qquad \pi(y_1 \mid x) = \frac{x+1}{n+2},$$

as discussed in Section 5–6. From this we obtain the values of actions a_0 and a_1:

$$V(a_0, x) = 0,$$

$$V(a_1, x) = l\pi(y_1 \mid x) - k = l\frac{x+1}{n+2} - k.$$

Thus we shall introduce the treatment if and only if $x + 1 > k(n+2)/l$.

We may draw the reader's attention to the fact that this is precisely the model, with a somewhat different utility function, which was appropriate in the no-data decision problem of introducing a new product. Thus we have a means of extending the analysis of that problem to the case in which we may have a trial run with the new process to seek information about the probability of an effective article.

Comparison of Two or More Treatments   Consider the case of two treatments first; the extension to more than two treatments is easy. On the supposition that we have to choose one or other of the treatments, there are just two actions possible:

$$a_1: \quad \text{adopt treatment 1,}$$
$$a_2: \quad \text{adopt treatment 2.}$$

The method of analysis is then simply to evaluate as in the preceding paragraph the value for each treatment separately. From the results there, on the assumption that we have the same form of prediction analysis for each of the success probabilities, we have the values

$$V(a_1, x_1) = l\frac{x_1+1}{n_1+2} - k_1, \qquad V(a_2, x_2) = l\frac{x_2+1}{n_2+2} - k_2.$$

Thus we adopt treatment 1 if and only if

$$\frac{x_1+1}{n_1+2} - \frac{x_2+1}{n_2+2} > \frac{k_1 - k_2}{l}.$$

For more than two treatments we simply compute the values associated with each treatment, as above, and select one with the greatest value.

EXERCISES

1. In a trial with a completely new treatment 27 out of a total of 40 applications have proved successful. The future cost of treatment is estimated at 5 per application and

the gain (loss) from a successful (unsuccessful) application at 8 (0). Follow the analysis of this section to decide whether the treatment is worth adopting.

2. In a comparative trial for two treatments 1 and 2, treatment 1 was applied 23 times with 15 successes and treatment 2 scored 26 successes in 38 trials. The reward for a future success is reckoned to be 25 and for failure 0. The costs per application of treatments 1 and 2 are 11 and 12. Which is the better treatment to adopt?

   A third treatment was applied under similar conditions 18 times with 13 successes, so it appears to be more effective than the other two treatments. Is this effectiveness more than offset by its greater cost, estimated at 13 per future application?

3. Two synthetic industrial dyes were compared for effectiveness in a trial in which dye 1 was applied to 48 standard pieces of material with 37 successes, and dye 2 to 98 pieces with 81 successes. On the assumption that the success of a future dyeing operation will give a return of 200 and failure a loss of 100, and that the costs per operation are 105 for dye 1 and 120 for dye 2, which dye do you recommend?

7–8   APPLICATION TO SELECTING A QUALITY IMPROVER

Since individuals vary it seems sensible to ask whether they display differential responses to different treatments. Two patients suffering from the same ailment do not necessarily react satisfactorily to the same drug because of other differing circumstances. Can we devise a procedure which will allow us, by examining the present state of an individual, to prescribe the "best" treatment, one which takes account of the prognosis, and balances this in some way against the cost of treatment? Problem 8 of Section 1–8 is such a case, for it essentially recognizes that before treatment there are two possible conditions of the experimental unit, and that treatment may make no change or cause different extents of improvement. The analysis is again relatively simple once the groundwork of the preceding section is available, since we can evaluate, *for each present condition*, the corresponding values of introducing treatment 1 and treatment 2. The higher of these will indicate which treatment is the more appropriate for that condition. Again we adopt the prediction analysis of earlier paragraphs. For example, for initial condition 1 with treatment 1 applied, the success probability may be regarded as the probability of an improvement to level 3. From a success we gain $3 - 1$ for the improvement in quality but at a cost 0.1, so the utility is 1.9; from a failure the utility is $(2 - 1) - 0.1 = 0.9$. Out of 7 applications of treatment 1 to units of initial quality 1 we have 2 successes. From a naive prognosis analysis we therefore have that the value of adopting treatment 1 for initial quality 1 is

$$\tfrac{3}{9} \times 1.9 + \tfrac{6}{9} \times 0.9 = 1.233.$$

Application to Selecting a Quality Improver

Table 7–16 gives the complete picture of values for the various possibilities. From this table we see that for units of initial quality 1 we should adopt treatment 1, and for units of initial quality 2 we should adopt treatment 2.

TABLE 7–16

Values of treatments for different initial qualities

Initial quality	Treatment	
	1	2
1	1.233	1.229
2	0.300	0.371

EXERCISES

1. The following table (a condensed form of that in Problem 8) relates to another investigation of quality improvement, in which the costs of treatments 1 and 2 are 0.3 and 0.5 per unit and the selling prices of qualities 2 and 3 are 2 and 4 per unit.

Initial quality	Number of untreated units	Treatment applied	Number of treated units reaching quality	
			2	3
1	23	1	16	7
2	48	1	13	35
1	23	2	11	12
2	48	2	9	39

How should treatments be allocated to units? If 60 percent of untreated units are of quality 1, what is the mean profit per unit with the best treatment allocation policy?

Would your treatment policy change if the cost of treatment 1 increased by 0.05 per unit?

2. The relative effects of a fumigant and an aerosol spray on rot in timber has been studied at a building research center. The timbers were classified into three degrees of rot and the effect of the treatment assessed by whether or not rot was arrested. The table below shows the results of treatments on 170 timbers.

Degree of rot	Number of timbers	Treatment	Number of timbers in which rot was arrested
1	28	Fumigant	24
1	28	Aerosol	22
2	34	Fumigant	20
2	34	Aerosol	23
3	23	Fumigant	7
3	23	Aerosol	12

The costs per timber of fumigant and aerosol treatments are 6 and 17. The advantage of saving a timber rather than having to replace it is assessed at 100. What treatment policy do you advise?

7–9 SEQUENTIAL DECISION-MAKING: CONSTRUCTION OF A STOPPING RULE

We turn now to the first part of Problem 11 (Attempting to reach a target, Section 1–10). How do we decide how many operations of the process to undertake? We could attempt to answer this question in terms of the technique of choosing among experiments as developed in Section 6–11. We suppose that there are just six possible experiments available to us, namely

$$e_0: \quad \text{undertake no operations,}$$
$$e_1: \quad \text{undertake one operation,}$$
$$\cdots$$
$$e_5: \quad \text{undertake all five operations.}$$

Note that there is no unknown state of nature in the present problem; we know which particular model is operating, and therefore the risk and Bayesian risk coincide. We shall use the term risk for definiteness. If we undetake n operations and finish with a quality index z_n, then the loss is $(z_n - 9)^2 + 10n$. If x_1 denotes an addition to quality from a single operation, we can express the risk as

$$
\begin{aligned}
N_n &= \mathscr{E}\{(z_n - 9)^2 + 10n\} \\
&= \mathscr{E}\{(z_n - 9)^2\} + 10n && \text{by Theorem 3–9–1} \\
&= \mathscr{V}(z_n) + \{\mathscr{E}(z_n) - 9\}^2 + 10n && \text{by Theorem 3–9–3} \\
&= n\mathscr{V}(x_1) + \{n\mathscr{E}(x_1) - 9\}^2 + 10n && \text{by Theorem 3–9–4} \\
&= 0.8n + (2n - 9)^2 + 10n \\
&= (2n - 9)^2 + 10.8n.
\end{aligned}
$$

TABLE 7–17

Risks associated with *n* operations

n	0	1	2	3	4	5
N_n	81.0	59.8	46.6	41.4	44.2	55.0

Table 7–17 gives these risks for $n = 0, \ldots, 5$. Clearly the best of these experiments is e_3 with associated risk 41.4. Can we do better than this?

Let us translate this problem into a more picturesque setting. You are a golfer standing on the tee with the hole 9 units away; take one unit equal to 50 yards, say. You have a golf bag with just one club, say an iron. Your problem is: How many shots up to a maximum of five allowed by the rules of this target golf should you have with your iron before deciding that you are close enough to the hole to accept a "putting score." Each stroke with the iron costs you 10 points, and the putting score finally added if you stop play at a distance l from the hole is assessed as l^2. It is quite clear to any golfer that it would be madness to decide on the tee how many shots to play. You know that although you send the ball reasonably straight down the fairway, you are very variable in the distance you can achieve with your iron. You realize therefore that a more reasonable procedure is to try, after each shot when you know how far you are still from the target, to decide between settling for a putting score now or playing more shots to reduce the putting score at the cost of more strokes. To be able to make a decision you must have some information about the variability of distance of your iron shots. To get a complete analogy with the production problem we suppose that the distances you make are distributed according to the probability model for the quality additions at an operation.

While intuition may lead you to the best procedure in this very simple situation, the formal resolution of this decision problem is interesting and by no means trivial, since it requires you to look ahead and undertake the sizable task of enumerating all the future possibilities. For example, suppose that you have already taken two shots and have gone a distance $z_2 = 4$ from the tee. If you stop now your total score is 45. If you decide to play on you may go a distance l at the next shot ($z_3 = 5$) and if you decide to stop then your score would be 46, an increase; if you had third and fourth shots and stopped, having had two l's, your score would have risen to 49. On the other hand, you may be lucky enough to go a distance 3 with your third shot; if you stop then your score would be dramatically reduced to 34; and so on. The reader can imagine some of the other possibilities for himself. What sort of crystal ball do you need to resolve such an involved set of possibilities?

The answer is found in the recognition of an extremely simple property of an optimum procedure for such a sequential decision problem.

Principle of Optimality   It is a property of a best sequential decision procedure that, whatever the position reached at a particular stage in the process, this best sequential procedure applied to the remaining decision problem at this stage must be the best procedure for that remaining decision problem.

In terms of the golf competition, if you find yourself at position $z_2 = 4$ after two strokes the best procedure for the problem as a whole applied to your present position will coincide with the best procedure you can devise for the reduced problem now facing you, of getting as low a score as possible for a hole of length 5 units in at most three strokes. From the position reached you have to do the best you can in order to implement a best procedure for the problem as a whole. This is a restatement in golfing terms of what has been called by its principal exponent, Richard Bellman, the *principle of optimality*. It is a fairly self-evident principle but its clear statement in sequential decision problems is one which eludes many decision-makers. The idea is of earlier origin and is implicit in the work of Wald, particularly in the use of "backward induction."

The principle of optimality emphasizes that there are a number of inter-related decision problems, a typical one being the problem that remains after you have had n strokes and reached position z_n. The great simplification brought about is the awareness that the sensible way of tackling the problem is not to stand quivering on the tee looking at the complexity of the problem ahead, but to imagine yourself down the fairway with a simpler decision problem ahead. In fact, start from a study of the simplest aspect of the decision problem you may be faced with, that of choosing whether to stop after four shots and accept the present putting score or to take another shot. For this simple problem you should be able to find what the best course of action is for each possible z_4 and the associated minimum expected addition to the already accumulated score. Denote by $F_4(z_4)$ the minimum expected addition to the score from the best action taken from position z_4 after four shots. You know that you must stop at the latest after the next shot, so that the enumeration of future possibilities is easy. The choices open to you are to stop now, "action a_0," with the putting score of $(z_4 - 9)^2$ the only addition to your score, or to take another shot and then stop. If you do take another shot and if it takes you a further distance y, then you incur an addition to your score of $(z_4 + y - 9)^2 + 10$, the sum of the final score and the stroke score. In fact, $(z_4 + y - 9)^2$ may be denoted by $F_5(z_4 + y)$ since it is the minimum expected addition to your score from position $z_4 + y$ after five shots in the trivial sense that it is the score forced on you at that position by the rules of the competition. Looking forward from position z_4 after four shots you will assess the effect of taking another shot by computing the expected additional score from the shot, namely

$$\sum_Y F_5(z_4 + y)p(y) + 10.$$

Since $F_4(z_4)$ is the minimum expected addition to the score from position z_4,

$$F_4(z_4) = \min \left\{ (z_4 - 9)^2, \ \sum_Y F_5(z_4 + y)p(y) + 10 \right\}.$$

You can thus run through all the possible values of z_4, computing both terms inside the braces, selecting the smaller value as the appropriate value if $F_4(z_4)$ and recording whether the optimum action at this stage is to stop (action a_0) or to continue (action a_1). For example,

$$F_4(5) = \min \{(5 - 9)^2, \ F_5(5 + 1)p(1) + F_5(5 + 2)p(2) + F_5(5 + 3)p(3) + 10\}$$

$$= \min \{16, \ 9 \times 0.4 + 4 \times 0.2 + 1 \times 0.4 + 10\}$$

$$= \min \{16, 14.8\} = 14.8.$$

If you have gone 5 units after four shots you will opt to take another shot with an expected addition of 14.8 to your present score of 40. Thus you can complete the column headed $n = 4$ in Table 7–18. For the sake of completeness the table includes the column headed $n = 5$, showing the final addition (the putting score) for the various possible positions which may be reached after five shots.

Now that you know the best way of proceeding from each possible position z_4 and the minimum expected addition to your score accruing from such a best action, you can move back to the position z_3 after the third shot and consider how you should act. Denote by $F_3(z_3)$ the minimum expected addition to your score from position z_3 by the operation of an optimum procedure from that position. If you stop now the only addition to your score is the putting score $(z_3 - 9)^2$. If you take another shot and go an additional distance y you will have reached a position $z_3 + y$ after four strokes and you know from your previous analysis that the minimum expected addition to your score from this position is $F_4(z_3 + y)$. Looking ahead from position z_3 the decision to have another shot brings with it a minimum expected addition to your score of

$$\sum_Y F_4(z_3 + y)p(y) + 10.$$

Since $F_3(z_3)$ is the minimum expected addition to the score from position z_3 it must be the smaller of the two expected additions just considered. Thus

$$F_3(z_3) = \min \left\{ (z_3 - 9)^2, \ \sum_Y F_4(z_3 + y)p(y) + 10 \right\}.$$

From the information in the column headed $n = 4$ of Table 7–18 you can construct both the quantities inside the braces, pick out the smaller as the value of

TABLE 7–18

Table of $F_n(z_n)^\dagger$

z_n	n					
	5	4	3	2	1	0
0						$39.38\ a_1$
1					$34.42\ a_1$	
2				$29.58\ a_1$	$29.50\ a_1$	
3			$24.48\ a_1$	$24.29\ a_1$	$24.29\ a_1$	
4		$19.8\ a_1$	$19.32\ a_1$	$19.32\ a_1$		
5	$16\ a_0$	$14.8\ a_1$	$14.80\ a_1$	$14.80\ a_1$		
6	$9\ a_0$	$9.0\ a_0$	$9.00\ a_0$	$9.00\ a_0$		
7	$4\ a_0$	$4.0\ a_0$	$4.00\ a_0$			
8	$1\ a_0$	$1.0\ a_0$	$1.00\ a_0$			
9	$0\ a_0$	$0.0\ a_0$	$0.00\ a_0$			
10	$1\ a_0$	$1.0\ a_0$				
11	$4\ a_0$	$4.0\ a_0$				
12	$9\ a_0$	$9.0\ a_0$				
13	$16\ a_0$					
14	$25\ a_0$					
15	$36\ a_0$					

$\dagger\ a_0 = $ stop, $a_1 = $ continue.

$F_3(z_3)$, and record what the appropriate best action is at this stage. For example,

$$F_3(6) = \min\{(6 - 9)^2,\quad F_4(6 + 1)p(1) + F_4(6 + 2)p(2) + F_4(6 + 3)p(3) + 10\}$$

$$= \min\{9,\quad 4 \times 0.4 + 1 \times 0.2 + 0 \times 0.4 + 10\}$$

$$= \min\{9, 11.8\} = 9;$$

and the optimum action if you have gone a distance of 6 units after three strokes is to stop and accept the addition of the putting score of 9 to your accumulated stroke score of 30. It is clear that you can proceed backward toward the tee shot in this way. The general relation (commonly referred to as the *dynamic programming equation* for the problem) is

$$F_n(z_n) = \min \left\{(z_n - 9)^2,\quad \sum_Y F_{n+1}(z_n + y)p(y) + 10\right\}, \qquad (7\text{--}9\text{--}1)$$

where $F_n(z_n)$ denotes the minimum expected addition to the score from position z_n after n strokes from the operation of an optimum procedure. The table can thus be completed, and from it you can then see how to operate an optimum strategy from the tee. For example, you certainly play off the tee, and also certainly take a second shot. However, if you have been fortunate enough to push ahead to position 6 after two shots, then you stop; and so on for other possibilities. Indeed you can construct for yourself a convenient chart (Fig. 7–9) which allows you to plot your progress and see what the appropriate action is after each shot. In this particularly simple situation the best procedure can even be easily described in words: Continue taking shots until the distance gone is at least 6 or all five shots have been used up. Since this target golf problem is mathematically equivalent to the production process problem, we have also solved the latter problem with an obvious interpretation of Fig. 7–9.

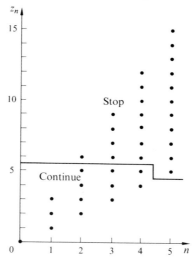

Fig. 7–9 Chart showing appropriate action for each possible position (n, z_n).

The advantage of the sequential decision procedure is now apparent; it yields a smaller risk or Bayesian risk. From the tee your minimum expected score with a predetermined number of shots is 41.4. With the sequential decision procedure with its construction of a best stopping rule your minimum expected score is 39.38. It should be noted, however, that the stopping rule may turn out to be a fixed-number rule with the continuation region of the graphic representation including all the possible positions until the final stage. For example, for a distance competition in which the golfer is allowed to take up to five shots with no penalty per shot and a final reward of z_n, where n is the number of shots taken by the golfer before he stops, the player will clearly decide to take his full five shots. The optimum sequential decision rule is to continue until the five shots have been used, giving a fixed-number stopping rule.

EXERCISES

1. Consider Problem 11(1) of Section 1–10 with the following alterations.
   a) At most four operations of the process are allowed.
   b) Each operation costs 1.4.
   c) The additions to the quality index at each of the independent operations are 0, 1, 2 with probabilities 0.3, 0.4, 0.3.
   d) The target quality index is 6, with lossess for final quality index q as follows:

Final quality	0	1	2	3	4	5	6	7	8
Loss	9	8	7	5	3	2	0	2	3

   Carry out the analysis of this section, providing a table of $F_n(z_n)$ and a chart (Fig. 7–9) showing the appropriate action for each possible circumstance.

2. The temperature level of a chemical process is the crucial factor in determining the quality of the chemical produced. The following table gives the returns obtained from operations at the seven possible temperature levels.

Temperature level	1	2	3	4	5	6	7
Return	0	1	4	9	18	30	20

   Temperature level is easily ascertained and is known to be 4 initially. It is possible to carry out independent adjustments in an attempt to reach a more desirable temperature level, but each adjustment has a variable effect, adding 1, 0, -1 to the level attained before the adjustments with probabilities 0.4, 0.4, 0.2. The cost (taking account of time lost) of each adjustment is 2.7. Given that a maximum of three adjustments can be made, devise a set of suitable instructions for the most profitable manufacture of the chemical.

   What would your advice be if at most two adjustments are allowed from a starting level 4?

3. The economics of the control of fungal disease in fruit bushes is being studied. Eight degrees 0, 1, . . . , 7 of fungal infestation have been recognized. Standard practice allows up to four applications of fungicide, at increasing strengths, the costs per bush with the first, second, third, fourth applications being 8, 10, 12, 14. Successive applications are assumed to effect independent reductions of 1, 2, 3, 4 in the attained degree of infestation with probabilities 0.4, 0.3, 0.2, 0.1 (any "negative" degree so produced being identified with degree 0). If fungal control is abandoned while the degree of infestation is i, then the eventual damage to the crop is figured to be $10i$.

   What fungal control policy do you advise for bushes initially infested to degree 7?

4. Instead of being offered for immediate sale at 500 per gem, four rough gems may be subjected to an expensive cutting and polishing process one after the other at a cost of 1000 per gem. Sets of polished gems are highly priced, the price depending on the

number in the set as follows:

Number z of gems in set	1	2	3	4
Selling price $g(z)$	1000	3000	6000	10,000

Unfortunately the cutting process is far from foolproof, and there is a probability 0.3 that a gem will be ruined and rendered valueless. A decision can be made at any point in processing to sell any cut set already produced and all remaining unprocessed gems.

Let z_n denote the number of cut gems produced after n gems have been subjected to the process, and $F_n(z_n)$ the maximum expected final return (less any future costs) from the adoption of an optimum policy from that position (n, z_n). Show that

$$F_n(z_n) = \max \{g(z_n) + 500(4 - n), 0.3F_{n+1}(z_n) + 0.7F_{n+1}(z_n + 1) - 1000\} \quad (n = 0, 1, 2, 3),$$

$$F_4(z_4) = g(z_4).$$

Hence complete a table of the form of Table 7–18 and provide instructions for implementing the best policy in the form of a chart.

7–10 A PROBLEM OF PROCESS CONTROL

The golfing reader may have felt disappointed with the analysis of the preceding section in that his judgment was being called into play simply to decide when to stop and accept a putting score. Every golfer knows that he carries more than one distance club in his bag. The problem will be more realistic if we allow him to play any shot with whichever of three distance clubs he cares to choose. The distances achievable with these three clubs are variable, this variability being described in Table 7–19 by the three probability models or functions, where $p_i(y)$ refers to club i. The penalty per shot with each club is also shown in the table. A maximum of five shots is still allowed, and the putting score is, as before, the square of the final distance from the hole when the player opts to stop. It is clear that a new order of difficulty is now presented, and that the problem is

TABLE 7–19

Table of $p_i(y)$

Club i	Distance y			Penalty
	1	2	3	
1	0.7	0.1	0.2	1
2	0.2	0.6	0.2	2
3	0.1	0.3	0.6	3

precisely the same as part 2 of Problem 11 (Attempting to reach a target, Section 1–10). We could again restrict the analysis to fixed strategies off the tee—for example, a predetermined two shots with club 1 and three shots with club 2. The expected score with this fixed strategy could readily be calculated along the same lines as before, but again we would find that a sequential decision procedure is better.

The technique of determining an optimum decision procedure is in fact only a little more complicated than that of the preceding section. Define $F_n(z_n)$ to be the minimum expected addition to the score obtainable from position z_n after n strokes from the use of a future optimum strategy. Note that by the definition of $F_n(z_n)$ in terms of future play and score there is no need to worry about which clubs have been used up to this point. We again work from the green back to the tee to discover the optimum strategy. The only additional complication is the relatively trivial one that in his look forward the golfer has to choose between four courses of action, namely

a_0:   stop now,
a_1:   take another shot with club 1,
a_2:   take another shot with club 2,
a_3:   take another shot with club 3.

Following the argument of the preceding section we see that if he takes club i from position z_n after n shots, then the minimum expected addition to his score is

$$\sum_Y F_{n+1}(z_n + y)p_i(y) + i.$$

From stopping now the additional score is $(z_n - 9)^2$. Since $F_n(z_n)$ is the minimum attainable expected score, it must be the smallest of these four expressions just obtained. We can express this in the following way:

$$F_n(z_n) = \min\left[(z_n - 9)^2, \min_i \left\{ \sum_Y F_{n+1}(z_n + y)p_i(y) + i \right\} \right]. \quad (7\text{–}10\text{–}1)$$

Again he can start with the easiest of these decision subproblems, namely the determination of the best action from position z_4 after four shots. He can solve this since he knows what he must do at position z_5 after five shots: by the rules of the competition he must stop, so

$$F_5(z_5) = (z_5 - 9)^2.$$

As before, he can work his way back to the tee position.

As an example, we shall determine the best action from position 4 after three shots, and compute the corresponding minimum expected addition to the score from that position, namely $F_3(4)$. We have

$$F_4(5)p_1(1) + F_4(6)p_1(2) + F_4(7)p_1(3) + 1$$
$$= 5.7 \times 0.7 + 3.4 \times 0.1 + 1.9 \times 0.2 + 1$$
$$= 5.71.$$

Similarly,

$$F_4(5)p_2(1) + F_4(6)p_2(2) + F_4(7)p_2(3) + 2 = 5.56,$$
$$F_4(5)p_3(1) + F_4(6)p_3(2) + F_4(7)p_3(3) + 3 = 5.73.$$

Hence

$$\min_i \left\{ \sum_Y F_4(4 + y)p_i(y) + i \right\} = \min \{5.71, 5.56, 5.73\}$$
$$= 5.56.$$

Hence, by (7–10–1),

$$F_3(4) = \min \{(4 - 9)^2, 5.56\} = 5.56,$$

and the best action from position 4 after three shots is to take a shot with club 2. The reader should verify some of the other steps for himself. From the completed table (Table 7–20) he can again construct a suitable handy chart in the form of Fig. 7–10, which the reader will find self-explanatory after the similar one of the preceding section.

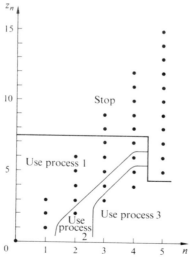

Fig. 7–10 Chart showing appropriate action for each possible position (n, z_n).

TABLE 7-20

Table of $F_n(z_n)^\dagger$

z_n	5	4	3	2	1	0
				n		
0						8.00 a_1
1					7.77 a_1	
2				7.63 a_2	6.08 a_1	
3			7.72 a_3	5.76 a_1	4.78 a_1	
4		9.7 a_3	5.56 a_2	4.26 a_1		
5	16 a_0	5.7 a_3	3.77 a_1	3.09 a_1		
6	9 a_0	3.4 a_2	2.43 a_1	2.43 a_1		
7	4 a_0	1.9 a_1	1.90 a_1			
8	1 a_0	1.0 a_0	1.00 a_0			
9	0 a_0	0.0 a_0	0.00 a_0			
10	1 a_0	1.0 a_0				
11	4 a_0	4.0 a_0				
12	9 a_0	9.0 a_0				
13	16 a_0					
14	25 a_0					
15	36 a_0					

$\dagger$ a_0 = stop, a_1 = use club or process 1, a_2 = use club or process 2, a_3 = use club or process 3.

The best strategy is to move along steadily with club 1 since it costs fewer points, but if there is a run of bad luck and the golfer begins to trail, it is worth his while to pay the extra cost of using club 2 or, if his plight is really desperate, club 3 to catch up by exploiting their higher probabilities for distances 2 and 3.

EXERCISES

1. For its finished products a refinery aims at a target quality index of 7, the penalties arising from under- and over-refining being as follows:

Terminal quality index	0	1	2	3	4	5	6	7	8	9
Penalty	40	20	10	7	5	4	2	0	2	4

The raw material input has quality index 0, and two refining processes, 1 and 2, are available. The effect of an operation of a process is uncertain, process 1 giving an addition of 1, 2, 3 to the attained index with probabilities 0.4, 0.2, 0.4; for process 2 the corresponding probabilities are 0.2, 0.6, 0.2. A maximum of three such operations is allowed and at each operation either process may be chosen. The additions to quality index at different operations are independent, and the costs of processes 1 and 2 are 1 and 1.7 per operation.

Design an efficient method of organizing the refining of raw material.

2. A new method of adjusting the temperature level of the chemical process of Exercise 2 of Section 7–10 has been devised. Its characteristics are similar to those of the previous method but the probabilities that an adjustment adds 1, 0, -1 to the level attained before the adjustment are 0.5, 0.1, 0.4. The cost is 2.3 per adjustment.

Devise an adjustment scheme which makes the best use of the two available methods.

3. In the problem of gem-cutting (Exercise 4 of Section 7–10) a cheaper alternative cutting method is available at a cost of 300 per gem, but unfortunately it is less reliable with a probability 0.5 of ruining a gem.

What cutting policy makes the most effective use of these two cutting methods?

4. An international medical committee, interested in devising a regime for the relief of an arthritic condition, has available two treatments 1 and 2. For any patient a maximum of three courses of treatment applied consecutively is permissible and each course may be of either treatment 1 or treatment 2. The authority has divided the severity of the condition into seven grades 0, 1, ..., 6. Analysis of a controlled clinical trial has suggested the following prognosis pattern for patients initially in grade 3. A course of treatment 1 reduces by 1, leaves unchanged, increases by 1 the severity grade at the start of the course with probabilities 0.7, 0.1, 0.2; the corresponding probabilities for a course of treatment 2 are 0.5, 0.4, 0.1. Changes due to successive courses are assumed to be independent.

Much discussion has taken place in the committee weighing up the relative advantages of reducing the severity grade and the costs in money, time, and discomfort to the patient in applying courses of treatment. Eventually the committee has agreed on the following scales (measured in the same units) for costs of courses of treatment and for costs of leaving a patient in a particular severity grade at the end of the regime.

Treatment	Cost of course
1	3.5
2	3.0

Severity grade	0	1	2	3	4	5	6
Cost	0	10	30	50	80	120	200

Devise a regime best suited to relieve patients who are initially in severity grade 3.

7–11 SEQUENTIAL STATISTICAL DECISION-MAKING

In our examples so far we have made the assumption either that the informative experiment is of predetermined size or, in the case of sequential decision-making, that we know which specific probability model is in operation. Let us now remove these restrictions and so obtain the flavor of a full sequential statistical decision problem, where we decide between different courses of action in sequence after each observation becomes available and where the exact probability model is not known to us.

To do this we return to Problem 7 (Introducing a new treatment, Section 1–8) which we previously tackled in a nonsequential way in Section 7–7. We saw there how to analyze this problem for the case of a fixed number n of observations. For example, for the case $n = 5$ the terminal decision is to adopt the treatment if and only if the number z_5 of successes in the five trials is greater than $7(k/l) - 1$.

To compare experiments of different sizes it is clearly necessary to consider in the construction of the utility function not only what may happen to a single individual in the future. Such a restriction would make the relative cost of experimentation to utility so large that we would probably not experiment at all. Presumably, if and when we introduce a treatment we shall apply it to a number I of individuals, so in the notation of the previous analysis we should take the utility function to be as in Table 7–21. The cost of experimentation per

TABLE 7–21

Table of $U(a, y)$

Action	Typical future result	
	y_0 (failure)	y_1 (success)
a_0 (do not introduce)	0	0
a_1 (introduce)	$-Ik$	$I(l - k)$

individual can then be regarded as the cost of treatment, together with any extra administrative costs. For the sake of definiteness, let us suppose that $I = 1000$, $k = 0.45$, $l = 1$, and that the cost of experimentation is 5 per individual.

Hence in the fixed ($n = 5$) experiment we shall adopt the treatment if and only if the number of successes in the five trials is 3 or more. The Bayesian worth for this case can in fact be shown to be 107.1.

Can we do better than this if we allow the possibility of action being taken after any one of the observations becomes available? For a fair comparison we shall, of course, restrict our attention to a maximum of five observations. And again we shall make use of plausible predictions based on a uniform prior plausibility function for the success probability; see Section 5-6 and, in particular, (5-6-3) and (5-6-4).

Again we shall be forced to apply the dynamic programming technique. Let us denote by $F_n(z_n)$ the maximum (using an optimum decision procedure) expected future return (terminal gain less any future costs of observation) from a position where we have taken n observations and observed z_n successes. We may now look ahead and say that we can either stop and take one of the actions a_0 (do not introduce) or a_1 (introduce) or take another observation (action a_2) and assess the position after that observation. If we stop now, then our utility is $U(a, y)$ as displayed in the table and, as before, we have

$$V(a_0, z_n) = 0,$$

$$V(a_1, z_n) = 1000\left(\frac{z_n + 1}{n + 2} - 0.45\right).$$

If we take another observation at cost 5, this may be y with plausibility $\pi(y \mid z_n)$ and our *subsequent* maximum expected future return will be $F_{n+1}(z_n + y)$, so our maximum expected future return *from our present position* is

$$\sum_Y F_{n+1}(z_n + y)\pi(y \mid z_n) - 5.$$

Since $F(z_n)$ is the maximum attainable from the present position by the operation of a best procedure, it is the maximum of the three quantities above. We can express this by writing

$$F_n(z_n) = \max\left\{0, 1000\left(\frac{z_n + 1}{n + 2} - 0.45\right), \sum_Y F_{n+1}(z_n + y)\pi(y \mid z_n) - 5\right\}. \quad (7\text{-}11\text{-}1)$$

As in previous dynamic programming analyses, since we must stop and act after five observations at the latest, we know that

$$F_5(z_5) = \max\left\{0, 1000\left(\frac{z_5 + 1}{5 + 2} - 0.45\right)\right\},$$

and we can easily pick out the greater of the two quantities for the various possible z_5. The column headed $n = 5$ in Table 7-22 gives the value of $F_5(z_5)$ for each z_5. For example, by (7-11-1),

$$F_5(1) = \max\{0, 1000(\tfrac{2}{7} - 0.45)\} = 0.$$

We can then work backwards, as in previous applications, to consider what the best action is from stage $n = 4$. To do this we have to compute, for each z_4, all

TABLE 7–22

Table of $F_n(z_n)^{\dagger}$

z_n	n					
	5	4	3	2	1	0
0	$0\,a_0$	$0\,a_0$	$0\,a_0$	$0\,a_0$	$21.2\,a_2$	$116.2\,a_2$
1	$0\,a_0$	$0\,a_0$	$17.3\,a_2$	$78.6\,a_2$	$221.2\,a_2$	
2	$0\,a_0$	$55.7\,a_2$	$150.0\,a_1$	$300.0\,a_1$		
3	$121.4\,a_1$	$216.7\,a_1$	$350.0\,a_1$			
4	$264.3\,a_1$	$383.3\,a_1$				
5	$407.1\,a_1$					

$^{\dagger}\, a_0 =$ do not introduce, $a_1 =$ introduce, $a_2 =$ take another observation.

the quantities in the braces in (7–11–1), the last sum being evaluated as

$$F_5(z_4)\left(1 - \frac{z_4 + 1}{4 + 2}\right) + F_5(z_4 + 1)\frac{z_4 + 1}{4 + 2}$$

from the values already obtained in the column $n = 5$. Again for each z_4 it is easy to record the value of the greatest term in the braces and to note beside it the

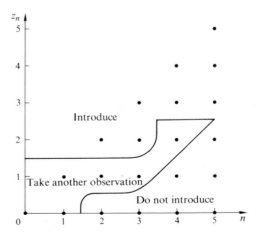

Fig. 7–11   Chart showing appropriate action for each possible position (n, z_n).

appropriate action that leads to that maximum value. For example, by (7–11–1)

$$F_4(3) = \max \{0, \quad 1000(\tfrac{4}{6} - 0.45), \quad \tfrac{2}{6} \times 121.4 + \tfrac{4}{6} \times 264.3 - 5\}$$
$$= \max \{0, 216.7, 211.7\} = 216.7,$$

with action a_1, which explains the entry $216.7\,a_1$ in column $n = 4$. When column $n = 4$ is completed, we then apply the dynamic programming equation to the construction of column $n = 3$, and then back to $n = 2, 1, 0$. Thus the complete sequential statistical decision problem is solved.

We can set out the decision procedure in a convenient graphic form. In the application of Fig. 7–11 we move horizontally one step if a failure is recorded and we move one step diagonally upward to the right if a success is recorded. We start at the origin 0 and so long as we stay in the region marked "Take another observation" we move on to the next observation. If we cross one of the boundaries we stop and take the action indicated. While the decision problem may seem quite a difficult one and may require careful analysis, it is easy to give instructions in this graphic form so that they can be readily carried out by someone who does not understand the underlying problems.

EXERCISES

1. Reconsider the problem of introducing a new treatment as discussed in this section with the following changes: $I = 2000, k = 0.58, l = 1$; the maximum number of observations is three and the cost of each observation is 10.

   What difference in your sequential plan emerges when the cost of each observation can be reduced to 4?

2. A group of veterinary surgeons is concerned about the economics of introducing a new operation for a serious horse disease. The probability of effecting a cure by the operation is unknown. The veterinary hospital can accept for surgery each week just three horses. At the development stage the operation costs 800 per horse, but if introduced as a routine the estimated cost per horse is 40. The financial advantage in curing a horse is 100. It is assumed that if introduced the operation would be applied to some 400 horses before any further substantial advance in treatment could be brought to trial stage.

   The hospital board requires a recommendation within the next two weeks. What is the most economical plan of investigation and of reaching a conclusion?

3. Socks are manufactured in pairs, and of all pairs produced one-half have both socks perfect, one-third have one sock imperfect, one-sixth have both socks imperfect. You are asked to construct a rational inspection plan for each pair and are provided with the following information.

   The socks of a pair may be inspected in sequence at a cost of 3 per sock. Any sock found imperfect may be completely repaired before sale at a rectifying cost of 4 per sock. The selling price of a perfect sock is 10 more than its original cost of manufacture; the loss arising from the replacement of a sold imperfect sock is 15. The socks of a pair must be sold as a pair but it is not necessary to inspect both, or even any, socks before placing the pair on the market.

4. Problem 5 (Choice of a batch sentencing rule, Section 1–6) was analyzed in Section 6–13 from a fixed sample-size point of view. What advantages, if any, would there be in carrying out the sampling inspection sequentially?

CHAPTER 8

HISTORY, PRESENT EXTENSIONS,
AND FUTURE TRENDS

The purpose of this final short chapter is threefold: first, to provide a brief history and a recapitulation of the nature of decision-making under uncertainty as we have developed it, to point out some straightforward extensions, and so to allow the reader to survey what he has read; second, to relate the field to other disciplines; and third, to suggest further reading and to indicate probable future trends of research in, and applications of, statistical decision theory.

8–1 A BRIEF HISTORY

The natural place for any brief history of a subject is at the end of an exposition rather than at the beginning, since an understanding of the present state of knowledge will make the history more intelligible and the implications of the history for the subject and its future clearer. Statistical decision theory is essentially a synthesis of a number of different branches of knowledge, and the student can only benefit from the realization that these various historical strands of development form a very natural basis for its logical as well as its chronological development. An awareness of this separation of the subject into component parts and their eventual synthesis should add to the reader's appreciation of statistical decision theory. Once he has read this section he is invited to review the subject matter of this book in the light of his accumulated knowledge.

The subject matter of statistical decision theory stems from three main streams of development—the theory of preference and utility, the theory of probability, and statistical inference—which have joined forces at various points in its history.

Preference and Utility Terms such as preference, indifference curves, value, and utility have been in common usage by economists certainly since the turn of this century, and indeed the ideas can be traced back to Ricardo, Mill, and even Smith. In his *The Theory of Political Economy*, published in 1871, Jevons had already made explicit use of the concept of cardinal utility (scales of preference) and was even bold enough to develop his theory in mathematical notation. Much of twentieth-century economic theory has been influenced by Marshallian economics, as set out in Marshall's *Principles of Economics*, published in 1901. A main element of this theory is the concept of ordinal utility (orders of preference) through the analysis of indifference curves. While there had thus been for some considerable time a common language and indeed a highly developed though controversial theory of utility and value, there was no sign of integrating this with the uncertainties inherent in such situations. It is true that there was an awareness of the feature of uncertainty and risk. The economist's solution to this problem was twofold. First, and quite reasonably, he pointed to the possibility of insuring against calculable risks such as fire, flood, etc. For other uncertainties he swept the problem under the carpet by subsuming the existence of an entrepreneur whose function it was to know what risks to take and who had presumably profound business acumen. Now while this theory may at some time have been of some relevance, it can hardly be maintained in the fast-moving, complex, technological world of today. It is becoming increasingly necessary to investigate as fully as possible, and to attempt to quantify, the uncertainties of any given situation before reaching a conclusion. The massive increase of expenditure, time, and manpower on operational and market research and on business studies and management training is a clear indication of an awareness of this need.

We have not studied the theory of utility as a separate subject in this book. Our consideration of orders and scales of preferences, often referred to as ordinal and cardinal utilities, in Chapter 1 has been sufficient for our purposes.

Uncertainty While man's awareness of uncertainty must date back almost to prehistory, his first successful attempts to quantify it came as late as the seventeenth century. The story of the gambling Chevalier de Méré's request in 1654 to his mathematician friend Pascal to help him decide on what is a fair division of the stakes in an interrupted game of chance is now a familiar one. Although there are indications of earlier understanding by others, Pascal's work was the most systematic and showed signs of appreciation of the role of the applied mathematician in the analysis of these betting problems. From the subsequent correspondence between Pascal and Fermat to the present day the subject of probability has had a steady uninterrupted development to reach the position of a highly integrated central theory with many ramifications in its applications. The names of some famous mathematicians appear in the list of its developers. James Bernoulli was the first to note explicitly the "addition law," our property (3) of Definition 2–7–1(b), and the "multiplication law," our Definitions 3–2–1 and 3–3–1, a significant piece of abstraction, and to provide a general formula for binomial counting experiments (Definition 3–6–2). De Moivre, Lagrange, Laplace, and Gauss made very significant contributions by their development of normal theory, at the heart of much present-day work, and the magnificent approximation, now known as the central limit theorem or the law of errors, which allows one of the few escapes from intractability in many complex applications.

A special comment is required about the role of the Reverend Thomas Bayes and his posthumous *An essay towards solving a problem in the doctrine of chances* (1763) in this development. His contribution to probability theory can be simply described as the discovery of one of the basic laws of conditional probability. This so-called Bayes's theorem has been the center of at times bitter controversy, not over its mathematical correctness, but over its appropriateness as a tool of statistical inference. This controversy has been at its liveliest in recent years. While the main stream of modern statistical inference was emerging during the period 1920–40, the attitude adopted by the vast majority of statisticians was frequentist, with probability tied firmly to the notion of the limit of long-run relative frequency. During this period of rapid technical statistical advances there were indeed some voices in the wilderness. Jeffreys, in his *Theory of Probability* (1939) and earlier papers, and Keynes, in his *Treatise on Probability* (1921), propounded the viewpoint of probabilities as "degrees of belief"; Ramsey, in his *Truth and Probability* (1926), and de Finetti, in his *Foresight: its Logical Laws, its Subjective Sources* (1937), presented the concept of subjective probability, in which each person must formulate his own probabilities in terms of his willingness to accept imagined bets. It has, however, been only recently that the achievements of these pioneers have met with full recognition. For the revival of interest during the last two decades in subjective probability and in the Bayesian argument, in general the main credit must go to L. J. Savage. It is largely due to his work (see References 17, 18) and enthusiasm that interest in the Bayesian form of analysis has developed to the extent that it is now recognized as an important practical tool.

The most significant technical advances of this century lie in the development of stochastic processes and in the axiomatic approach initiated by Kolmogorov. Stochastic processes may be described as the dynamic theory of probability, where the probabilistic pattern develops over time or in space. The publication of Kolmogorov's book *The Foundations of Probability* in 1933 clearly demonstrated how the whole, by then complicated, structure of probability theory could be derived from a few extremely simple and acceptable axioms. There is little doubt that the insight into the subject given in this book drew attention to the advantages to be gained from the clear formulation of problems, and gave statisticians and other users of probability theory a greater appreciation of their role as model-builders or applied mathematicians. The basis of all applied mathematics is a clearly formulated model of the particular aspect under consideration; failure to appreciate this fact, in both teaching and practice, is at the heart of many of the difficulties and controversies arising in the assessment of uncertainties.

The study of the construction of a language of uncertainty formed the subject matter of Chapters 2 and 3.

Inference Man has for a long time been able to make inferences from his observation of nature. For example, many of the old sayings about weather, such as "A red sky at night is a shepherd's delight," are expressions of this ability to see a pattern, albeit an uncertain one. Any attempt at quantifying inference, other than for nearly deterministic mechanisms, had clearly to await the development of a suitable language of uncertainty, and we have seen that this came as late as the seventeenth century. Therefore, it comes as no surprise that the first investigations of any real substance into the problem of making inferences from variable data appear as late as the eighteenth century. The great pioneers in this field were undoubtedly Bayes, Laplace, and Gauss, with their theories of the probabilities of causes, of errors, and of the combining of "inconsistent" data by least-squares estimation. The application of the last of these to astronomical problems, such as the positioning of stars, and to surveying was a major advance still in common use today.

There was little further development until the late nineteenth century, when the demands of the evolving biological sciences, with their greater display of variability in their raw material, demanded the search for a satisfactory means of estimation and hypothesis-testing. Galton and Karl Pearson were pioneers in this field, but the founding of the more modern approach to inference was to await the arrival of the genius of R. A. Fisher in 1925. The principles underlying the problem of estimation were evolved and methods of estimation and a large number of standard statistical tests were derived. Later the principles of testing hypotheses were more clearly formulated by Neyman and E. S. Pearson in the period 1930–40. Much of contemporary statistical inference is a development of the ideas of Fisher, Neyman, and E. S. Pearson. However, as already mentioned in our discussion on uncertainty, recent years have seen a swing of the pendulum back to the ideas of Bayes and Laplace.

The relation of probability theory to inference should be clearly understood. Probability theory provides the means of describing the real-world situation under consideration by the provision of a whole class of possible models. It is then the purpose of statistical inference to examine the data available from the real situation and to assess through principles of inference which of the possible models are reasonable and which unreasonable. Probability theory is thus one of the main pure mathematical tools used by applied mathematicians who call themselves statisticians.

The main concepts and principles of statistical inference have been outlined in Chapter 5.

The First Synthesis: The Theory of Games Probability and statistics, on the one hand, and economic theory and its applications, on the other, continued to have a largely separate development until very recently. The pioneer work of Ramsey and de Finetti remained unknown and unrecognized until the recent past. Another breakthrough came with the min-max theorem of von Neumann in 1927, but the influence of this also was not felt until the publication by von Neumann and Morgenstern of their *Theory of Games and Economic Behavior* in 1944. This theory combined the concepts and techniques of probability and economic theory. The feature of uncertainty was now boldly incorporated in a theory of utility through the identification of utility with the payoff or reward in a game of chance. A whole theory of competition under uncertainty was developed and the repercussions of the novelty of the approach are still being felt in economic theory and other disciplines.

Some of the simpler aspects of the theory of games have been considered in Chapter 4.

The Second Synthesis: Statistical Decision Theory The theory of games provided a means of describing how decisions could be taken or patterns of behavior explained in a prescribed situation. What was still lacking was a means of exploiting any information which was available from sources outside this prescribed situation. Where the theory of games had combined utility theory and probability theory, what was now required was a combination of utility theory and statistical inference. This was recognized by Wald who in his *Statistical Decision Functions* of 1950 presented a well-developed analysis of the subject. The subject of our study is thus barely 20 years old. It has greatly enhanced our understanding and knowledge of statistics, although it is only in the last few years that the theory has had really successful application. There are good reasons for this. Wald was working in a period when frequentism was in its heyday. Frequentism may be described as the belief that probabilistic statements should refer only to events and not to the "causes" postulated by Bayes and Laplace; or, in other words, that the only concept of probability that should be admitted is that which is the abstraction of the fact that the relative frequency of an event is fairly stable when the number of repetitions of the "experiment" under question is large. Wald's approach was necessarily colored by the dominant statistical philosophy of his day, and although "Bayesian" solutions form an integral part of the development of the theory, no great emphasis was placed on their practical use. Gradually over the last 20 years there has been a reopening of interest in the Bayesian approach which admits probabilistic statements about "states of nature," based on some kind of empirical evidence or in very extreme Bayesianism on purely introspective subjective assessments of probabilities. The culmination of this revival is in the comprehensive volume *Applied Statistical Decision Theory* by Raiffa and Schlaifer of the Harvard Business School.

There has been, as is not uncommon in the statistical world, a great deal of controversy over the relative merits of opposing approaches. This is not an aspect which we have dwelt on unduly in this book but any writer must eventually declare his attitude to such a controversy. It is my belief that it is not particularly helpful in applied mathematics to attempt to produce some all-embracing creed which one can hope to apply in all situations. The individual situation should dictate what the appropriate statistical model should be. There are some situations which are decidedly frequentist; there are others which are certainly Bayesian. It is hoped that the discussion and analysis of particular problems in this book has helped to clarify the applicability of these different approaches. The main task of Chapters 6 and 7 has been to attempt to expose the nature and structure of statistical decision problems and how the statistician evolves a solution.

8–2 RECAPITULATION

Applied mathematics, the art of bringing a mathematical argument to bear on a real problem so that it makes a significant contribution to the solution, is largely a matter of attitude. It involves the recognition that relevant entities of the real world may be represented symbolically by counterparts in a model, that the interrelations, forms, and functions of these entities can be represented by mathematical operations or instructions, and that sensibly directed mathematical development of the model may often lead to conclusions which help substantially in the resolution of the real problem.

The manner in which applied mathematics can help in the field of decision-making under uncertainty stems both from its analytic role of breaking down problems into sensible component parts and from its synthetic role of producing a suitable blending of these parts to produce an optimum course of action by mathematical operations.

The analysis of decision-making in the face of uncertainty first requires the decision-maker to recognize four facets of his problem:

1. the assessment of the consequences of the possible actions in the face of the possible but unknown states of nature,
2. the quantitative expression of the uncertainties of any situation,
3. the appreciation of the competitive aspect of decision-making and hence the study of competitive situations,

4. the use of data or information to provide some reduction in the amount of uncertainty present.

From some elementary discussion in a trivial situation in Chapter 1 we saw that we have little hope of making rational decisions between alternative courses of action unless we have a fairly clear picture of what our preferences would be if the uncertainty were removed, whatever that removal may lead to. This in effect requires the decision-maker to be able to specify a utility function (or, equivalently, a very elaborate list of preferences) which places a quantitative assessment of the benefit derivable from each action in the face of each possible though unknown state of nature. The necessity for such a detailed assessment is often not realized and the cause of much hesitation in decision-making is simply an expression of the absence of clear-cut objectives. To say this is not to infer that most decision-makers are faltering muddleheads who have their priorities confused, but rather to suggest that perhaps too little time, energy, money, and thought are spent on this aspect of the decision-making process. All the data in the world are of little use to a decision-maker if the objectives of the decision-making exercise are not clear. If the sole contribution of statistical decision theory were to draw attention to the central role played by the utility specification or its equivalent, then it would serve a useful purpose.

A very significant contribution to the analysis of decision-making under uncertainty is the construction of a model or language within which we can speak quantitatively about degrees of uncertainty. This quantification is possible because even in uncertain situations there is a form of stability whereby the relative frequency with which an event occurs in repetitions of the same situation settles down in the long run. We are thus able to tie our notion of the uncertainty of an event—its probability—with this long-run feature. From the simple properties of relative frequencies we see what the grammar of the language of probability should be, and so what structure a probability model should possess.

The delightful surprise in this form of model-building is that the structure turns out to be extremely simple. From this basic idea of a probability model we are then able to construct from models for component experiments a compound model for the overall experiment. For experiments which do not interfere or interact with each other this compound model takes a particularly simple form. This building of larger models from simple independent components is an important facility because of its wide applicability; it is called the *product model*, since its probability function is obtained by a multiplication of the probability functions of the component models. We also saw how to build up the structure of certain kinds of dependent experiments through the notion of staged experiments, the experiment undertaken at any stage being dependent on what has actually happened at the performance of the previous experiments. Again the model structure of the compound experiment is simply related to the description of the first-stage experiment and to the several descriptions of the possible second-stage experiments, and so on. We also saw that it is possible to use a vector record to represent an outcome which is many-faceted and that the recording of the many facets can conceptually be considered to take place in stages in different ways. From such a consideration one of the central results of conditional probability emerges, the so-called Bayes's theorem.

Usually there are many possible probability models contending for the title of true model for a given situation, and the main object of most experimentation is to try to reduce in some way this class of possible models. It is necessary to label the possible models in some convenient way, and this leads to the notion of the index set or the set of possible states of nature.

The competitive aspect of decision-making is highlighted by the study of the most primitive form, that in which two contestants confront each other in a game, each contestant having a specified set of available strategies defined by the rules of the game and there accruing a specified utility or loss of a magnitude depending on the selected strategies of the player and the opponent. To obtain a full analysis and to devise optimum strategies, we had to admit the possibility of randomized strategies whereby a contestant may choose one of his specified strategies by first performing a probabilistic experiment to determine which he should play. This brings about a simple integration of game theory and probability theory. For the case in which the opponent's randomized strategy is known to the player, the selection of an optimum strategy is straightforwardly obtained by computing the values associated with each strategy. An initial simplification can sometimes be obtained by the summary rejection of clearly bad or inadmissible strategies. When the opponent's strategy is not known to the player, he must resort to the pessimistic philosophy of max-min.

In such analyses of games we are in fact solving the problem of decision-making under uncertainty in the situation in which there are no data, where there is no possibility of performing an informative experiment.

Next we studied the problem of statistical inference. From an initial position of uncertainty about an unknown state of nature, how can we, using the data obtained from an informative experiment, take steps to remove some of that uncertainty? One form of answer is provided by the concept of a prior plausibility function for the various states of nature and its conversion by the routine application of the conditional probability argument of Bayes's theorem to a posterior plausibility function for the states of nature. This method shows the change in attitude to states occasioned by the information obtained. In effect, we can here regard the statistician as a box into which we feed our prior plausibility function and our information x. Using mathematical techniques of no direct interest to the decision-maker, the box must then give as output the posterior plausibility function. We also looked at some other aspects of statistical inference whereby attempts are made to provide a kind of working value for an unknown state of nature (estimation), most popularly through the concepts of minimum variance unbiasedness and maximum likelihood, and to distinguish between two (or only a few) states of nature (hypothesis testing) by principles which admit only the relative frequency interpretation of probability or plausibility.

Finally came the weaving together of the various strands in a synthesis of utility specification, probability model-building, competitive behavior and statistical inference into statistical decision theory. We recognized three basic sets of elements: the set S of unknown states of nature, the set X of possible outcomes of the informative experiment, and the set A of possible actions. These sets are interrelated in pairs. First, the prior plausibility function on the set S and the class of probability models on the record set X, and indexed by S, connect the sets S and X and provide the probability structure. The inference problem can then be immediately completed and is one of the components of the decision problem looked at from the Bayesian point of view. Second, the action set A and the index set S are tied together through the utility or loss function which plays the role of the payoff in the theory of games. Third, the record set X and the action set A are connected, since we want to know how to act when we know the simple record observed. To go from the record set X to the action set A we need a function on X taking values in A, a decision procedure. The synthesis is then completed by the principle of selecting as best action one which maximizes (minimizes) the expected utility (loss), the expectation being with respect to the posterior plausibility function. We saw that this is a relatively easy operation and that there are easy means within this framework of allowing a choice of alternative informative experiments, of permitting the utility structure to depend on the record of the informative experiment or even on the unknown outcome of some future, and as yet unperformed, experiment.

This kind of decision-making can be given further support by a theory of rational decision-making. If one postulates a rational man who makes his choices in a sensible, consistent way, then it can be shown that he acts as if he had a utility function, a plausibility function, and chooses an action which maximizes the associated Bayesian worth. Of course, this does not mean that this is precisely how a rational decision-maker must make his decisions; but it does show us that if we can persuade ourselves to construct these elements, we are on the way to being good decision-makers.

We pointed out also that there were inherent difficulties in the choice of an action in the decision-making process as envisaged by the frequentist school. It is possible to reduce the set of possible decision procedures to a set of sensible or admissible procedures, but this may still leave a large set of procedures.

Additional principles for the further reduction of this set are not always available, and the max-min approach may not be a very realistic one.

Our study of statistical decision theory has taken us right up to the present boundaries of the subject, although we confined our attention to simple finite examples. Even within this context, however, we were able to see how to handle the case of sequential decision-making in a reasonable, satisfactory way, where information reaches us in sequence and at any point of the sequence we have the option to stop collecting information and to decide what final action to take. We saw that such procedures can have advantages over the practice of fixing the size of the experiment in advance. This led us to the idea of control theory, where we have some power to intervene in a process, as we observe it developing, to direct its final product toward some desirable goal.

8–3 EXTENSIONS

Throughout this book we have deliberately limited ourselves in theory and practice to situations which can be expressed in finite terms. By this limitation we were able to restrict the form of mathematics to the extremely simple instructions "sum the following finite set of numbers" and "choose the largest (or smallest) of the following finite set of numbers." We hope that even within this simple context we have succeeded in conveying clearly the analytic and synthetic aspects of decision-making under uncertainty. Let us now mention briefly a few extensions which help to widen the applicability of the theory.

Many practical problems require that some or all of the sets X, S, A should not be restricted to be finite sets. For example, for an informative experiment which records the number of particles emitted by a source of radiation in a given time interval, we would need to take $X = \{0, 1, 2, \ldots\}$, the infinite set of all nonnegative integers, since we cannot place an upper bound on the number emitted. Again, although we may record the lifetime of a component to the nearest second and so require only a discrete record set, it is mathematically more convenient to introduce the notion of a continuous record set, namely the set of all nonnegative real numbers. We may go even further and consider n components and so be involved in an n-replicate experiment, with a continuous n-dimensional record set. The only difference with continuous record sets is that we achieve accumulation of the quantity of probability assigned by a model to a record or subset by the mathematical technique of *integration* or multiple integration instead of the previous process of simple addition. We have already seen in our discussion of binomial trials that the index set S may be continuous. These extensions of the nature of X and S raise the question of what forms the probability functions $p(x \mid s)$ and the plausibility functions $\pi(s)$ and $\pi(s \mid x)$ may take for realism and practical use. There is much work on special forms bearing the names *normal model, Poisson model,* and *negative exponential model*, and suited to special situations. Matching the form of model to a given problem is largely a matter of experience and compromise. While the underlying physical, biological, technological, or economic mechanism may suggest an appropriate form, considerations of tractability are also relevant. No illumination is brought to a problem by the construction of a model which is so elaborate that it cannot be significantly developed. Again there may be an infinite number of possible actions. For example, in the problem of deciding at what strength to manufacture a pharmaceutical preparation, the possible actions corresponding to the possible strengths may conceptually best be described on a continuous scale.

Such generalizations of the nature of the sets X, S, and A do not alter at all the structure of the decision problem. The only difference is that the form of mathematics involved in the construction of a best action or decision procedure is more sophisticated but usually remains within the scope of modern methods and computation.

In our study of sequential decision-making we confined our attention to the case in which the maximum number of steps was limited. Since it may be inconvenient to have this limitation or difficult to preassign a realistic maximum to the number of steps, it is necessary to study more general sequential processes. Much work in this more difficult area has been done, some of the most fruitful results stemming from a very general approximation theory, devised by Wald, for evaluating absorption probabilities at boundaries of a random walk.

8-4 RELATION TO OTHER DISCIPLINES

The complex structure of modern society, with its ever-increasing speed of communication and its spectacular advances in scientific knowledge and technology, demands the interdependence of disciplines once almost completely separated. Problems of decision-making under uncertainty which are of any magnitude are already, and will increasingly become, resolvable only by the bringing together and cooperation of many disciplines. In this section we suggest briefly the role that some of these disciplines may play in the decision-making process.

Economics In recent years economics has become much more quantitatively oriented. This quantification has been largely stimulated by the obvious need in a world of rapidly expanding population and trade to understand more deeply the nature of an economy and to discover suitable and acceptable means of regulating it. Commonly quoted phrases such as "another economic crisis," "delicately balanced position," "balance of payments difficulties," "inflationary spiral" all evidence the existence of difficult decision problems. The economist's contribution is largely to help in the construction of economic models of the economy of interest. His special training and study is directed toward identifying what aspects and entities of the economy are relevant and to postulating how these may be interconnected. The testing of the adequacy of the resulting economic models to explain the past and their subsequent use for predicting future development is the subject matter of econometrics. Much work in this discipline has been undertaken in the last 25 years, and there have even been bold attempts to construct models for the entire economy of the United Kingdom or the United States. The economist's role is, however, not confined to the mechanism of the nation's finances, and he has much to contribute in the economic and financial operation of smaller units in industry, insurance, and business. One of the major drawbacks in much of his work is the lack or scarcity of reliable data. It is not the least of the economist's tasks to ensure that information is collected in a relevant form.

Accountancy There is already strong evidence that a revolution is under way in the discipline of accountancy, where the task of the accountant is no longer the traditional keeper and balancer of books. Much more emphasis is now being placed on sampling techniques, cost analysis, and stock control. All of these are directed toward the kind of information collection required for the assessment of the costs of, and likely returns from, the operation of a decision procedure. This trend will certainly continue, fostered by the availability of the high-speed retrieval of information now possible with modern computing systems and by the need for more frequent assessment of the state and feasibility of a financial undertaking. Possibly one of the most valuable contributions which the accountant can make is to help in the construction of realistic utility functions. His understanding of the effects of past decisions and his ability to assess the present condition of the system place him in possession of invaluable knowledge.

Medicine, Science, and Technology It is tautological that where the decision problem is concerned with a medical, scientific, or technological process the appropriate expert must be involved. The problem of which, if any, of a number of different drugs should be manufactured clearly requires careful assessment of advice from the medical profession and pharmacologist in addition to that of the pharmaceutical technologist, economist, and accountant. The question of which of a number of proposed steel-making processes to adopt requires the steel technologist's assessment of the relative feasibility of available choices as large-scale processes and the metallurgist's assessment of the qualities of the finished product. The point is so obvious that further examples are unnecessary.

Operations Research The recent discipline of operations research, which may be loosely described as the application of quantitative techniques to industrial, business, and government processes, is clearly one whose boundaries are ill-defined. The mathematical contributor to an operations research team has the same applied mathematical attitude as the statistician. The early pre-occupation of the mathematicians in operations research has naturally been with deterministic situations (apart from some probabilistic problems such as queueing), and the very successful mathematical programming techniques evolved (such as linear, convex, and dynamic programming) reflect this. As operations research develops and concentrates more on stochastic aspects and as statisticians begin to see the many opportunities for the application of their discipline in a most interesting field, the boundaries will blur even more.

Computing Our concentration on simple finite situations has unfortunately disguised the fact that there are often sizable computational problems that remain after the decision problem has been fully formulated. There is, however, strong evidence that many of the decision problems that beset us today are certainly capable of being solved within the foreseeable future. This is not because of any miraculous thinking powers of "electronic brains." It is simply that the number of calculations needed to solve a problem of moderate size is essentially very large, and to complete these in a finite time the high speed with which computers can add, multiply, and discriminate in a directed way between alternative routes of computation can be very useful. Much remains to be done to build up libraries of reasonably general programs which can be immediately available for the feeding in of prior plausibility functions, information, and utility functions.

Management In business and industrial decision-making it is generally regarded as the privilege of those engaged in management to have the final choice of the course of action to be adopted. Such a privilege carries with it the responsibility of ensuring that information and views from all relevant sections of the organization are sought and coordinated. It is clear, therefore, that a full awareness by management of the structure of decision-making under uncertainty cannot but be beneficial to the quality of the decision procedure adopted. The role of management is to assign appropriate divisions of labor in the formulation, where necessary, of a prior plausibility function, in the design and conduct of any informative experiment undertaken, and in the assessment of the utility structure. Accountants, economists, market research workers, scientists, and technologists must all be directed to their respective tasks. The retaining of the final decision in the separate hands of management is a safeguard against the enthusiasms of individual disciplines.

Psychology Great interest has been shown by many psychologists in statistical decision theory as a basis for the psychological study of behavior. It is obvious that many decisions are made on what appear to be highly irrational grounds.

The great attraction that gambling has for many people, with its display of a preference for an infinitesimal chance of a huge prize rather than a steady small return from a safe investment, is a well-known phenomenon. Such decision-making is not made on the basis of minimizing the calculated risk. The explanation of this form of apparently irrational behavior in psychological terms may lead to interesting developments and adjustments in statistical decision theory. Part of the explanation may be in terms of concepts of subjective probability, and, since it is at least interesting to explore the feasibility of allowing very subjective judgments to form the basis of the prior plausibility function, the psychologist may be a very useful participant in the process of abstracting information from the individual in a usable form.

Philosophy   Throughout this book we have at various times made mild philosophical comments on the meaning and interpretation of probability and on the nature of applied mathematics. Philosophers have long been interested in the fundamental nature of the concept of probability, and statisticians have engaged in many philosophical arguments within their ranks, often to the extent of bitter controversy. Much of this argument has been of a general nature, where the pros and cons of an approach or interpretation are fought over with no specific problem in mind. It is often remarkable to see how a specific practical problem can cause the argument to subside into the activity of resolving the particular problem. There is little doubt that clarification of the interrelationship of philosophy and statistical practice is required. We confine ourselves here to the following brief comments.

The approach of statistical decision theory is an applied mathematical approach, for it uses a mathematical model to represent a real situation, each symbol and relationship of the model having some counterpart or conceptual counterpart in the real situation. It is the duty of the decision-maker to establish for his particular problem the nature of this correspondence between reality and model. He should thus be aware, for example, of how well founded any prior plausibility function is, and so be in some position to judge how meaningful a Bayesian form of analysis may be, or whether the circumstances enforce the caution of a max-min approach. The *particular* situation and not any general philosophy dictates what form of model is most appropriate. The clash between Bayesians and frequentists is idealogical; differences in statistical practice are not so frequent and usually much more marginal than many of the protagonists care to admit. Another philosophical red herring is a long-fought battle over the distinction between statistical inference and decision theory. "Does decision theory contain the whole of statistical inference?" "Does statistical inference contain the whole of decision theory?" These are favorite questions. The answers clearly must vary according to the definitions of the terms "statistical inference" and "decision theory" and the whole problem is largely one of semantics. The argument continues mainly because the protagonists seldom wish to waste their breath in defining terms.

To sum up, any branch of applied mathematics can be tested only by its application in the situations it purports to depict. Whether or not it is good applied mathematics will depend on its usefulness in practice as a tool to a solution of the real problem or the insight it provides as a step toward a solution. Whether or not it survives will depend on how important the real problems are regarded by mankind. The young branch of statistical decision theory is now finding application to many varied situations. What adjustments to its present form may prove necessary will depend on the assessment of these applications. There can, however, be little doubt that the need to face decision-making under uncertainty will remain for many generations and that statistical decision theory in some form or other will play an important role in resolving these problems.

8–5 FUTURE TRENDS

In the preceding section we talked about the interdisciplinary type of research which it is necessary to conduct to exploit the existing structure of statistical decision-making. Within the field of statistical decision theory itself much remains to be done. Sequential decision theory is still in the early stages of its development. In the examples we studied we placed an upper limit on the number of observations allowed. When this is removed another order of difficulty emerges, and although some progress has been made on this aspect, a number of substantial problems remain. In the field of design of experiments much research is still needed. For instance, in the very simple experiment in which we are testing only two treatments, the fully sequential problem (for example, in what order should the treatments be tested) is far from solved. One of the most interesting and challenging modern problems is that of statistical control, where information about the true unknown state of a process is gradually accumulated and has to be fed back into the efficient control of the process toward some ideal or to minimize some eventual loss. The problems of automatic flight are familiar examples in this field.

The exploration of techniques for the collection of information which will allow the construction of realistic utility functions is a crucial step toward the more routine application of statistical decision theory. Without some such means of quantifying the desirable goals a decision problem is scarcely formulated. Associated with this field of investigation is the study of how decisions are actually made rather than how they should be made. Much insight into the process of human decision-making, especially in situations in which it is difficult to construct direct utility functions (for example, medicine), might be obtainable if the possibility of estimating utility functions actually used from a sequence of observed decisions were investigated.

The great impetus to the development of any branch of knowledge is undoubtedly the strident demands of the practical problems which beset men, and the long-term course of statistical decision theory will certainly be dictated by these needs. When one thinks of the high speed with which technological innovation advances, one soon realizes that there will be no shortage of interesting problems for many years to come for those who find them intellectually stimulating. I hope that the reader, by being stimulated by this book, may find himself one of the instigators of such exciting new developments.

FURTHER READING

FURTHER READING

The following is a brief annotated list of books for the reader who wishes to widen his understanding of statistical decision theory.

1. Blackwell, D., and M. A. Girshick (1954). *Theory of Games and Statistical Decisions.* New York: Wiley.

   A highly mathematical account of the theory of games and its relation to statistical decision theory. Only readers with understanding of advanced mathematical techniques should attempt to read this account.

2. Chernoff, H., and L. E. Moses (1959). *Elementary Decision Theory.* New York: Wiley.

   An excellently organized account of statistical decision theory with many illustrative examples at a slightly higher mathematical level than the present book. An excellent choice of follow-up reading.

3. Edwards, W., and A. Tversky (1967). *Decision Making: Penguin Modern Psychology Readings No. 8.* Harmondsworth, Middlesex: Penguin Books.

   A collection of papers, mainly on the more psychological aspects of decision-making, which are scattered throughout books and journals. It contains in particular excellent accounts of the development and theory of utility and subjective probability. No sophisticated mathematical techniques are required for its appreciation.

4. Ferguson, T. S. (1967). *Mathematical Statistics: A Decision Theoretic Approach.* New York: Academic Press.

   A recent good exposition at a sophisticated mathematical level of statistical decision theory pushing right to the frontiers of present knowledge, including an excellent account of sequential decision-making. This will undoubtedly prove a useful text over the next few years.

5. Hodges, J. L., and E. L. Lehmann (1964). *Basic Concepts of Probability and Statistics.* San Francisco: Holden-Day.

   A delightfully clear exposition of basic probability model-building and its application to estimation and hypothesis testing. Little mathematical knowledge is required since attention is confined to discrete mathematics. Emphasis is given to the motivation and clarification of the concepts and many simple illustrations are used to drive home the basic structure of the problems.

6. Kolmogorov, A. (1933). *Grundbegriffe der Wahrscheinlichkeitsrechnung.* English translation (1950): *Foundations of the Theory of Probability.* New York: Chelsea.

   The first axiomatic treatment of probability theory, now a classic of mathematical probability. While this book is now mainly of historical interest, it remains for the mathematician a clear, concise account of the fundamentals of probability model-building.

7. Lindgren, B. W. (1962). *Statistical Theory.* New York: Macmillan.

   An undergraduate text developing probability theory, statistical inference, and decision theory in a clear, unhurried way. A more advanced book than 8.

8. Lindgren, B. W., and McElrath, G. W. (1966). *Introduction to Probability and Statistics.* New York: Macmillan.

   An elementary readable account of probability theory and statistical inference (estimation and hypothesis testing) mainly from the frequentist viewpoint, with one short chapter on the selection of procedures. Much more elementary than 7.

9. Lindley, D. V. (1965). *Introduction to Probability and Statistics from a Bayesian Viewpoint.* Cambridge: Cambridge University Press.

   The first volume contains a straightforward account of probability theory at the undergraduate level. The second volume is a Bayesian derivation of the standard estimation and hypothesis-testing procedures of the long-established frequentist approach. Much emphasis is laid on the search for prior plausibility functions which lead to frequentist practice.

10. Loève, M. (1960). *Probability Theory.* Princeton: D. van Nostrand.

    A basic mathematical textbook on probability theory and its ramifications, giving an extremely clear and well-motivated development. While the book contains a splendid section on the mathematical aspects of measure theory, only readers with previous mathematical training are liable to benefit from this.

11. Meyer, P. L. (1966). *Introductory Probability and Statistical Applications.* Reading, Mass.: Addison-Wesley.

    An extremely clear account of probability model-building at the advanced undergraduate level, with two final chapters giving the essentials of estimation and hypothesis testing. Concepts are well motivated and there are many worked illustrative examples and exercises for the reader.

12. Mode, E. B. (1966). *Elements of Probability and Statistics*. Englewood Cliffs, N. J.: Prentice-Hall.

At a slightly lower mathematical level than, but similar in content and approach to, 11.

13. Mosteller, F., R. E. Rourke, and G. B. Thomas (1961). *Probability and Statistics*. Reading, Mass.: Addison-Wesley.

Originally the official text for a television course, this is a very readable account of elementary probability theory and statistical inference. Well illustrated by examples, it has all the advantages of a text by authors of experience who have thought deeply about the teaching of their subject.

14. Raiffa, H. (1968). *Decision Analysis*. Reading, Mass.: Addison-Wesley.

A fascinating elementary account of statistical decision theory with much more emphasis on the aspects of utility and plausibility assessment than the present volume. It thus makes an excellent companion to *Choice against Chance*.

15. Raiffa, H., and R. Schlaifer (1961). *Applied Statistical Decision Theory*. Boston: Harvard Business School.

Destined to become a classic of the Bayesian approach to decision-making, this comprehensive volume has been the stimulus to much of present research in decision theory. Its emphasis is on an applied mathematical approach to business problems, but the treatment is general. It unfortunately suffers from an over-elaborate notation which has a slowing effect on the reader.

16. Schlaifer, R. (1959). *Probability and Statistics for Business Decisions*. New York: McGraw-Hill.

The predecessor of 15 and much more readable, with many useful illustrative examples.

17. Savage, L. J. (1954). *The Foundations of Statistics*. New York: Wiley.

A fundamental analysis of subjective probability, utility theory, and the theory of the rational decision-maker, and a treatment much referred to in the literature. The mathematical level is advanced undergraduate.

18. Savage, L. J., *et al.* (1962). *The Foundations of Statistical Inference*. London: Methuen.

An interesting, stimulating, and very readable account of a seminar held in London which gives a very clear picture of the various philosophical camps, frequentist and Bayesian.

19. Schmitt, S. A. (1969). *Measuring Uncertainty*. Reading, Mass.: Addison-Wesley.

An elementary account of Bayesian inference and decision-making, skilfully illustrated and extremely rich in penetrating remarks. Forms an excellent sequel at the next level of mathematics to the present book.

20. Vajda, S. (1956). *The Theory of Games and Linear Programming*. London: Methuen.

A clear presentation of the theory of games and the techniques of their solution at a fairly elementary mathematical level.

21. Von Neumann, J., and O. Morgenstern (1944). *Theory of Games and Economic Behavior*. Princeton: Princeton University Press.

   The classic of the theory of games, a large comprehensive volume of nondata decision-making, and containing an extensive treatment of the theory of utility. The mathematics used is at the advanced undergraduate level.

22. Wald, A. (1950). *Statistical Decision Functions*. New York: Wiley.

   The first coherent advanced treatment of statistical decision theory, now largely of historical interest because it makes difficult reading at a sophisticated mathematical level. It contains most of the fundamental ideas and results of present-day statistical decision theory.

23. Williams, J. D. (1954). *The Compleat Strategyst*. New York: McGraw-Hill.

   A popular and entertaining account at the elementary level of the theory of games.

The following list refers the reader wishing to study more deeply some particular aspect of statistical decision theory to appropriate books on the above list.

Utility theory	3, 14, 17, 21.
Probability	5, 6, 7, 8, 9, 10, 11, 12, 13, 17, 19.
Theory of games	1, 20, 21, 23.
Statistical inference	5, 7, 8, 9, 11, 12, 13, 18, 19.
Statistical decision theory	1, 2, 3, 4, 7, 8, 14, 15, 16, 17, 18, 19, 22.

APPENDICES

APPENDICES

1. FUNCTIONS

A clear understanding of the simple but very general concept of *function* will greatly help to make clear the structure of decision-making under uncertainty. To define a function we need two recognizable collections of objects or *sets* of *elements*.

Examples

1. The set $X = \{1, 2, 3\}$ consists of the elements or integers $1, 2, 3$. The set Y consists of all real numbers; each of the numbers $0.4, 57, \frac{4}{3}$ is a member or element of Y.

   When we wish to refer to an unspecified element of X we may use the symbol x, and speak of "x in X." Similarly, the phrase "for every y in Y" means "for all the elements in the set Y."

2. The sets X and Y may both contain the same elements. For example, X and Y may both be the sets consisting of all the positive real numbers.

3. There is no need for X and Y to have elements with numerical associations. For example, we can consider $X = \{s, f\}$, where s symbolizes success in an examination and f failure; and $Y = \{a_1, a_2\}$, where a_1 is a symbol representing the action "throw a party" and a_2 the action "study harder."

   A *function p* is then simply an instruction on how to assign to *each* element x in X one corresponding element, say $p(x)$, of Y. We then say that p is a function on X taking values in Y. Not all elements of Y need be used up in this correspondence. To return to our three examples:

1. The elements of Y corresponding to the elements of X can be shown, for such *finite* sets, in tabular form. For example,

x	1	2	3
$p(x)$	0.4	0.1	0.5

defines a function p on X taking values in Y. This is an example of a probability function on a record set X. Similarly,

x	1	2	3
$d(x)$	1	4	9

defines a different function d on X taking values in Y.

2. Here we could define a function d on X and taking values in Y by setting $d(x) = x^3$ for every x in X. The function d would then provide a suitable instruction for calculating the volume of a cube from the known length of an edge, that is, from a given element of X.

3. An example of a function d_1 on X and taking values in Y is specified in the table

x	s	f
$d_1(x)$	a_1	a_1

This would be an instruction to throw a party regardless of the outcome of the examination. Another, and perhaps more sensible, function would be d_2 assigning $d_2(s) = a_1$, $d_2(f) = a_2$.

From two functions defined on X taking numerical values, for example p and d of Example 1, we can easily derive a product function on X, taking value $d(x)p(x)$ again in Y. For Example 1,

x	1	2	3
$d(x)p(x)$	0.4	0.4	4.5

2. SUMMATION INSTRUCTIONS

To avoid the repetition of long-winded instructions, it is often worth while to introduce a convenient shorthand notation. The summation instruction is an excellent example of such a device. The capital Greek letter sigma, Σ, is used to provide this instruction, and throughout this book is always accompanied by a subscript which denotes a set. This subscript, for example X in Σ_X and

R in Σ_R, gives information about the extent of the addition. The notation Σ_X is an instruction to evaluate the (numerical) function that follows for each x in X and then to add together the values obtained. Thus in Example 1 of Appendix 1,

$$\sum_X p(x) = p(1) + p(2) + p(3) = 0.4 + 0.1 + 0.5 = 1.0,$$

$$\sum_X d(x)p(x) = d(1)p(1) + d(2)p(2) + d(3)p(3) = 0.4 + 0.4 + 4.5 = 5.3.$$

If R is the subset $\{1, 3\}$ of X, then

$$\sum_R p(x) = p(1) + p(3) = 0.4 + 0.5 = 0.9,$$

$$\sum_R d(x) = d(1) + d(3) = 1 + 9 = 10.$$

3. MAX AND MIN INSTRUCTIONS

A second basic operation which requires a shorthand notation is that of optimization (minimization or maximization).

The notation min applied to a set is an instruction to pick out the smallest element of the set. Thus

$$\min \{1, 2, 3\} = 1.$$

The notation extends in an obvious way, $\min_X$ being an instruction to evaluate the function that follows for each x in X and to choose the smallest of the values so obtained. Thus in Example 1 of Appendix 1,

$$\min_X p(x) = \min \{0.4, 0.1, 0.5\} = 0.1,$$

$$\min_X d(x)p(x) = \min \{0.4, 0.4, 4.5\} = 0.4.$$

The instructions max and $\max_X$ are similar to min and $\min_X$ but instruct us to pick out the largest instead of the smallest. Thus

$$\max \{1, 2, 3\} = 3,$$

$$\max_X d(x)p(x) = \max \{0.4, 0.4, 4.5\} = 4.5.$$

These instructions can be combined to form a sequence of instructions. Thus in Example 1 of Appendix 1,

$$\min \left\{ \sum_X d(x)p(x), \max_X d(x) \right\} = \min \{5.3, 9\} = 5.3,$$

since

$$\sum_X d(x)p(x) = 5.3 \quad \text{and} \quad \max_X d(x) = \max \{1, 4, 9\} = 9.$$

4. WEIGHTED AVERAGES

If 1, 2, 3 are the possible lengths of components from a manufacturing process and if the proportions of total production which are of these lengths are 0.4, 0.1, 0.5, then the average length of components is

$$1 \times 0.4 + 2 \times 0.1 + 3 \times 0.5 = 2.1. \tag{A}$$

This operation of averaging can be expressed formally in terms of a weighted average. First a weighting function must be defined. A weighting function on X is a function p on X taking nonnegative values or weights such that $\sum_X p(x) = 1$. The weighted average of x is then $\sum_X xp(x)$. More generally, the weighted average of $d(x)$, where d is some numerical function on X, is $\sum_X d(x)p(x)$. For Example 1 of Appendix 1, the weighted average of $d(x)$ for the given weighting function p is

$$\sum_X d(x)p(x) = 1 \times 0.4 + 4 \times 0.1 + 9 \times 0.5 = 5.3. \tag{B}$$

In (A) above the weighted average 2.1 lies above

$$1 = \min \{1, 2, 3\} = \min_X x$$

and below

$$3 = \max \{1, 2, 3\} = \max_X x.$$

It is easy to show that the general result holds:

$$\min_X x \leq \sum_X xp(x) \leq \max_X x; \tag{C}$$

for

$$x \leq M = \max_X x \qquad \text{for every } x \text{ in } X,$$

so that

$$xp(x) \leq Mp(x) \qquad \text{for every } x \text{ in } X.$$

Summing the left-hand and right-hand sides over X, we have

$$\sum_X xp(x) \leq M \sum_X p(x) = M,$$

since p is a weighting function. This establishes the inequality on the right-hand side and the inequality on the left-hand side follows by a similar argument.
By a similar argument,

$$\min_X d(x) \leq \sum_X d(x)p(x) \leq \max_X d(x). \tag{D}$$

We have a verification of this result in Example 1, since 5.3 lies between 1 and 9.

Expectations (Definitions 3–7–1, 3–7–2), variances (Definition 3–8–1), values (Definitions 4–5–1, 6–7–1), worths (Definition 6–2–1), and Bayesian worths (Definition 6–5–1) are all examples of weighted averages.

The proof of Theorem 4–7–1 is essentially concerned with weighted averages, the weighting functions being randomized strategies of the opponent.

Theorem 4–7–1   A simple strategy a is inadmissible if and only if it is dominated by some other simple strategy.

Proof of the "if" statement. If a is dominated by a', then, by Definition 4–7–2,

$$U(a, s) \leq U(a', s) \qquad \text{for every } s \text{ in } S,$$

with strict inequality for s^*, say. Hence

$$U(a, s)\pi(s) \leq U(a', s)\pi(s) \qquad \text{for every } s \text{ in } S, \tag{E}$$

and for every possible weighting function π on S. By summing (E) for every s in S, we have

$$\sum_s U(a, s)\pi(s) \leq \sum_s U(a', s)\pi(s)$$

for every randomized strategy π of the opponent. Hence, by Definition 4–5–1,

$$V(a, \pi) \leq V(a', \pi)$$

for every randomized strategy π of the opponent. Also for the particular strategy which sets $\pi(s^*) = 1$, we have

$$V(a, \pi) = U(a, s^*) < U(a', s^*) = V(a', \pi).$$

Hence, by Definition 4–7–1, a is inadmissible.

Proof of the "only if" statement. Suppose that a is inadmissible. Then we have to prove that a must also be dominated.

If a is inadmissible, then, by Definitions 4–7–1 and 4–5–1, for some a'

$$\sum_s U(a, s)\pi(s) \leq \sum_s U(a', s)\pi(s) \tag{F}$$

for every weighting function π on S, with $<$ holding for some π^*, say. The particular weighting function with $\pi(s) = 1$ applied to (F) gives

$$U(a, s) \leq U(a', s) \tag{G}$$

and this can be established for every s in S.

Now, for π^*, we rewrite (F) as

$$\sum_s \{U(a', s) - U(a, s)\}\pi^*(s) > 0.$$

All the expressions in braces in this sum are, by (G), known to be nonnegative, and clearly they cannot all be zero, otherwise the sum could not be positive. Hence there is at least one s for which $<$ holds in (G), and we have established that a is dominated by a'.

EXERCISES

1. For the following function p on $X = \{1, 2, 3, 4\}$ and taking values in the set of real numbers

x	1	2	3	4
$p(x)$	0.1	0.2	0.3	0.4

   construct the functions $xp(x)$ and $x^2p(x)$. Evaluate

   a) $\Sigma_X\, p(x)$,   b) $\Sigma_X\, xp(x)$,   c) $\Sigma_X\, x^2p(x)$.

2. Patients attending a certain clinic can have any combination of three important symptoms—headache, high blood pressure, impaired vision. There are two possible treatments—hospitalization, and rest at home—and treatment allocation is made by the following rule: If at least two of the symptoms are present, hospitalize; otherwise treat at home. Define a suitable symptom set X, a treatment set T, and an appropriate treatment allocation function t on X taking values in T.

3. In Problem 6 (Estimating a number of cells, Section 1–7) let $X = \{0, 1, 2, 3\}$, the set of possible numbers of positive reactions in the three tests, and $S = \{0, 1, 2\}$, the set of possible numbers of intruder cells in the organism. A biologist believes it reasonable to conclude that any organism which gives no positive reaction contains no intruder cell, that any organism which gives exactly one positive reaction contains exactly one intruder cell, and that all other organisms have two intruder cells. Define a suitable function on X taking values in S which describes his method of estimation.

   How many different such estimating functions are there?

4. Evaluate

   a) min $\{5, 2, 6, 6\}$,   b) max $\{5, 5, 3, \frac{1}{2}\}$,
   c) max $\{6, 3, \text{min}\,(1, 7)\}$,   d) min $\{2, 3, \text{max}\,(1, 2)\}$.

5. Show that

   a) min $\{\text{max}\,(1, 2, 3), \text{max}\,(4, 5, 6)\} < \text{max}\,\{\text{min}\,(1, 2, 3), \text{min}\,(4, 5, 6)\}$,
   b) min $\{\text{max}\,(1, 4), \text{max}\,(2, 5), \text{max}\,(3, 6)\} = \text{max}\,\{\text{min}\,(1, 2, 3), \text{min}\,(4, 5, 6)\}$.

6. Three real-valued functions $p(x)$, $d_1(x)$, and $d_2(x)$ are defined on the set $X = \{0, 1, 2)$ as on page 275.

   Construct the functions $d_1(x)p(x)$ and $d_2(x)p(x)$ and evaluate $\Sigma_X\, d_1(x)p(x)$ and $\Sigma_X\, d_2(x)p(x)$. Hence evaluate

   a) min $\{\Sigma_X\, d_1(x)p(x), \Sigma_X\, d_2(x)p(x)\}$,
   b) max $\{\Sigma_X\, d_1(x)p(x), \Sigma_X\, d_2(x)p(x)\}$.

x	0	1	2
$p(x)$	0.5	0.3	0.2
$d_1(x)$	3	4	7
$d_2(x)$	2	3	10

INDEX

INDEX

ABCDE79876543210